Boyo G. Ockinga

A CONCISE GRAMMAR OF MIDDLE EGYPTIAN

Boyo G. Ockinga

A Concise Grammar of Middle Egyptian

AN OUTLINE OF MIDDLE EGYPTIAN GRAMMAR

by Hellmut Brunner revised and expanded

Second, revised edition

VERLAG PHILIPP VON ZABERN · MAINZ AM RHEIN

XVI, 180 pages

Bibliographic information published by Die Deutsche Bibliothek

Die Deutsche Bibliothek lists this publication in the Deutsche Nationalbibliographie; detailed bibliographic data is available on the Internet at <*http://dnb.ddb.de*>.

The text was written with Microsoft Word for Windows 2000, the hieroglyphic text with WinGlyph Professional

Cover design: scribes at work (from the tomb of Hesi/Seshemnefer, Saqqara)
Title page illustration: Thoth and Seshat (from Pylon I, Medinet Habu)

ISBN-10: 3-8053-3601-2
ISBN-13: 978-3-8053-3601-7

Printed in Germany by Philipp von Zabern
Printed on fade resistant and archival quality paper (PH 7 neutral) · tcf

For R. E. Cowlin
who first taught me hieroglyphs

CONTENTS

PREFACE TO THE SECOND EDITION

The positive response received by the *Concise Grammar of Middle Egyptian* and its German counterpart *Mittelägyptische Grundgrammatik* has made it possible to plan a new edition. In preparing the present revision, I am grateful to a number of users and readers for their observations, suggestions and corrections, which have been integrated into this version. In particular I would like to thank Professor Wolfgang Schenkel, Tübingen, for his continued support and for numerous constructive comments.

I am also again indebted to Susanne Binder for her unfailing support.

In this second edition, the Sign List and Vocabulary have been extended. Apart from corrections and improvements in points of detail, the presentation of the language here follows that of the first edition. The most significant changes are:

1. The abandonment of the so-called "Narrative Infinitive". Frank Feder ('Das Ende des "narrativen Infinitivs" in Sinuhe', *LingAeg* 12 [2004], 53–74) has convincingly argued that the examples interpreted as "narrative infinitives" in the story of Sinuhe are either ancient scribal errors, or that they can be understood as "konstatierende Überschrifts-Infinitive", i.e. in a narrative they serve as headings that set the scene for an event; the examples found in expedition reports are also to be understood in this way.

2. The acceptance of the existence of two *sḏm.n=f* forms – one nominal and one verbal. Based on the two *sḏm.n=f* forms of the verb *rḏi* (*rḏi* and *ḏi*), the possibility of the existence of two *sḏm.n=f* forms was raised in the first edition of this grammar (*Concise Grammar of Middle Egyptian* [Mainz, 1998], § 71). But *rḏi* and *ḏi* are not used consistently, making them doubtful indicators for the existence of two *sḏm.n=f* forms. In the meantime, however, Wolfgang Schenkel has identified a more reliable indicator in the Coffin Texts: the IIae gem. verbs show gemination in the nominal *sḏm.n=f* forms (see *Tübinger Einführung in die klassisch-ägyptische Sprache und Schrift* [Tübingen, 2005], 184–192).

3. The constructions dealt with under the heading "Emphasis" in the first edition have now been differentiated and appear under the headings "Focalisation" (§§ 118–122) und "Topicalisation" (§§ 123–129).

Finally, I would here also like to thank Dr Annette Nünnerich-Asmus and the Verlag Philipp von Zabern for their willingness to publish this second revised edition of the grammar.

Boyo Ockinga
Macquarie University, Sydney
July, 2005

PREFACE TO THE FIRST ENGLISH EDITION

This book is a slightly revised version of the German edition. Over several years I have been able to use parts of this grammar in classes in Sydney and Adelaide; thanks to all those students who persevered and whose enthusiasm for ancient Egyptian is a constant encouragement. Once again, many thanks to Susanne Binder for her unflagging support and help with editing and proofreading.

Boyo Ockinga
Heidenheim/Brenz, February 1998

PREFACE TO THE FIRST GERMAN EDITION

When the second edition of his *Abriss der mitteläygptischen Grammatik* went out of print, my former teacher, Professor Hellmut Brunner, encouraged me to write a new teaching grammar to replace it. I owe him an especial debt of thanks for his constant support. It is a particular sorrow to me that he did not live to see the completion of this book.

I would like to acknowledge the useful notes of Professor Wolfhart Westendorf to the second edition of Brunner's *Abriss*, which have been incorporated here. My particular thanks to Professor Wolfgang Schenkel for reading the manuscript of this work, for his many helpful comments and for the very constructive discussions with him. I would like to also express my appreciation to Dr Mark Collier for the invaluable discussions I was able to have with him on the Middle Egyptian verbal system.

Without the tireless assistance of my wife, Susanne Binder, the appearance of this book would have been delayed considerably. It has greatly benefited from her patience, her philological knowledge and her enthusiasm for grammar.

My thanks to Mr Franz Rutzen for his willingness to publish this grammar and to his colleagues, in particular Dr Klaus Rob, for their contribution towards its realisation as a book.

Boyo Ockinga
Macquarie University
Sydney, July 1997

INTRODUCTION

The language of Ancient Egypt has a history that can be traced for over three thousand years. Several stages of the language can be identified: Old, Middle and Late Egyptian, Demotic and Coptic.

Old Egyptian is the language in which, for example, the Pyramid Texts and the biographical and royal inscriptions of the Old Kingdom (ca. 2650–2100 BC) were composed. Middle Egyptian was the written language of Egypt during the Middle Kingdom (ca. 2140–1650 BC).

In the following periods, although the spoken language continued to develop, Middle Egyptian was regarded by the Egyptians themselves as a "classical" language and Middle Egyptian literature was used in the scribal schools throughout the New Kingdom. Monumental inscriptions and religious texts were still composed in Middle Egyptian down to the Graeco-Roman Period (the most recent hieroglyphic inscription, on a temple wall in Philae, dates from AD 394). This use of Middle Egyptian can be compared with that of Latin in Europe during the Middle Ages. As in the case of Medieval Latin, the later texts composed in Middle Egyptian no longer represent a pure form of the language since they are often influenced by the contemporary vernacular.

Late Egyptian, the spoken language of the New Kingdom, began to be used from the Amarna Period onwards for both literary and non-literary texts. Demotic is the term for a very abbreviated form of the script and language that was originally introduced for administrative purposes in the 7th century BC and continued in use down to the 5th century AD. Coptic, written with the Greek alphabet and supplemented by seven characters derived from the hieroglyphic script, is the latest stage of the language, which survives to the present day in the liturgy of the Coptic Church.

This book is an introduction to the hieroglyphic script and grammar of Middle Egyptian. It is offered as a successor to Hellmut Brunner's *An Outline of Middle Egyptian Grammar* and, like its predecessor, it is a teaching grammar and aims to provide the beginner with the essentials of the language in as compact a form as possible.

It is divided into four main parts: Script and Grammar, Sign List, Grammar Exercises and Reading Exercises, Vocabulary. In addition to texts of the Middle Kingdom, the Reading Exercises include examples of monumental inscriptions of the 18th Dynasty, which, as mentioned above, continued to be written in Middle Egyptian.

The arrangement of the material in the first part largely follows that of Brunner's grammar: after introducing the principles of the script, the various parts of speech are dealt with. Non-verbal sentences being an important feature of the Egyptian language, it is possible for beginners to thoroughly familiarise themselves with nouns, adjectives, pronouns and particles and yet still meet examples of complete sentences in the exercises. The verb and its usage, together with more complex sentence structures, form the last and largest section of the grammar section of the book. The sequence of the exercises, all taken from original texts, corresponds to the order in which the material is presented. Where forms or constructions not yet encountered appear, a reference to where they can be found in the grammar is provided.

Personal experience in language classes has shown that the student would benefit from more detail than that provided by Brunner's *Outline*, thus the content of this grammar and the method of presentation has been expanded (all examples include transliterations and translations; additional examples have been provided, tables included, and hieroglyphic writings have been added in the vocabulary). An attempt has also been made to take account of research done into the language over the last 35 years, in particular in our understanding of the verbal system, which has been advanced by the work of H.J. Polotsky and the representatives of the "Standard Theory". However, as a result of the work of M. Collier, the "Standard Theory" has in recent times been the object of critical review. This grammar follows these new developments and, although adopting individual observations of the "Standard Theory", it does not embrace the total system. Influenced by modern linguistics, a plethora of new grammatical terminology has been introduced for Egyptian. However, bearing in mind that this grammar is intended as an introduction, I have tried to be as economical as possible in the terminology used. Those who are particularly interested in Egyptian linguistics should consult the works of W. Schenkel and A. Loprieno listed in the following brief bibliography.

Further Literature:

The following is only a small selection of works on the subject. A more complete bibliography can be found in W. Schenkel (2005).

Works on Egyptian Language

James P. Allen, *Middle Egyptian. An Introduction to the Language and Culture of Hieroglyphs* (Cambridge, 2000): A detailed up to date introduction to the Egyptian script and language.

Elmar Edel, *Altägyptische Grammatik* (Rome, 1955/1965): A detailed and systematic presentation of the language of the Old Kingdom; very helpful with Middle Egyptian texts that use old forms, e.g. the Coffin Texts.

Alan H. Gardiner, *Egyptian Grammar* (Oxford, ^{3}1957). Although the first edition of this study appeared over 70 years ago, Gardiner's *Grammar* remains the most comprehensive presentation of Middle Egyptian available and is still an essential reference tool for all detailed work in the language. It should be noted, however, that Gardiner's interpretation of the verbal system no longer reflects our current under-standing. Also, the structure of Gardiner's *Grammar* follows his own particular didactic method and, unlike this grammar, is not ordered systematically according to parts of speech and syntax.

Wolfgang Schenkel, *Tübinger Einführung in die klassisch-ägyptische Sprache und Schrift* (Tübingen, 1994), is the first comprehensive post-"Standard Theory" grammar. It also provides an introduction to the "Standard Theory", as well as a comprehensive bibliography of works dealing with the study of the language. The latest edition, published in 2005, presents a new approach to the syntax of the verb.

Wolfhart Westendorf, *Grammatik der medizinischen Texte* (Berlin, 1962), is useful for more advanced work with Middle Egyptian texts since it analyses a complete corpus of texts and discusses obscure constructions which are not dealt with in general grammars.

Antonio Loprieno, *Ancient Egyptian. A Linguistic Introduction* (Cambridge, 1996), presents a comprehensive, linguistically oriented introduction to the Egyptian language, including the development of the language from Old Egyptian through Middle and Late Egyptian to Coptic.

Wolfgang Schenkel, *Einführung in die altägyptische Sprachwissenschaft* (Darmstadt, 1990). As well as grammar in the narrower sense, this work also deals with themes such as the history of the study of the language, vocalisation, and metre.

Henry G. Fischer, *Ancient Egyptian Calligraphy,* (New York, ^{3}1988). In addition to an excellent introduction to Egyptian calligraphy, this work also provides numerous observations on the palaeography of individual signs.

Dictionaries

Adolf Erman and Hermann Grapow (eds.), *Wörterbuch der ägyptischen Sprache*, 12 vols. (Leipzig and Berlin, 1926–1963). Although in part dated, this work is the only complete dictionary of the Egyptian language (excluding Demotic and Coptic) with references for the occurrence of words ("Belegstellen"). Work on the Berlin Dictionary is being continued by the Berlin-Brandenburgischen Akademie der Wissenschaften and is accessible on the internet under the following URL: http://aaew.bbaw.de

Raymond O. Faulkner, *A Concise Dictionary of Middle Egyptian* (Oxford, 1962): a compact work that deals specifically with Middle Egyptian and also includes references.

Rainer Hannig, *Die Sprache der Pharaonen* (Mainz, 1995): a dictionary that deals with the vocabulary of Egyptian from the Old Kingdom to the Third Intermediate Period (ca. 1000 BC). The lists of names of deities, kings and toponyms as well as the maps are particularly useful. References to the occurrence of words are not included.

Rainer Hannig, *Ägyptisches Wörterbuch I, Altes Reich und Erste Zwischenzeit* (Mainz, 2003): a detailed specialised dictionary of texts of the Old Kingdom and First Intermediate Period, which includes references.

Text Editions

Kurt Sethe, *Ägyptische Lesestücke* (Leipzig, 1924), provides a useful collection of Middle Egyptian hieroglyphic texts of all genres, including "classics" such as the story of Sinuhe and the tales from Papyrus Westcar.

Adriaan de Buck, *Egyptian Reading Book* (Leiden, 1948): an anthology of Middle Egyptian texts of the Middle and New Kingdoms with exercises.

Louis Zonhoven, *Middle Egyptian Texts*, Vol. I: *Literary Texts in the Hieratic Script* (Leiden, 2001). A compendium of all the major Middle Egyptian literary texts written in the cursive hieratic script, presented in hieroglyphic transcription. A compendium of monumental texts is planned.

In the textbook series *Einführungen und Quellentexte zur Ägyptologie*, Christian Leitz and Louise Gestermann (eds.), a collection of text editions with commentary, covering various genres is planned. The first volume deals with monumental hieroglyphic texts of the Graeco-Roman period: Christian Leitz, *Quellentexte zur Ägyptischen Religion*, Band I: *Die Tempelinschriften der griechisch-römischen Zeit* (Münster, 2004).

In the same series a useful textbook on the literature of the Old and Middle Kingdoms has appeared, which provides an introduction to the literary works of the period and bibliographic references to the text editions in which they are available: Günter Burkard, Heinz J. Thissen, *Einführung in die altägyptische Literaturgeschichte* I. *Altes und Mittleres Reich* (Münster, 2003).

Useful editions of a number of classical texts have appeared in the series *Kleine Ägyptische Texte* edited by Wolfgang Helck† and Hartwig Altenmüller.

I. SCRIPT AND TRANSLITERATION

A) SCRIPT § 1

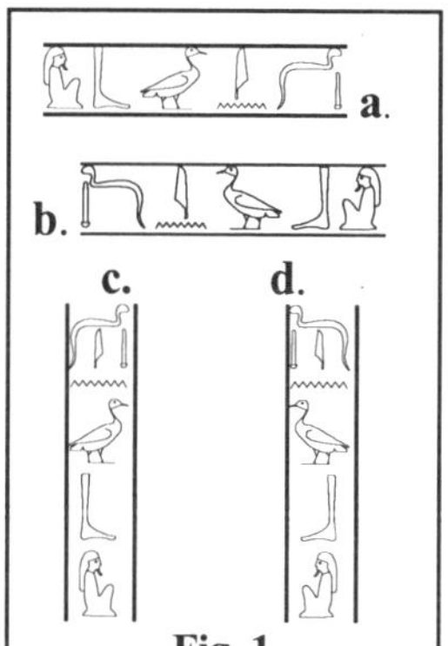

Fig. 1

There are basically two forms of script. Texts carved on monuments are written in hieroglyphic form, where the pictorial character of the sign is clearly recognisable (such as those used in this book). A cursive form of hieroglyphs (hieratic), was used for texts written in ink mainly on papyrus, writing boards or ostraca (pot shards or flakes of limestone).

Texts are mostly written from right to left (Fig. 1a. & 1c.), but also in the other direction (Fig. 1b. & 1d.), and they can run either horizontally (Fig. 1a. & 1b.) or vertically (Fig. 1c. & 1d.). In this book, they are written from left to right; the last of the reading exercises, however, runs from right to left. In Egyptian texts there are neither spaces between words nor punctuation. Although hieroglyphs are pictorial represent-ations, the Egyptian script is primarily phonetic and not pictorial, i.e. most of the signs have phonetic values. The semi-consonants *w* and *i* are not written at all in the earliest texts but appear more frequently over time, more often in word stems than in endings.

B) TRANSLITERATION § 2

Egyptian has 24 consonantal phonemes. For their transliteration and their approximate phonetic values see § 5. The uniliteral signs dealt with there form the Egyptian alphabet (as reconstructed by modern scholars) and their sequence is that used in dictionaries and vocabularies. Vowels were not written and are therefore not considered.

1) LOGOGRAMS (also called "Ideograms") § 3

Logograms can depict the object they designate:

 *rˁ.w* "sun";  *ḥw.t* "house";  *ḥr* "face"

or they can have symbolic meaning:

 *sš* (*sš3*, older *sẖ3*) (writing equipment) for "scribe", "to write"

 *dšr* (flamingo) for *dšr* "to be red", in *dšr.t* "the red land", i.e. "desert"

| | | (three strokes) designate plural

Some signs can both depict the object designated and have symbolic content:

𓇳 *rꜥ.w* "sun" or "day"; 𓄣 *ꞽb* "heart" or "thought", "understanding", "wish"

2) PHONOGRAMS

§ 4 **a)** LOGOGRAM AS A COMBINATION OF CONSONANTS (following the rebus-principle)

𓎟	*nb* ("basket")	in 𓎟𓏤𓀻	*nb* "lord"
𓁷	*ḥr* ("face")	in 𓂧𓁷𓂋𓄛	*dḥr* "leather"

When used in this way, the sign loses its logographic character and becomes a pure phonogram, in the examples above a bi-literal (cp. § 6).

§ 5 **b)** UNI-LITERALS (pointers to conventional pronunciation in brackets)

𓄿	*ꜣ*	(as in "h**a**rd", Semitic *aleph*)	𓐍	*ḫ*	(as in "lo***ch***")
𓇋	*ꞽ*	(as in "***i***n", Semitic *yod*)	𓄡	*ẖ*	(as in German "i***ch***")
𓇌, 𓏭	*y*	(as in "bab***y***")	𓊃	*z*	(voiced s as in "no***s***e")
𓂝	*ꜥ*	(glottal stop, Semitic *ayin*)	𓋴	*s*	
𓅱	*w*	(as in "***w***ay" or "p***oo***l")	𓈙	*š*	(as in "***sh***ape")
𓃀	*b*		𓈎	*ḳ*, *q*	(Semitic *kaf*)
𓊪	*p*		𓎡	*k*	
𓆑	*f*		𓎼	*g*	
𓅓	*m*		𓏏	*t*	
𓈖	*n*		𓍿	*ṯ*	(as in "i***tch***")
𓂋	*r*		𓂧	*d*	
𓉔	*h*		𓆓	*ḏ*	(voiced as in "***j***ungle")
𓎛	*ḥ*	(like Semitic emphatic h)			

By the Middle Kingdom, *z* and *s* are no longer distinguished phonetically; this applies in part to *t* and *ṯ*, as well as *d* and *ḏ*, so that, alongside historically correct writings, one finds cases where these signs have been interchanged. In this book 𓋴 and 𓊃 are transliterated as *s*. 𓇌 *y* at the end of a word can only be followed by the additional endings *t* (feminine), *w* (plural) and a determinative, but by no other phonetic sign. The

Egyptian script has no distinct sign for *l*, for which it uses *ꜣ*, *n* or *r* (also […] in the Late Period).

Further uni-literals:

[…] *w*, […] *m* (actually *im*), […] *n*, […] for *t* or *ṯ* (actually *ti*), […], […], […], […] *m* at the beginning of a word.

c) BI-LITERALS

§ 6

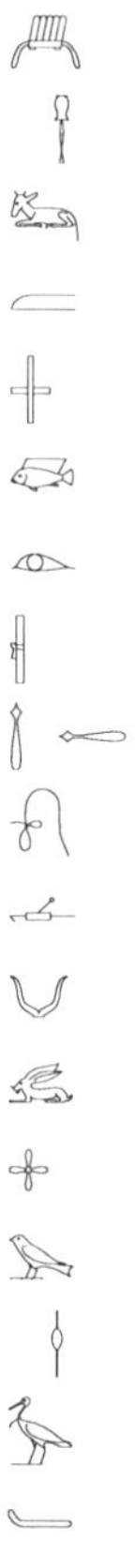	*ꜣw*		*pꜣ*	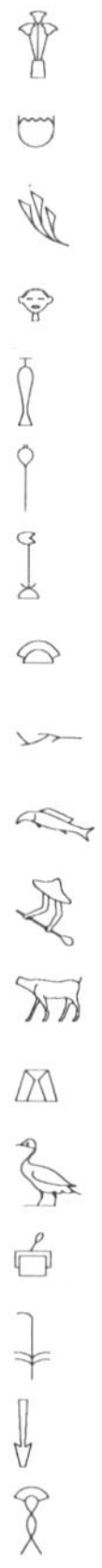	*ḥꜣ*	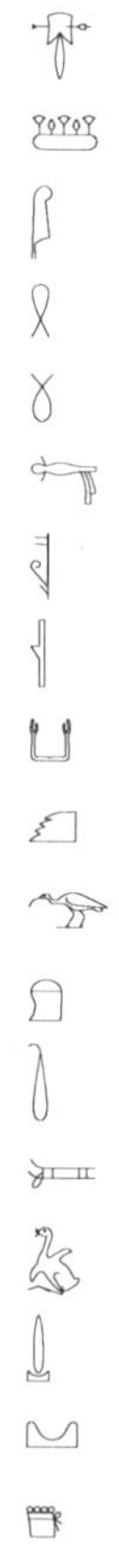	*st*
	ꜣb, mr		*pr*		*ḥm*		*šꜣ*
	iw		*pḥ*		*ḥn*		*šw*
	im, gs		*mꜣ*		*ḥr*		*šn*
	im		*mi*		*ḥs*		*šs*
	in		*mn*		*ḥḏ*		*šd*
	ir		*mr*		*ḫꜣ*		*ḳs*
	is		*mr*		*ḫꜥ*		*ḳd*
	ꜥꜣ		*mḥ*		*ḫt*		*kꜣ*
	wꜣ		*ms*		*ẖꜣ*		*km*
	wꜥ		*mt*		*ẖn*		*gm*
	wp		*nw*		*ẖn*		*tꜣ*
	wn		*nw*		*ẖr*		*ti*
	wn		*nb*		*sꜣ*		*tm*
	wr		*nm*		*sꜣ*		*ṯꜣ*
	wḏ		*ns*		*sw*		*ḏꜣ*
	bꜣ		*nḏ*		*sn*		*ḏw*
	bḥ, ḥw		*rw*		*sk*		*ḏr*

§ 7 **d)** TRI-LITERALS

ꜥnḫ	*wꜣḥ*	*ḥkꜣ*	*ḫpr*	*tw*
ꜥḥꜥ	*nfr*	*ḥtp*	*sḏm*	

§ 8 **e)** SIGN COMBINATIONS

nn *mw* *nw* *i* *tr* *wꜣḏ*

< *iyi* "to come"; (and) in *šm* "to go"

§ 9 3) DETERMINATIVES

The following is a selection of the most common determinatives:

man	embrace
woman	come, go
people	turn back
eat, drink, think, speak	leg, stride
load, carry	cross, tresspass
enemy, death	skin, quadruped
strength, action	bird, insect
praise, plead, greet	small, bad, weak
child	flutter, alight
god, king	tree
see	plant, flower
nose, breath, rejoice, anger	wood, tree
flesh, limb	heaven, sky, above
negation, nothing	night
like	sun, day, time

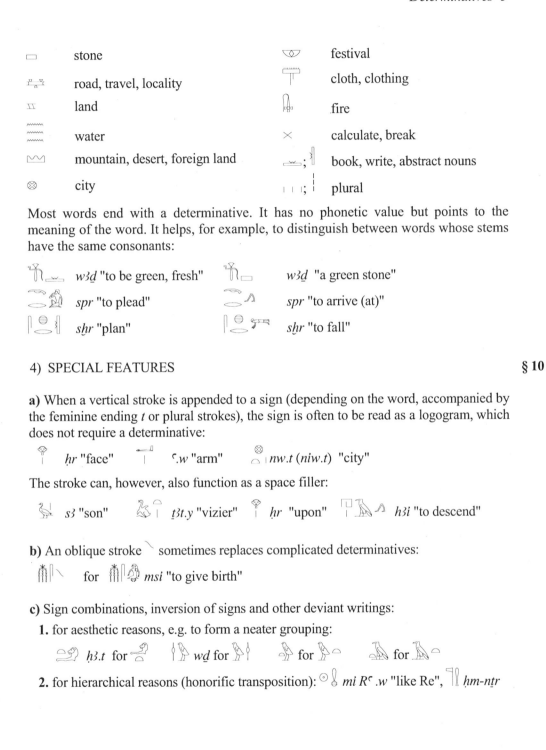

▭	stone	▽	festival
🜨	road, travel, locality		cloth, clothing
	land		fire
~~	water	×	calculate, break
⌒	mountain, desert, foreign land		book, write, abstract nouns
⊗	city		plural

Most words end with a determinative. It has no phonetic value but points to the meaning of the word. It helps, for example, to distinguish between words whose stems have the same consonants:

wȝḏ "to be green, fresh"   *wȝḏ* "a green stone"

spr "to plead"   *spr* "to arrive (at)"

sḫr "plan"   *sḫr* "to fall"

4) SPECIAL FEATURES §10

a) When a vertical stroke is appended to a sign (depending on the word, accompanied by the feminine ending *t* or plural strokes), the sign is often to be read as a logogram, which does not require a determinative:

ḥr "face"   *ꜥ.w* "arm"   *nw.t* (*niw.t*) "city"

The stroke can, however, also function as a space filler:

sȝ "son"   *ṯȝt.y* "vizier"   *ḥr* "upon"   *hȝi* "to descend"

b) An oblique stroke `⟍` sometimes replaces complicated determinatives:

for   *msi* "to give birth"

c) Sign combinations, inversion of signs and other deviant writings:

1. for aesthetic reasons, e.g. to form a neater grouping:

ḥȝ.t for   *wḏ* for   for   for

2. for hierarchical reasons (honorific transposition):   *mi Rꜥ .w* "like Re",   *ḥm-nṯr* "servant of god; priest"; *s3 nsw* "son of the king, prince"; *ḥw.t nṯr* "mansion of god, temple"

3. In historic writings:

a. Phonetic change *swr* > *swi* "to drink" (not *swri*!)

fsi > *psi* "to cook"

b. Archaic writings , , for *it* "father"; for *ir.y pʿ.t* "prince"

§ 11 5) PHONETIC COMPLEMENTS

a) In order to clarify the reading of multi-literal signs which have more than one phonetic value, uni-literal signs are often added:

in *3b* "to wish" and *mr* "to suffer"

in *w3ḥ* "to place, remain" and *ski* "to perish"

b) For aesthetic-graphic reasons (grouping of signs to form a neat block), uni-literal signs often accompany multi-literal signs even in cases where there can be no confusion:

ʿnḫ *nfr* *ḫpr* *mi*

Phonetic complements usually follow their signs, but they can also precede (e.g. *t* in front of *tw*) or precede and follow the sign (e.g. *t* before *tm* and *m*).

c) Phonetic Determinatives: Some words have determinatives that do not fit their meaning. They are written because they fit the context in another word where they have formed a close association with phonograms that appear in both words. From the Middle Kingdom onwards (for) is found as a determinative with *ḳd* and *d* in *ḳd* "to build, to form (pots)" and as a phonetic determinative in *sḳdi* "travel (by water)".

§ 12 6) CONVENTIONAL PRONUNCIATION

Since the Egyptian script does not indicate vowels, when pronouncing Egyptian words an e is conventionally inserted between consonants in cases where no *3*, *ʿ* or so-called semi-consonant (*w* or , , *i/y*) breaks up the sequence of consonants: *3ḫ* "akh", *ʿnḫ* "ankh", *mi* "mi", *wbn* "weben", *bw* "boo", *nfr* "nefer", *ḫpr* "kheper".

7) TRANSLITERATION – ADDITIONAL NOTATION § 13

In the transliteration of some Egyptian words, two morphological separators are used to clarify their structure:

. separates a word stem from a grammatical ending (e.g. plural *w*, feminine *t*) or a tense element (§§ 14ff, 22ff, 68ff)

= separates suffix-pronouns from a word stem, a grammatical ending or a tense element (§§ 28, 68 ff).

Other notations:

( ) brackets what is not written in hieroglyphs; added by editor for grammatical clarification

{ } brackets what the editor considers to be an error in the hieroglyphic text

< > brackets emendations by the editor

[ ] brackets damaged text in the original, but added by the editor

II. ACCIDENCE AND SYNTAX

A) THE NOUN

1) GENDER AND NUMBER § 14

There are two genders, masculine and feminine.

Abstract nouns are usually feminine, e.g.  *ḏw.t* "evil", 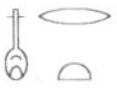 *nfr.t* "good".

Nouns have singular, plural and dual forms.

a) ENDINGS § 15

Masculine: two groups (1) without an ending, (2) with ending *-w* (often not written).
Feminine: with ending *-t*

NOUNS					
singular		**plural**		**dual**	
m. **ø**	 *sn* "brother"	.*w*	 *sn.w*	.*wy*	 *sn.wy*
m. .*w*	 *ḥfȝ.w* "snake"	.*ww*	 *ḥfȝ.ww* "snakes"	.*wwy*	 *ʿ.wwy* "(the two) arms"
f. .*t*	 *sn.t* "sister"	.*wt*	 *sn.wt*	.*ty*	 *sn.ty*

§ 16 **b)** WRITINGS:

1. The masculine ending *-w* is usually not written:

pr.w "house" *Rꜥ.w* "(god) Re" (occasionally)

It can also be indicated by a plural writing:

nfr.w "perfection" *mn.w* "monument" *ḥtp.w* "peace"

2. The feminine ending *-t* is sometimes not written.

3. The plural can be written in the following ways:

Three logograms – an archaic writing *pr.ww* "houses"

Three groups of phonograms *rn.w* "names"

Three determinatives *nh.wt* "sycamores"

or (predominantly) with the plural determinative or , e.g. *ḥm.wt* "women".

4. The dual is indicated by the reduplication of signs:

Two logograms *pr.wwy* "(the) two houses"

Two determinatives *ṯḫn.wy* "(the) two obelisks"

Or phonetically with *w* and dual determinative (phonetic value *y*) *ꜥ.wwy* "(the) two arms".

5. Collective nouns are written like plurals but are grammatically singular:

šꜥy "sand" *mnmn.t* "herd"

mw "water" is usually construed as a singular, rarely as a plural.

6. When followed by a suffix-pronoun, some feminine nouns have an additional *-w* that precedes the feminine *t* ending: *dp.t* "boat" and *dpw.t=f* "his boat".

§ 17 **c)** SPECIAL FEATURES

1. *rmṯ* (m. sg.) means "person"; *rmṯ.w* (m. pl.) "people" can sometimes also be found as a writing for the collective *rmṯ.t* (f. sg.) "humankind" (*t* is rarely written) or for the singular *rmṯ* "person".

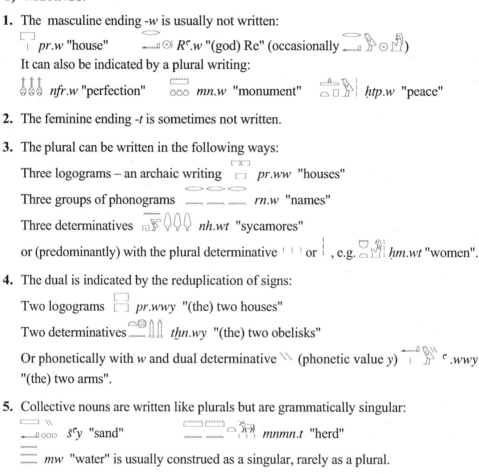

2.  *iḫ.t* "thing" is feminine, but when used with the meaning "something" or "property" it is masculine.

3. Foreign place names are construed as feminines:

 *Rṯnw ḥr.t* "Upper-Retenu" (part of Syria-Palestine)

2) GENITIVE

a) DIRECT GENITIVE **§ 18**

In this construction, which expresses possession or belonging, two nouns are juxtaposed. The first is the *nomen regens* (noun of possession), the second the *nomen rectum* (noun of the possessor):

 *s3 wꜥb* "son of a / the priest"

 *nb.t pr.w* "lady of the house"

b) INDIRECT GENITIVE **§ 19**

In the indirect genitive construction, rather than being directly juxtaposed, the *nomen regens* and the *nomen rectum* are linked by the *nisbe*-adjective of the preposition *n* (§ 23) which functions as the genitive-adjective:

	GENITIVE-ADJECTIVE	
	masc.	**fem.**
sg.	*n(.y)*	 *n.t*
pl.	 *n.w*	 *n.(w)t*

 *r3 n.y Km.t* "the language of Egypt"

 *ḥm.wt n.(w)t wr.w* "the wives of the princes"

If the *nomen rectum* is separated from the *nomen regens* by another word (e.g. an adjective or direct genitive), then the indirect genitive is generally used:

 *s.t Ḥr.w n.t ꜥnḫ.w* "the Horus-Throne of the living"

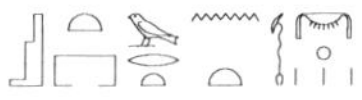 *s.t wr.t n.t ḏꜥm* "the great throne of (i.e. made of) gold"

3) COORDINATION AND DISJUNCTION

§ 20 **a)** COORDINATION: there is no specific word for "and". Coordination is expressed by

1. Juxtaposition (the rule):

ỉ3w.wt=ṯn pr.ww=ṯn "your offices and your houses"

2. Prepositions *ḥr* "upon " or *ḥnꜥ* "with", both used for "and":

dꜥ ḥr ḥy.t "storm and rain"

ms.w=ỉ ḥnꜥ sn.w=ỉ "my children and my kin"

§ 21 **b)** DISJUNCTION: "or" is either not expressed or is indicated by a following *r3-pw*

ṯs.w nb ḥ3.ty-ꜥ.w nb "every commander or every prince"

m nb m sn m ḫnms r3-pw "as lord, as brother or as friend" (*m* is here the "*m* of predication", § 43.1a).

B) THE ADJECTIVE

1) FORMS

Adjectives have feminine and plural forms like nouns (§ 14ff). They are derived either

§ 22 a) from verbal stems, usually without an ending in the masculine:

nfr "perfect, beautiful, good" *bỉn* "bad, evil"

§ 23 or b) from nouns and prepositions to which is added the ending *y,* the so-called *nisbe*:

nṯr.y "god-like, divine" *ẖr.y* "which is under"

ḥr.y "which is above, upper" *ỉm.y* "which is in"

	Nisbe-ENDINGS	
	masc.	**fem.**
sing.	*.y*	*.yt*
plur.	*.yw*	*.ywt*

Note the writings of the following *nisbe*-adjectives:

1. *ỉm.y* "which/who is in" – from the preposition *m* "in" (see § 35):

	masculine	feminine
sing.	*ỉm.y* or	*ỉm.yt*
plur.	*ỉm.yw*	*ỉm.ywt*

2. *ḫnt.y* "which/who is in front of" – from the preposition *ḫnt* "in front of" (see § 35):

	masculine	feminine
sing.	*ḫnt.y* , or	*ḫnt.yt*
plur.	*ḫnt.yw*	*ḫnt.ywt*

3. Some writings of these adjectives are based on dual forms (on the rebus-principle):

nṯr nw.ty "city god" (not "god of the two cities")

Ḥr.w ꜣḫ.ty "Horus of the horizon" (not "Horus of the two horizons")

2) USAGE OF THE ADJECTIVE **24**

a) As the attribute to a noun, it follows the noun and agrees with it in gender and number:

ḥrr.t nfr.t "the beautiful flower".

b) As a noun: *ḏw.t* "evil" (fem./ abstract noun)

ẖft.y "opponent, the enemy" (*nisbe*)

c) As a predicate: in the *nfr sw* - Sentence (§ 56).

d) In epithets adjectives can be qualified by a noun; their gender and number are determined by the antecedent: "Amun, *ỉḳr sḫr.w* excellent of counsels", "(The goddess) Hathor, *nfr.t ḥr* beautiful of countenance".

e) Combined with the preposition *r,* it functions as the comparative, there being no special form of the adjective in comparisons: *wr r ỉt=f* "greater than his father".

3) SPECIAL FEATURES **§ 25**

a) or *ỉr.y* (prepositional adverb from *r* "to") "belonging to" (invariable) can replace the third person suffix-pronoun when used to express possession (§ 28 end).

b) *nb* "every, all" is only used as an adjective, never as a noun. In place of "all" as a noun:  *si nb* "every man",  *wꜥ nb* "everyone",  *iḫ.t nb.t* "everything". In formulaic expressions the endings (fem. and pl.) are often not written:  *iḫ.t nb(.t) nfr.t wꜥb.t* "every good (and) pure thing".

c)  *ky* "other" precedes the noun and has the following forms:

	masculine	feminine
sing.	*ky* 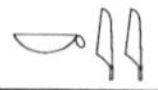	*k.t* 
plur.	*ky.wy* 	*k.t* 

 *ky sp* "another time"; 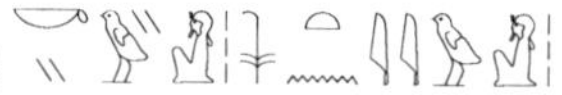 *ky.wy nsy.w* "other kings". The expression 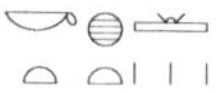 *k.t iḫ.t*, lit. "other thing(s)", can replace the plural form. It regularly precedes the noun. It is often used as a noun with the meaning "other (people), others": 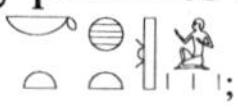; also  *k.t ḫy*.

d) An indirect genitive can replace an adjective as the attribute of a noun: 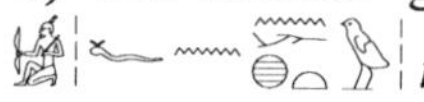 *mšꜥ=f n(.y) nḫt.w* "his army of victory", i.e. "his victorious army".

C) PRONOUNS

1) PERSONAL PRONOUNS

§ 26 **a)** INDEPENDENT PRONOUNS

singular		plural	
1.c.	*ink*  "I"	**1.c.**	*inn* , 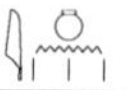 "we"
2.m.	*ntk*  "you" (older form *ṯwt* )	**2.c.**	*nṯṯn* , (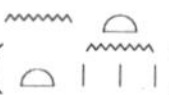) "you"
2.f.	*ntt* ,  "you" (older form )		
3.m.	*ntf*  "he" (older form *swt* )	**3.c.**	*ntsn*  "they"
3.f.	*nts* ,  "she"		

Usage:

1. In Nominal Sentences:

a. as the subject of an *ink*-Sentence (§§ 50–52)

b. as the predicate of a *pw*-Sentence (§ 53)

2. As subject of the infinitive (§ 83 b)

3. As the pronominal subject in the *in*-Construction (§§ 119–120)

b) DEPENDENT PRONOUNS **§ 27**

singular		plural	
1.c.	*wi* "I, me"	**1.c.**	*n* "we, us"
2.m	*ṯw* ( ) "you"	**2.c.**	*ṯn* , ( ) "you"
2.f.	*ṯn* ( ) "you"		
3.m.	*sw* "he, him"	**3.c.**	*sn* ( ) "they, them"
3.f.	*sy* ; (,) "she, her"		
neuter	*st* "it"		

Usage:

1. As the object of all forms of the verb (which it follows), including participles (§§ 98–104), the Future Verbal Adjective (§ 112) and, in exceptional cases, the infinitive (§ 83d). It can also have reflexive meaning since there is no distinct reflexive pronoun.

2. As the subject in an Adverbial Sentence (§ 44 c), following the particles , , , (§ 37) or (less frequent) without introductory particle. Here, the indefinite pronoun *tw* "one" can also serve as the subject.

3. After (§ 37) in the negated Adverbial Sentence (§ 47).

4. As the subject in an Adjectival Sentence (§ 56).

5. *st* can serve as the object of an infinitive (§ 84).

§ 28 c) SUFFIX-PRONOUNS

singular		plural		dual	
1.c.	*=i* also fem. "I, me, my" ; woman; , king	**1.c.**	*=n* "we, us, our"	**1.c.**	*=ny*
2.m.	*=k* [1.] "you, your"	**2.c.**	*=ṯn* ( ) "you, your"	**2.c.**	*=ṯny*
2.f.	*=ṯ* ( ) "you, your"				
3.m.	*=f* [2.] "he, him, his"	**3.c.**	*=sn* ( ) "they, them, their"	**3.c.**	*=sny*
3.f.	*=s* [3.] ( ) "she, her"				
"one"	*=tw*				

Note: With dual nouns [1.] *ky* [2.] *fy* [3.] *sy*

Usage:

1. Expresses possession after a noun: *s3=f* "his son"

2. As the subject of the finite verb in the suffix-conjugations: *sḏm=f* "he hears" (§§ 68ff).

3. After prepositions (§§ 35–36)

4. After infinitives: with *intransitive* verbs – subject (§ 83);

with *transitive* verbs – object (subject only if the infinitive has both an object and a subject, § 84).

5. The word ( ) *ḏs* "self, own" is only used with a suffix: *ḏs=f* "himself", *nsw ḏs=f* "the king himself", *rn=k ḏs=k* "your own name."

***Note*:**

1. The suffix-pronoun *=i* is sometimes not written, e.g. when followed by a dependent pronoun used with reflexive meaning (§ 27).

2. *ir.y* ( ) / (§ 25 a) can replace suffixes of the 3rd person (possessive): "His majesty had sent an army, *s3=f smsw m ḥr.y ir.y* his eldest son was its commander (lit.: the commander thereof)."

2) DEMONSTRATIVES

a) ADJECTIVAL DEMONSTRATIVES **§ 29**

		singular	plural	dual
known	**m.**	*pw*, *pwy* "this"	*ipw* "these"	*ipwy* "these (two)"
	f.	*tw*, *twy* "this"	*iptw* "these"	*iptwy*
near	**m.**	*pn* "this"	*ipn* "these"	*ipny*
	f.	*tn* "this"	*iptn* "these"	*iptny*
far	**m.**	*pf* "yon, that"	*ipf* "those"	*ipfy*
	f.	*tf* "yon that"	*iptf* "those"	*iptfy*

b) NOMINAL DEMONSTRATIVES **§ 30**

GROUP 1 (without)		
known	**c.**	*nw*
near	**c.**	*nn*
far	**c.**	*nf*

GROUP 2 (with)		
near	**m.**	*pꜣ*
	f.	*tꜣ*
	c.	*nꜣ*
far	**m.**	*pfꜣ*
	f.	*tfꜣ*
	c.	*nfꜣ*

Note: The pronouns with *n* are singular and are often used for the neuter:

pty nꜣ "What is this?"

c) ARTICLE **§ 31**

pꜣ, *tꜣ* and *nꜣ* (§ 30) lose their demonstrative force and function as definite articles ("the"); in spoken Egyptian probably as early as the Middle Kingdom.

For the very rarely expressed indefinite article "a" Egyptian uses the numeral *wꜥ* "one".

§ 32 d) POSSESSIVE ADJECTIVE

		masculine	feminine	common/ plural
1.c.	**my**	*p3y=i*	*t3y=i*	*n3y=i*
2.m.	**your**	*p3y=k*	*t3y=k*	*n3y=k*
2.f.	**your**	*p3y=ṯ*	*t3y=ṯ*	*n3y=ṯ*
3.m.	**his**	*p3y=f*	*t3y=f*	*n3y=f*
3.f.	**her**	*p3y=s*	*t3y=s*	*n3y=s*
1.pl.	**our**	*p3y=n*	*t3y=n*	*n3y=n*
2.pl.	**your**	*p3y=ṯn*	*t3y=ṯn*	*n3y=ṯn*
3.pl.	**their**	*p3y=sn*	*t3y=sn*	*n3y=sn*

§ 33 e) USAGE OF THE DEMONSTRATIVES (§§ 29–32)

1. Position

a. Adjectival demonstratives **follow** the noun:

hrw.w pwy n.y wḏʿ mdw.t "this day of judgment".

"Then she repeated for him *mdw.t tn* this matter."

b. The nominal demonstrative, the article and the possessive adjective **precede** the noun:

"... and give *nn i3d.wt n nn ḥm.wt* these nets to these women..."

Re-Weser says to Isis, Nephthys and Heket: "Please give *p3 it n p3y=tn ẖr.y-ḳni* the grain to your porter."

2. Singular and plural

a. The adjectival demonstratives occur almost only in the singular.

b. The plural and dual forms of the adjectival demonstratives are only commonly found in Old Egyptian and in religious texts. In place of the plural forms, a nominal demonstrative followed by the genitive-adjective *n.y* "of" (§ 19) is used. The noun is normally in the plural, sometimes in the singular:

nn n.y sr.w "these officials"

nw n.y nṯr.w	"these gods"
nꜣ n.y ẖrd.w	"these children"
nꜣ n.y mw n.y pꜣ š	"these waters of this lake"

3. Absolute usage of the nominal demonstratives (i.e. as a noun):

ḫr m-ḫt hrw.w swꜣi(.w)(§ 81) *ḥr nn* "Now, after days had passed after this (event)… "

4. The adjectival demonstratives *pf* and *tf* are used to refer to something with either respect or disdain: *ḫr pf* "that (vile) enemy"; *ẖnw pf šps* "that noble Residence".

3) INTERROGATIVES (for their usage see § 148) **§ 34**

	in, in-iw	introduces a question, remains untranslated
	išst	"what?"
	m	"who, what?"
	ḥr m	"why?"
	r m	"why, to what purpose?"
	ḥr sy išst	"why?"
	mi m	"how?"
	ptr/pti	"who, what?" (< *pw tr*)
	si	"who, what, which?"
	iḫ	"what?"
	ṯn	"where, whence, where to?"

D) PREPOSITIONS and their *nisbe* forms

Prepositions precede not only nouns or suffix-pronouns but also clauses (like conjunctions) since verb-forms can be nominalised, i.e. used as nouns.

§ 35 1) SIMPLE PREPOSITIONS

 *imytw* "between"

 *m* (with suffix-pronoun )
"in, out of, through (instrumental), with"
introduces a predicate (§§ 43.1a): "*m* of predication"
before infinitives: with verbs of movement replacing *ḥr* (§§ 85, 86, 93)
with Aorist *sḏm=f* : "as, as truly as" (§ 70.2c)
with (Historic) Perfect *sḏm=f* : "when" (§ 72.2)
nisbe:  *im.y* (§ 23)

 *mi* "like, according to"
with Aorist *sḏm=f*: "as when, according as" (§ 70.2c)
with *sḏm.t=f* : "like" (§ 73)

;  *n* "to, for, because of" (indicates dative / indirect object)
temporal: "within"
with infinitive: "because of"
with (Historic) Perfect *sḏm=f* (§ 72.2): "because"
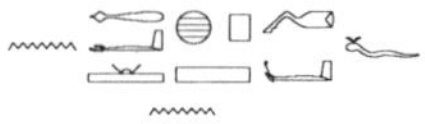 *n ꜥꜣ ḫpš=f* "because his might was great"
nisbe:  *n.y* (§ 23)

 r (with suffix-pronoun )
"towards, against, away from"; temporal: "at" (a time)
with a noun: "concerning"
with an adjective-verb: comparative "the god let me do it,  *mi ꜥꜣ=f r nṯr nb* according as he is greater than every god" (see also § 24 e)
with infinitive: "in order to", purpose, future (§ 85.2)
with Aorist *sḏm=f* : "according as, until" (§ 70.2c)
with *sḏm.t=f* : "until" (§ 73.2)
nisbe:  *ir.y* (§ 23)
 introducing conditional and temporal clauses: (§§ 127–131).

 *ḥ3* "behind, around"

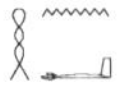 *ḥnꜥ* "together with"; "and" (§ 20)
with infinitive: continues previous verb-form (cf. § 87 2a)

 *ḥr* (with suffix-pronoun also  or )
"upon, in, because, regarding, for"
with infinitive: "while, on" (§ 85)
with Aorist *sḏm=f* : "because" (§ 70.2c)
nisbe:  *ḥr.y* (§ 23)

 *ẖr* "under, with" (also with sense of "carrying something")
nisbe:  *ẖr.y* (§ 23)

 *ḫr* "near, with, under (temporal, e.g. a king), to (a person)"

 *ḫft* "opposite, in front of, in accordance with"
with infinitive: "at the time of" (§ 85.2)
with Aorist *sḏm=f* : "when (temporal), according as" (§ 70.2c)
nisbe:  *ḫft.y* (with det.  or  : "enemy") (§ 23)

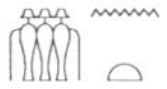 *ḫnt* local: "in front of, from, among"
temporal: "before"
nisbe: *ḫnt.y* "foremost" (§ 23)

 *tp* "upon"
nisbe: *tp.y* "who/which is upon, first, chief" (§ 23)

 *ḏr* "since, because"
with (Historic) Perfect *sḏm=f*: "since, because of" (§ 72.2)
with *sḏm.t=f* : "since, before, until" (§ 73.2)

2) COMPOUND PREPOSITIONS **§ 36**

 *m-ꜥ.w* "in the hand of, together with, from, with (in the possession of), through"

 *m-b3ḥ* "in front of, in the presence of"

	*m-m*	"among"
	*m / r / ḫr-ḥ3.t*	"in front of"
	*m-ḫt*	"behind, after" with (Historic) Perfect *sḏm=f* (§ 72.2): "after" with infinitive: "after"
	*m-s3*	"behind, after"
	*r-gs*	"beside"
	*ḫft-ḥr*	"in the presence of, in front of"

E) PARTICLES

§ 37 1) NON-ENCLITIC PARTICLES always take first position in a clause

 *iw* a) "it is the case"; introduces clauses that make a statement of fact: in Complex Verb Forms (§§ 90–94), in Adverbial Sentences (§ 44);
b) semantically and syntactically neutral "prop"-word for a pronominal subject in embedded Adverbial Sentences (§ 46 b) and in the Pseudo-verbal Construction (§§ 86–88);
c) "circumstantial converter" (§ 46 b).

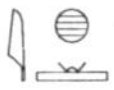 *iḫ* introduces a wish (§ 75.1): "oh" (usually not translated); see also § 140 a.

 *isṯ* (also *sṯ*, *ist*; older form  *isk, sk*) "while, as, in the meantime"; introduces main and subordinate clauses (§ 46 a, 97 b):

 *ti* same meaning as *isṯ*

 *wn.t* conjunction "because" (< *n wn.t*, see *n.tt*)

 *m=k* < particle (?) *m(i)* "behold" + suffix-pronoun
further forms: (f.) ; *m=ṯ/m=t*, (pl.)  *m=ṯn /m=tn*;
meaning: Presentative – "Behold! Look!" (§§ 44 c, 88.2, 97 a)

 n,  *nn* negative particle: negative equivalent of *iw* (§ 47);

ỉw + suffix-pronoun, but *nn* + dependent pronoun (§ 27).

n.tt introduces an object clause following some verbs (e.g. *rḫ* "to know"): *rḫ n.tt* "know that ..."; also conjunction "because" (< *n n.tt*). Often combined with prepositions to form a conjunction: *ḏr ntt* "since", *ḥr n.tt*, *n-n.tt* "because".

ḥ3 var. *ḥwy*, *ḥw*: with Subjunctive *sḏm=f* (§ 75.1) introducing wishes "Would that …" (or left untranslated).

k3 (also) "so", "then"; with Future (Prospective) *sḏm=f* (§ 74.5); with Subjunctive *sḏm=f* (§ 75.1).

2) ENCLITIC PARTICLES always "lean" (Grk. *enklitikos*) upon a preceding word. § 38

ỉs	"truly"
wnnt	"indeed, really"
m	"pray, do"
(ỉ)r=f	indicates emphasis; suffix-pronoun originally variable
ḥm	"assuredly, indeed"
swt	"but, however"
grt	"now"
tr	"indeed, truly"

F) NUMERALS

1) CARDINAL NUMBERS § 39

a) WRITINGS:

ones (in dates often)	ten thousands
tens (in dates often ⊂)	hundred thousands
hundreds	millions
thousands	

b) READING:

1	*wꜥ.w*	6	*sis.w*	100	*š.t* (fem.)
2	*sn.wy*	7	*sfḫ.w*	1,000	*ḫꜣ*
3	*ḫmt.w*	8	*ḫmn.w*	10,000	*ḏbꜥ*
4	*fd.w*	9	*psḏ.w*	100,000	*ḥfn*
5	*di̓.w*	10	*mḏ.w*	1,000,000	*ḥḥ*
				10,000,000	*šn*

c) USAGE

- The number follows its noun (cp. "$20"), which is usually in the singular, less frequently in the plural (never plural with the numbers 1 and 2).
- The numbers 1 and 2 are treated as adjectives (§ 24). All other numerals are nouns.
- The numbers 3 – 10 also have feminine forms ending in *-t*.
- *ḫꜣ* and *ḥḥ* can also precede the noun, which is introduced by the "*m* of predication" (§ 43.1a) or the genitive-adjective (§ 19).

§ 40 2) ORDINAL NUMBERS

- "first": , *tp.y* (*nisbe* of the preposition *tp* "upon", § 35).
- "second" to "ninth": with ending *nw* *fd.w-nw* "fourth".
- "Tenth" and higher ordinal numbers: with participle *mḥ* "that which fills",

  mḥ 10 "that which fills ten" = "tenth".

§ 41 3) DATES

"year" *rnp.t,* in dates *rnp.t sp* (alternative reading: *ḥꜣ.t-sp*).

"day" *hrw.w* (*rꜥ.w* in the combination *rꜥ.w nb* "every day"), in dates *sw* .

Seasons:

	ꜣḫ.t	"inundation"
	pr.t	"harvest"
	šm.w	"dryness, summer"

Months:

	*tp.y*	"first (month)"
	*ꜣbd 2*	"second month"
	*ꜣbd 3*	"third month"
	*ꜣbd 4*	"fourth month"

Example: 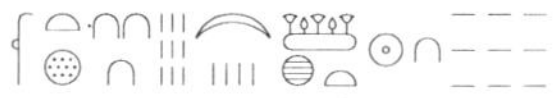 *rnp.t-sp 39 ꜣbd 4 ꜣḫ.t sw 19*

"Year 39, fourth month of the inundation, day 19"

G) NON-VERBAL SENTENCES

The **predicate** of a non-verbal sentence can be formed by 1) an adverbial phrase [Adverbial Sentence], 2) a nominal phrase [Nominal Sentence], or 3) an adjectival phrase [Adjectival Sentence].

The **subject** is always nominal, i.e. a noun, an independent pronoun or a nominalised verb form.

Non-verbal sentences indicate a state. Their tense is non-specific but determined by their context as present, past or future.

1) ADVERBIAL SENTENCES **§ 42**

WORD ORDER: subject – predicate

The predicate is formed by an adverb or its syntactic equivalent, i.e.
- preposition + nominal expression (noun, suffix-pronoun or infinitive) or
- Old Perfective (§ 81).

Adverbial Sentences are either *independent* (main clauses) or *embedded* (translated as subordinate clauses).

A further distinction is made between *simple* and *extended* Adverbial Sentences.

a) INDEPENDENT ADVERBIAL SENTENCES

§ 43 **1.** Simple adverbial main clauses

a. Basic form: noun (+ adjective) + preposition + noun

At the end of a medical prescription:  *pḫr.t nb.t mi sn.wt=s* "Every (other) remedy is like its second (i.e. inferior)."

 *šw m ẖr.t m nb ꜥḥꜥ.w* "He who was empty of possessions is (now) a lord (i.e. possessor) of treasures."

Most such sentences are sentence names:

 *Nb.t=i-m-nbw* "My mistress (is) the Golden One (i.e. Hathor)."
(The preposition *m* in the last two examples is the so-called "*m* of predication".)

 *Ỉmn(.w)-m-ḥ3.t* "Amun is at the forefront."

 *Sn=i-ḥnꜥ(=i)* "My brother is with me."

b. The focus is on the subject, which takes the form of a marked independent personal pronoun (§ 26); infrequent.

 *ink ds(=i) m ḥꜥ.wt* "I myself was in joy."

***Note*:**

Negation of such sentences with  in place of  (§ 37, 47):

 *ḥ3.ty=i n ntf m ẖ.t=i* "My heart, it was not in my body."

§ 44 **2.** Extended adverbial main clauses

a. Introduced by  *iw* (§ 37):

 *iw wdp.w nb ḥr ir.t=f* "Every butler was at his duty."

A pronominal subject is expressed by a suffix-pronoun (§ 28):

 *iw=i ḫr ḥs.wt n.t ḫr nsw* "I am/was under the favour of the king (lit. of by the king)."

Omission of the subject is possible:

 *iw mi sḫr nṯr* "(It) was like the plan of god."

b. Introduced by the verb *wnn* "to exist", which specifies the tense by converting the non-verbal sentence into a verbal sentence.

wnn + subject + adverbial predicate expresses future:

 *wnn b3k m-s3 nb=f* "The servant will be behind his master."

A pronominal subject is expressed by a suffix-pronoun (§ 28):

 *wnn=f m ḫbd n(.y) Rˁ(.w)* "He will be in the disfavour of Re."

c. Introduced by *m=k* (§ 37):

 *m=tn šps.wt ḥr šd.w* "Lo, noble (ladies) are (now) on rafts."

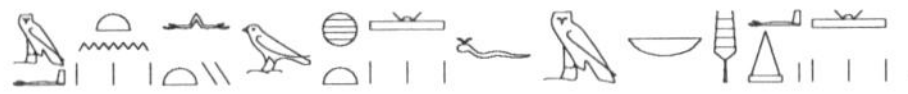 *m=tn iw.ty (i)ḫ.wt=f m nb ˁḥˁ.w* "Lo, he who had nothing is (now) a possessor of treasures."

A pronominal subject is expressed by a dependent personal pronoun (§ 27):

 *m=k wi r gs=k* "Lo, I am at your side."

 *m=k tw ˁ3* "Lo, you are (now) here."

b) EMBEDDED ADVERBIAL SENTENCES

An Adverbial Sentence can be embedded within or attached to a main clause. Here it expresses a circumstance that can be understood as a temporal, causal or modal subordinate clause.

§ 45 **1.** Simple embedded adverbial clauses

"The gods set out, having disguised themselves as dancers, *Ḫnm.w ḥnꜤ=sn ḥr ḳni* Khnum with them carrying the baggage". (modal)

"I spent three days alone, *ib=i m sn.nw=i* my heart (alone) as my companion". (modal)

§ 46 **2.** Extended embedded adverbial clauses

a. Introduced by *ỉst* / *ỉsṯ* / *sṯ* / *st* (§ 37) (also / , after Dyn. 12 also / *ti*):

ḥww=sn[§70] *n=f šnt.yw=f (ỉ)st ḥm=f m Ꜥḥ=f* "They (Re and Amun) smite for him (King Thutmosis II) his enemies, *His Majesty being in his palace.*" (modal – *st* introduces the emphasised adverbial adjunct of an Emphatic Construction – see § 70.1)

ỉt=i pw ntf ink s3=f wḏ.n=f[§71] *n(=i) wnn(=i) ḥr ns.t=f isk wi m im.y sš=f* "He (Amun) is my (Thutmosis III's) father, I am his son. He decreed for me that I should be upon his throne *while I was still a fledgling.*" (temporal – *isk* introduces the emphasised adverbial adjunct of an Emphatic Construction – see § 71.1)

"Year 8, *ỉst ḥm=f ḥr ḫ3s.t Rtnw* while His Majesty was in the hill country of Retenu." (temporal)

"I spent many years under King Intef *ỉsṯ t3 pn ḥr s.t-ḥr=f* while/when this land was under his charge." (temporal)

A pronominal subject is expressed by a dependent personal pronoun (§ 27):

The previous example continues: " ... *sṯ w(i) m b3k=f* " (and) I was his servant." (modal)

"I spent many years under my mistress *ỉsṯ s(y) m s3.t nsw* while she was (held the position of) King's Daughter." (temporal)

b. Introduced by *iw* (only with pronominal subject, i.e. suffix-pronoun):

"Men and women rejoice,  *iw=f m nsw* (now that) he is king." (causal)

"I became an officer in place of my father,  *iw=i m šri* (when) I was (still) a youth." (temporal)\

Note:
In the course of time, *iw* develops into a so-called "circumstantial converter" and then also introduces adverbial subordinate clauses with noun subjects. This only occurs regularly in Late Egyptian, but is already attested in the 11th Dynasty: "It (the gazelle) gave birth upon it (i.e. on the rock), 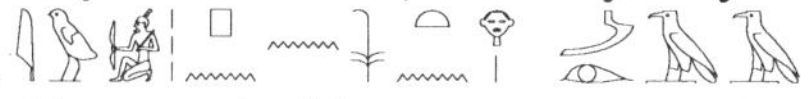 *iw mšꜥ pn n.y nsw ḥr m33* (§ 86) while this army of the king watched."

c) NEGATION of ADVERBIAL SENTENCES **§ 47**

1. Introduced by  *nn* ("it is not the case that", § 37):

 *nn sḫ3(.w)=f ḫr tp(.yw)-t3* "The memory of him is not (will not be) with those who are upon earth."

 *nn rn=f m-m ꜥnḫ.w* "His name is not (will not / shall not be) amongst the living."

A pronominal subject, expressed by a dependent personal pronoun (§ 27), follows the negation:

 *nn wi m ḥr(.y)-ib=sn* "I was not in their midst."

 *nn s(y) m ib=i* "It (the flight) was not in my heart (mind)."

2. Introduced by 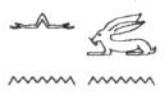 *nn wn* or  *n wn.t*

 *nn wn ḥn.t m ḫ.t=f* "There was no greed in his body."

 *n wn.t iwms im* "There was no lie therein."

3. An embedded adverbial clause is also negated by  *nn*:

"That means that his heart has descended, dropped down,  *nn sw m s.t=f* it (the heart) not being in its place."

§ 48 2) NOMINAL SENTENCES

Nominal Sentences are sentences whose subject and predicate are both formed of nominal expressions. Here, only sentences are dealt with which do not have a nominalised verb form, i.e. a participle, as one of their elements. The latter are dealt with under the *in*-Construction (§ 119–120).

There are three groups of Nominal Sentences:

a) those where both elements of the sentence are formed by nouns (§ 49);

b) those where the first element is an independent pronoun (§§ 50–52);

c) those formed with *pw* (§§ 53–55).

§ 49 **a)** NOMINAL SENTENCES WITH TWO NOUNS

Sentence names:

 *sn.t=f Spd.t* "His sister is Sothis."

 *Ptḥ ṯs.w=n* "Ptah is our commander."

Inalienable matters:

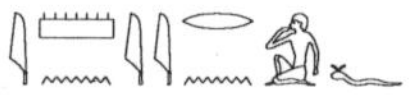 *Ỉmn.y rn=f* "Ameni is his name."

 *it=f ꜥꜣꜣbw* (?) "His father is Aabu."

In the so-called Balanced Sentence:

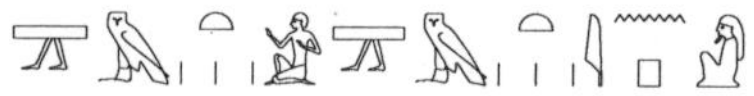 *šm.wt=i šm.wt Ỉnp.w* "My ways are the ways of Anubis"

 *mk.t=t mk.t Rꜥ(.w)* "Your protection is the protection of Re."

b) INDEPENDENT PRONOUN + NOUN/ADJECTIVE: THE *ink*-SENTENCE

There are two groups of *ink*-Sentences: with *unstressed* and *stressed* subject.

1. The *ink*-Sentence with an unstressed subject § 50

Where the subject is not stressed, but merely identified, it only appears in the form of an independent pronoun for the 1st or 2nd person. In the case of the 3rd person, either the *nfr sw*-Sentence (§ 56) or the *pw*-Sentence (§ 53–55) is used:

1st pers.: *ink (I)tm(.w)* "I am Atum."

3rd pers.: NN *(I)tm(.w) pw NN pn* "This NN is Atum."

ink nb i3m.t "I am a lord (possessor) of charm."

ink ḳb "I am quiet."

2. The *ink*-Sentence with a stressed subject § 51

The subject appears in the form of an independent pronoun in the 1st, 2nd and 3rd person:

swt nb=n "*He* is our lord."

ntf s3 Wsir "*He* is the son of Osiris."

Note: In the case of the 1st and 2nd person, one cannot always distinguish between a stressed and an unstressed subject. Sometimes the context makes this possible:

The eloquent peasant says to the chief steward Rensi: "Do not speak falsehood,

ntk iwsw you are the balance."

Sometimes the stressed subject is followed by the enclitic particle *is* (§ 38):

The snake declines the shipwrecked sailor's offers of gifts: "You are not rich in myrrh,

ink is ḥḳ3 Pwnt but *I* am the ruler of Punt."

3. Negation of the *ink*-Sentence § 52

The *ink*-Sentence is negated by ... *n ... is*:

n ink is m(w)t "I am not a dead one."

n ink is ḳ3i s3 "I am not arrogant (lit.: high of back)."

c) THE *pw*-SENTENCE

There are two types of *pw*-Sentences: bi-partite and tri-partite *pw*-Sentences.

WORD ORDER (in both cases): predicate – subject.

§ 53 **1.** The bi-partite *pw*-Sentence

The subject is a demonstrative pronoun (§§ 29–30), as a rule *pw*, which is invariable, and is further qualified by the predicate.

The predicate is formed either by a noun (a) or an independent pronoun (b):

	*it=k pw*	"It/he is your father." (a)
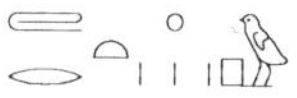	*pẖr.t pw*	"It is a remedy." (a)
	*dp.t m(w)t nn*	"This is the taste of death." (a)
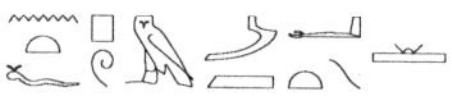	*ntf pw m m3ˁ.t*	"It is really him." (b)
	*ink pw*	"It is me." (b)

When the predicate is formed by an indirect genitive construction, *pw* often splits the genitive construction and immediately follows the *nomen regens*:  *iẖ.t=i pw n.w pr.w it=i* "It is my property of the house (estate) of my father." (Here *iẖ.t* is construed as a masc. plural – see § 17.2).

§ 54 **2.** The tri-partite *pw*-Sentence: noun – *pw* – noun

This sentence is an extension of the bi-partite *pw*-Sentence. Originally, the second noun stood in apposition to the subject *pw*:

 *tẖ pw ns=k* "It is the plummet (of the balance), namely your tongue."

But *pw* merely serves as the copula between the predicate and the subject: "Your tongue is the plummet".

 *dmi pw imn.t* "The west (i.e. the realm of the dead) is a dwelling."

 *bw.t=i pw nm.t nṯr* "The execution block of god is my abomination."

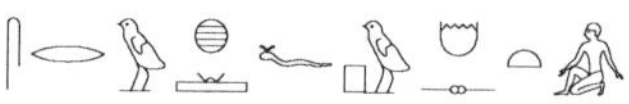 *srwẖ=f pw ḥmsi.t* "Sitting is his treatment."

3. Negation: both types of *pw*-Sentences are negated by ....  *n ... is* **§ 55**

 *iḫ.t=i pw n.w pr.w it=i n iḫ.t is pw pr.w ḥ3.ty-ʿ.w* "It is my property of the estate of my father, it is not the property of the estate of the prince."

 *n wr is pw wr im ʿwn-ib* "The great one there, the greedy one, is no (true) great one."

3) ADJECTIVAL SENTENCES (*nfr sw* - SENTENCES) **§ 56**

WORD ORDER : predicate – subject

Predicate: invariable adjective (§ 22f.) or participle (§ 98–104)

Subject: (1) noun, or (2) dependent pronoun (§ 27, usually 2nd or 3rd person, rarely 1st person).

 *nfr ḥrr.t tn* "This flower is beautiful." (1)

 *nfr tw ḥnʿ=i* "You are/will be happy/well-off with me." (2)

Often, the ending , the "admirative *wy*", is appended to the adjective or participle:

 *nfr.wy sw* "How beautiful it is!" (2)

 *rwḏ.wy sw ib=i* "How firm it is, my heart!" (2)

An interrogative (§ 34) can also take the place of the adjective or participle:

 *ptr (i)r=f* (§38) *sw* "Who, then, is he?" (2)

4) THE ADJECTIVAL SENTENCE with  *nn* or  *nn wn* (see also § 59) **§ 57**

In this sentence type,  *nn* ("it does/did not exist") takes the place of the adjective.
WORD ORDER: predicate – subject. The tense is dependent upon the context.

 *nn m3ʿ.tyw* (§ 23) "There are no just ones."

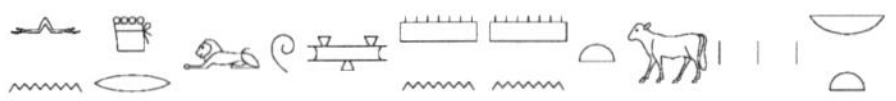 *nn ḏr.w mnmn.t nb.t* "There was no end to all (kinds of) cattle."

 *nn wn pḥ.wy=fy* "His / its end does not exist."

3. Negation: Beide *pw*-Sätze werden negiert durch .... *n ... is* § 55

iḫ.t=i pw n.w pr.w it=i n iḫ.t is pw pr.w ḥ3.ty-ʿ.w "Es ist mein Besitz vom Hause meines Vaters, es ist nicht Besitz (vom) Hause des Fürsten."

n wr is pw wr im ʿwn-ib "Der Große da, der habgierig ist, ist kein (wahrhaft) Großer."

3) ADJEKTIVALSATZ (*nfr sw* - Satz) § 56

WORTSTELLUNG: Prädikat – Subjekt

Prädikat: invariables Adjektiv (§ 22) bzw. Partizip (§§ 98–104)

Subjekt: Substantiv (1) oder abhängiges Personalpronomen (§ 27, meist 2. oder 3. Person, nur selten 1. Person) (2).

	nfr ḥrr.t tn	"Diese Blume ist schön." (1)
	nfr tw ḥnʿ=i	"Du hast es gut bei mir." (2)

Oft wird an das Partizip oder Adjektiv die Endung , das "admirative *wy*", angehängt:

	nfr.wy sw	"Wie schön ist es!" (2)
	rwḏ.wy sw ib=i	"Wie stark ist es doch, mein Herz!" (2)

An Stelle des Partizips kann auch ein Fragepronomen (§ 34) treten:

ptr (i)r=f (§38) *sw* "Wer ist er denn?" (2)

4) ADJEKTIVALSATZ mit *nn* , (vgl. auch § 59): § 57

Hier steht *nn* ("es gibt/gab nicht") an Stelle des Adjektivs bzw. Partizips.

WORTSTELLUNG: Prädikat – Subjekt

Die Zeitstufe ist abhängig vom Kontext.

nn m3ʿ.tyw (§ 23) "Gerechte gibt es nicht."

nn ḏr.w mnmn.t nb.t "Ein Ende von Vieh aller Art gab es nicht."

nn wn pḥ.wy=fy "Sein Ende gibt es nicht."

§ 58 5) EXPRESSIONS OF POSSESSION

Egyptian does not have a verb for "to have/belong to". Possession is expressed by

a) the invariable *nisbe*-adjective *n.y* (§ 23):

n.y ꜥnḫ W3ḏ.yt (§ 10 c) "Life belongs to Wadjet (Uto)."

A pronominal subject is expressed by a dependent pronoun (§ 27):

n.y wi Ḥr.w "I belong to Horus."

n.y sw Ḥr.w "He belongs to Horus." (NB the writing with , phonetic *ns*, is influenced by the close relationship between the *nisbe*-adjective and the pronoun.)

b) the preposition *n* (§ 35) (dative):

wr n=f irp r mw "To him belongs more wine than water."

iw n=k ꜥnḫ "To you belongs life."

c) the preposition *n* + suffix-pronoun + *im* or *im.y*:

n=k im.y ḥḏ "To you belongs silver."

d) the *nisbe n.y* + independent pronoun (§ 27):
(*n.y* + *ink* > *nnk*; the initial *n.y* is not written with the other pronouns.)

nnk p.t "To me belongs the sky."

ntk ꜥnḫ "To you belongs life."

ntk nḥḥ ḏ.t "Yours are eternity and everlastingness."

e) *nb* "lord / possessor of" + direct genitive (§ 18):

ink nb pr.w "I am the lord/owner of a house."

§ 59 6) NON - POSSESSION

Non-possession is expressed by Adjectival Sentences (§ 57).

nn + "dative" (§ 58 b): *nn n=k st* "It does not belong to you."

or *nn wn* + noun + genitive: *nn wn ib n.y si* "Man has no understanding (lit.: there does not exist the heart / understanding of a man)."

H) THE VERB

TERMINOLOGY: radical, root, stem

As in the case of the Semitic languages, the meaning of a word is dependent upon an abstract grammatical entity known as the "root" which comprises a number of radicals (root consonants). The stem is formed from the root, which can be modified, e.g. by reduplication of a radical, by addition of the causative prefix *s*, and (unwritten) vowels. Grammatical endings (fem. *t* and plural *w*) and other elements (see e.g. §§ 68, 76, 80) are appended to the stem.

1) VERB CLASSES

The formal classification of a verb is dependent on three criteria:

a) THE NUMBER OF ROOT CONSONANTS **§ 60**

Verbs are classified according to the number of radicals in their root. They form the following classes (in order of frequency):

3 radicals  *sḏm* "to hear"

2 radicals  *ḏd* "to speak"

4 radicals 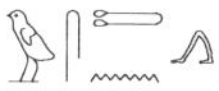 *wsṯn* "to stride"

There is one verb with 1 radical:  *i* "to say"

and several with 5 radicals, e.g.  *nhmhm* "to roar".

b) CAUSATIVE *S* **§ 61**

A verb is given causative meaning through the addition of the prefix *s*:

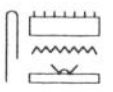 *s* + *mn* "cause to remain" (< *mn* "remain")

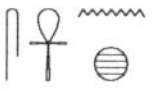 *s* + *ʿnḫ* "cause to live, vivify" (< *ʿnḫ* "to live")

In the case of verbs that have *w* as their first consonant, this consonant is usually elided in the causative:

 *s* + *ʿb* "purify" (< *wʿb* "to be pure")

§ 62 c) MODIFIABILITY OF THE ROOT

1. Strong verbs are invariable; they have two, three or four radicals.

2. Weak verbs are variable and one distinguishes three groups as follows:

§ 63 a. Ultimae infirmae verbs (ult. inf.)

The final radical is weak (*i*, *y*, or *w*).

tertiae infirmae (IIIae inf.):  *mri* "to love"

 *msi* "to give birth"

 *ršw* "to rejoice"

quartae infirmae (IVae inf.):  *msḏi* "to hate"

 *m3wy* "to be new"

Note: Some verbs with *i* as their final radical are strong, and therefore their root remains unchanged, e.g. 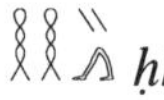 *ḥḥi* "to seek",  *tni* "to age".

§ 64 b. Ultimae geminatae verbs (ult. gem.)

These are verbs whose last radical is the same as the penultimate radical:

secundae geminatae (IIae gem.):  *ḳbb* "to be cool"

tertiae geminatae (IIIae gem.):  *pḥrr* "to run"

§ 65 c. Irregular verbs:

These verbs belong to one of the above classes of weak verbs but, in certain forms, they differ from the other verbs in their group:

 *iwi* "to come" (IIIae inf.)

 *ini* "to bring" (IIIae inf.)

 *wnn* "to be" (IIae gem.)

 *m33* "to see" (IIae gem.)

 *rḏi* "to give" (IIIae inf.)

2) VERB GROUPS **§ 66**

Verbs are classified into the following groups on the basis of their syntactic properties:

Transitive (trans.) verbs, those that can take a direct object;

Intransitive (intrans.) verbs are those that do not take a direct object. The verbs of movement ("to come", "to go", etc.) and verbs expressing a quality or adjective-verbs (e.g. "to be sweet", "to be cool", etc.) belong to this group.

Voice – Active and Passive: All verbs can form the passive, apart from the adjective-verbs (see §§ 76–79).

3) IMPERATIVE **§ 67**

a) FORMS

Only forms for the 2nd person singular and the plural are attested, no gender is discernible.

sg.  *sḏm* "hear!" pl.  *sḏm(.w)* ;  *sḏm.w* "hear!"

Irregular imperative forms:

rḏi:  (also , ) *imi* "give!"

iwi:  *mi* "come!"

Other special forms:

 *m* "take" followed by the reflexive dative *n=* (see below) is regularly written with the bi-literal sign :  *m n=k* "take to yourself!"

b) REINFORCING THE IMPERATIVE

1. With a dependent pronoun (§ 27):

 *wḏꜣ.w tn* "go!"

2. By means of the so-called reflexive dative (directs the action to the interest of the implied subject):

 *sḫꜣ n=k hrw.w n.y ḳrs* "Remember the day of burial!"

3. *ir* + suffix-pronoun > invariable *(i)r=f* ,  (§ 38):

 *sḏm.w r=f ṯn* "Hear ye!"

4) FINITE VERB FORMS

§ 68 THE SUFFIX CONJUGATION

The subject follows the stem or, in some cases, a grammatical ending. Elements such as *n* (§ 71), *tw* (§ 76) or *in, ḫr, k3* (§ 80) appear between the stem and the subject. A pronominal subject is expressed by one of the suffix-pronouns of § 28. For transliteration conventions see § 13.

1. ACTIVE VOICE

§ 69 a. CIRCUMSTANTIAL (PRESENT) *sḏm=f* / *iri=f*

Form of the weak stem:

IIae gem.: *ḳbb* "to be cool"  *ḳbb*

m33 "to see"  *m33*

IIIae inf.: *iri* "to do" *iri*

iwi "to come"  *iwi* (regular), but also  *iyi*

rḏi "to give"  *ḏi*

Usage:

The Circumstantial *sḏm=f* is a verbal verb form.

1. Normally, the bare Circumstantial *sḏm=f* is only found in non-initial position in a sentence, namely in adverbial subordinate clauses (but see also §§ 123, 126):

Modal clause:

 *iw iri.n=i* (§ 91.1) *pri.t Wpi-w3.wt wḏ3=f r* (§ 85.2) *nḏ it=f* "I conducted the procession of (the god) Wepwawet as he goes forth in order to protect his father."

Temporal clause:

 *iri=t* (§ 75) *hrw.w nfr wn=t tp t3* "May you(§ 75) spend a happy day while you are on earth."
(See also the second example of Perfective *sḏm.n=f*, § 71.1).

2. When used in a main clause in initial position, the Circumstantial *sḏm=f* is always preceded by a particle, e.g. *iw* (§ 92 Complex Aorist I) or *m=k* (§ 97 Presentative).

b. AORIST *sḏm=f / irr=f* § 70

Form of the weak stem (characteristic feature: gemination of the last radical):

IIae gem.:	*ḳbb*	"to be cool"	 *ḳbb*
	m33	"to see"	 *m33*,  *m3*
IIIae inf.:	*iri*	"to do"	,  *irr*
	iwi	"to come"	,  *iww*
	rḏi	"to give"	,  *ḏḏ*

Usage:

The Aorist *sḏm=f / irr=f* is a nominal verb form. It expresses something that is generally valid, or a recurring event. The tense required in a translation is determined by the context. It is found in initial position in a main clause and serves as a noun.

1. In initial position in main clauses

a. In the Emphatic Construction. Here the focus of interest is not on the verbal action of the main clause but rather on a following adverbial expression (§ 118, 122; also first example in § 46).

 *prr=i ḥsi.kw m ꜥḥ* "I (regularly) went forth, having been praised in the Palace." (The emphasised adverbial expression takes the form of the modal clause *ḥsi.kw* (§ 81) *m ꜥḥ*). To indicate the emphasis, this construction can be translated as a cleft sentence (§ 118): "That I used to go forth was having been praised in the palace."

 *ḏḏ tw ḫ3s.t n ḫ3s.t ḫr sḫ n.y ib=k n=k* "That one foreign land gave you to (another) foreign land was under the counsel of your own heart." (The modal clause *ḫr sḫ n.y ib=k n=k* is the emphasised adverbial expression.) ***Note:***  for  and for  as often the case in hieratic texts.

b. In the so-called Balanced Sentence (§§ 49, 71.1d, 132):

 *prr=ṯn r p.t m nr.wt prr=i ḥr tp.t ḏnḥ.w=ṯn* "(If) you ascend to the sky as vultures, I ascend upon the top of your wings."

 *m3 sw nṯr.w ḏḏ=sn n=f i3w* "(If) the gods see him, they give him praise."

2. In the position of a noun

a. As the object of another verb, i.e. in object clauses, particularly after *rḫ* "to know", *m33* "to see", *wḏ* "to command" and *mri* "to desire / wish":

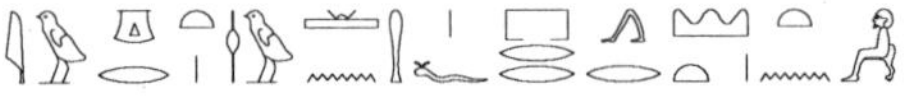 *iw gr.t wḏ.n ḥm=f prr(=i) r ḫ3s.t tn šps(.t)* "Now, his Majesty commanded that I go forth to this noble foreign land."

b. As subject of an Adjectival Sentence (§ 56)

 *ḳsn mss=s* "Her giving birth is difficult."

c. Following certain prepositions, e.g. *m* "as, in as much as", *mi* "as when, like", *r* "as", "until", *ḥr* "because", *ḫft* "when":

"As for every *wab*-priest, every priest, every phylarch and every female phylarch who will be in this city,  *m mrr=ṯn Wpi-w3.wt nṯr=ṯn bnr mrw.t* (§ 24 d) in as much as you love Wepwawet, your dearly beloved god, (so may you speak an offering prayer for me)."

"It was like a dream, 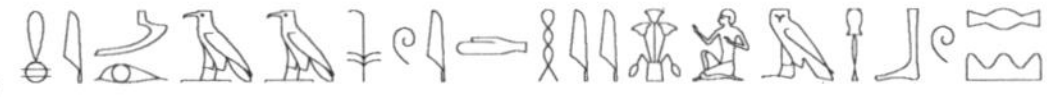 *mi m33 sw* (§ 27.1) *idḥ.y m 3bw* like a marsh-dweller seeing himself in Elephantine."

§ 71 **c. (PRESENT) PERFECT *sḏm.n=f* / *iri.n=f***

Corresponding to the Aorist *sḏm=f* / *irr=f* and the Circumstantial Present *sḏm=f* there are two *sḏm.n=f* forms – one nominal and one verbal (also called "Circumstantial-*sḏm.n=f*") – that cannot always be clearly distinguished morphologically (see Preface).

Form of the weak stem:

IIae gem.:	*ḳbb*	"to be cool"		*ḳbb.n*[1] ; *ḳb.n*[2]
	wnn	"to exist"		*wn=f* [1] (in place of **wnn.n*)
			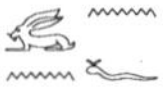	*wn.n=f* [2]
	m33	"to see"		*m3.n=f* [2]
IIIae inf.:	*iri*	"to do"	 (rare)	*iri.n=f*
	iwi	"to come"	 (usual)	*iyi.n*
			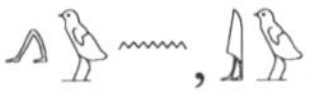 (rare)	*iwi.n*
	rḏi	"to give"		*rḏi.n=f* [3]
				*ḏi.n=f* [4]

Notes:

[1] Nominal verb form.

[2] Verbal verb form; *m33* irregular.

[3] Often nominal verb form; regularly after negative *n* (see § 71.3).

[4] Often verbal verb form (see § 71.2) and in performative statements (see § 71.4).

Usage:

1. Nominal verb form

a. In the **Emphatic Construction** (cp. § 70.1) the *sḏm.n=f* stands at the beginning of a section of text or in an independent sentence (see also second example in § 46):  *ḏd.n=i m m3ʿ.t* "*In truth* have I spoken."

 *iyi.n=i m ḫnt ḫr ḥm=f ḏi=f sip=i it.w nṯr.w* "I have come from the presence of His Majesty, he ordaining that I inspect the fathers of the gods." (Emphasis on the adverbial subordinate clause; *ḏi=f* Circumstantial Present *sḏm=f* [§ 69.1] followed by *sip=i* Subjunctive *sḏm=f* [§ 75]).

 *pšš.n s(y) mw.t=k Nw.t ḥr=k m rn=s n(.y) Štpt* "*In her name Shetepet (=Wadi Natrun)* has your mother Nut spread herself over you." (Note geminating form of IIae gem. verb *pšš*.)

b. In an object clause (uncommon):  *ir gmi=k*(§ 131) *ṯs.n=f* "If you should find that it (the stomach) has knotted ...".

c. After prepositions (e.g. *m-ḫt* "after", *r* "until", *mi* "like", *ḫft* "according to"):

The daughter of the nomarch ruled  *r ḫpr.n s3=s m nḫt-ʿ.w* "until her son had become an adult (lit.: one strong of arm)."

"You will act in the afterlife  *mi iri.n=k tp t3* like you did on earth."

d. In the Balanced Sentence:  *pri.n=sn r p.t m bik.w pri.n=i ḥr ḏnḥ(.wy)=sn* "(If) they went up to the sky as falcons, I went up on their wings." (cp. §§ 49, 70.1b, 118, 132)

2. Verbal verb form (in verbal main clauses and subordinate clauses):

a. Usually, the *sḏm.n=f* only takes initial position in a main clause as **part of a Complex Verb Form** (§§ 91a and 95.1, but see also §§ 123, 126).

b. Paratactically in a main clause:
In a main clause, which is part of a longer section of text, the verbal *sḏm.n=f* can paratactically follow a verb form at the head of a section of text:

i. Following the Complex Verb Form *ꜥḥꜥ.n sḏm.n=f* (§ 95.1):

Sinuhe recounts what he did after his victory over the hero of Retenu:  *ꜥḥꜥ.n ini.n=i iẖ.t=f ḥ3k.n=i mnmn.t=f* "Then I fetched his property and plundered his herd."

ii. Following the Complex Verb Form *iw sḏm.n=f* (§ 91a):

iw ḫrp.n=i k3.t m nšm.t msi.n=i in.w=s iri.n=i h3kr n nb=f "I directed the work on the *Neshmet*-barque (of Osiris); I made its ropes, I performed the *Haker*-festival for its lord (Osiris)."

iii. Following the Complex Verb Form *iw(=f) sḏm=f* (§ 92 Complex Aorist I):

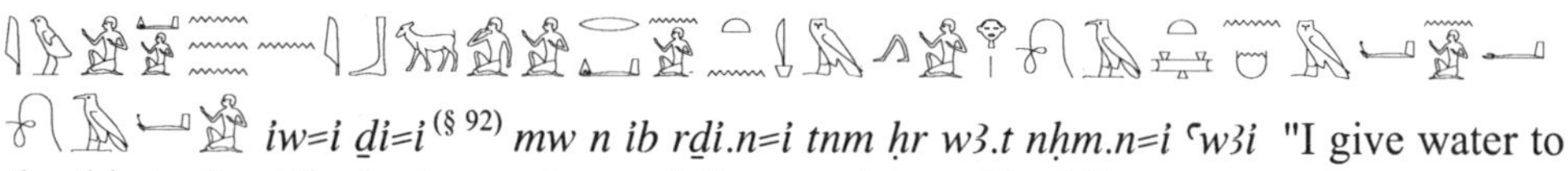 *iw=i ḏi=i* (§ 92) *mw n ib rḏi.n=i tnm ḥr w3.t nḥm.n=i ꜥw3i* "I give water to the thirsty, I set the lost upon the road, I rescued the robbed."

c. In verbal subordinate clauses:

In subordinate clauses the verbal *sḏm.n=f* is only used with ***transitive*** verbs. In the case of ***intransitive*** verbs the Old Perfective (§ 81) is utilised:

Following the king's letter Sinuhe continues:  *spr.n wḏ pn r=i ꜥḥꜥ.kw m ḥr(.y)-ib wḥw.t=i šdi.ntw=f n=i ḏi.n(=i) wi ḥr ẖ.t=i* "This letter reached me *as I was standing in the midst of my tribe*; it was read to me *I having placed myself on my belly* (as a mark of respect for the king)." Two nominal *sḏm.n=f* forms (§ 71.1) in Emphatic Constructions (the second a *tw*-passive, § 76) are followed by emphasised verbal subordinate clauses, the first an Old Perfective, since the verb is intransitive, the second a verbal *sḏm.n=f*. The emphasis is on the contrast between Sinuhe's postures: *standing* in the midst of his tribe, *prostrate* when the king's letter is read to him.

The caravan leader Sabni says: 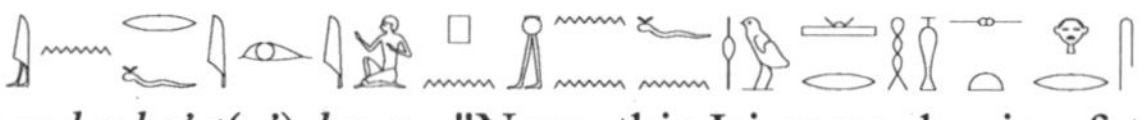 *iyi.n (i)r=f Iri pn* (§ 71.1) *ini.n=f n(=i) wḏ r ḥsi.t(=i) ḥr=s* "Now, this Iri came, having fetched for (me) a decree to praise (me) because of it." (*ini.n=f* in a temporal subordinate clause)

King Sesostris III writes to Ikhernofret:  *iri.n ḥm=i* (§71.1) *nw m3.n=i ṯw m iḳr sḫr* "My Majesty has done this (entrusted Ikhernofret with a task), after I recognised (lit.: saw) you as one excellent of counsel." (*m3.n=i* in a temporal subordinate clause)

3. Following the negation ***n*** **:** *n sḏm.n=f* ("He does not/can not hear").

This is the negative equivalent of both the Circumstantial Present *sḏm=f* and the Complex Aorist I *iw(=f) sḏm=f* (§§ 136 a, 142 b; see Table 3 – p. 85).

4. In performative statements: In captions accompanying the representations of the king with the gods on temple walls, the verbal *sḏm.n=f* appears where one of the persons (king or god) speaks in the 1st person:

In a scene where Amun hands King Sesostris the sign of life: "Words spoken by Amun-Re, King of the Gods: *di.n=(i) n=k ꜥnḫ wꜣs nb r šr.t=k nṯr nfr* I have (herewith) given you all life and dominion to your nose, perfect god."

d. (HISTORIC) PERFECT *sḏm=f* / *iri=f* § 72

Form of the weak stem:

IIae gem.:	*ḳbb*	"to be cool"	, *ḳb, ḳbb*
	mꜣꜣ	"to see"	*mꜣꜣ* (frequent); *mꜣ*
IIIae inf.:	*iri*	"to do"	*iri*
	iwi	"to come"	*iwi*, *iyi*
	rḏi	"to give"	, *rḏi*

Usage:

The (Historic) Perfect *sḏm=f* is an Old Egyptian form which is occasionally used in Middle Egyptian as a past tense form in main clauses:

In a biographical text of the Middle Kingdom: *rḏi wi ḥm=f r sš n.y tmꜣ* "His Majesty appointed me scribe of the cadaster."

The Perfect *sḏm=f* is mainly used in specific constructions:

1. After the Negative *n*, in the negative equivalent of the Perfect *sḏm.n=f*: *n sḏm=f* "he did not hear" (§ 138).

2. After certain prepositions, e.g. *ḏr* "since", *m-ḫt* "after", *m* "when" and *n* "because:

ḏr grg.tw(§ 76) *tꜣ pn* "since this land was founded."

The priest will bring offerings *m-ḫt pri=f* "after he has gone forth (and has performed the rituals in the temples)."

"I was a priest with my father *m wn=f tp tꜣ* when he was upon earth."

§ 73 e. The Form *sḏm.t=f*

Form of the weak stem:

IIae gem.:	*wnn*	"to be"		*wn.t*
	m33	"to see"		*m3n.t*
IIIae inf.:	*iri*	"to do"		*iri.t*
	iwi	"to come"		*iyi.t*
	rḏi	"to give"	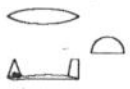 *rḏi.t*, 	*ḏi.t*

Usage:

The *sḏm.t=f* is used in only a limited number of constructions:

1. Following the negative *n*, to express an action that has not yet occurred: *n sḏm.t=f* "he has not yet heard / before he heard".

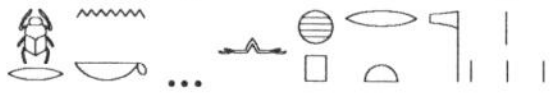 *ḫpr.n=k ... n ḫpr.t nṯr.w* "You came into being ... before the gods came into being."

2. After the prepositions *r* "until" and *ḏr* "since, until":

"A torch is lit for you in the night,  *r wbn.t šw ḥr šnb.t=k* until the sun shines on your breast."

"I was in this land under his (the king's) command, 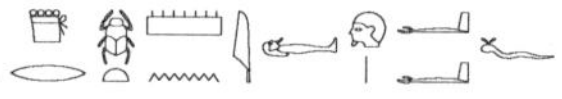 *ḏr ḫpr.t mni tp ꜥ.wy=f(y)* until death came to pass upon his arms (i.e. he died)."

§ 74 f. FUTURE (PROSPECTIVE) *sḏm(.y/w)=f / iri(.y/w)=f*[1]

Form of the weak stem:

IIae gem.:	*ḳbb*	"to be cool"		*ḳbb*
	wnn	"to be"		*wnn*
	m33	"to see"		*m33*
IIIae inf.:	*iri*	"to do"		*iri, iri.y*
	iwi	"to come"		*iwi*
	rḏi	"to give"		*rḏi*
	ḫdi	"travel downstream"		*ḫdi.w*

Note: [1]The endings are often not written. When the subject is a noun, the ending *w* is sometimes found in place of *y*. In the course of time the distinction between the Future and Subjunctive *sḏm=f* (§ 75) was lost.

Usage:

The Future (Prospective) *sḏm=f* is used both as a nominal and a verbal form. A morphological distinction between the two has not been identified.

1. Nominal verb form

a. In the Emphatic Construction (see also §§ 70.1a, 71.1):

 *sʿm.y=k ir=f m išst* "*What*, then, will you eat (lit.: swallow)?"

 NN  *sʿm.w NN m ḥ(n)k.t n.t bd.t dšr.t* "*Beer of red barley* will NN drink (lit. swallow)."

b. In an object clause, serving as the object of certain verbs, e.g. *rḫ* "to know", *m33* "to see", *wḏ* "to command", *mri* "to desire/wish", *sḫ3* "remember":

The king says of the god: 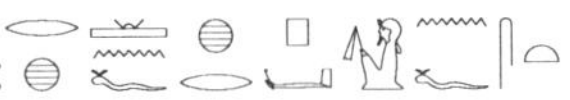 *rḫ.n=f ḫrp=i n=f st* "He knows that I will govern it (the land) for him."

 ...  ... *m mrr=ṯn* (§ 70.2c) ... *sḏd.w=ṯn mšʿ=ṯn n ḥm.wt=ṯn* "in as much as you wish ... that you will tell your wives about your expedition ..."

2. Verbal verb form

a. In main clauses

Maat (justice) will take its place, disorder having been cast out;  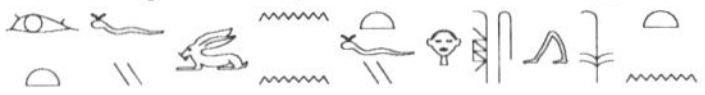 *ršw.y gmḥ.t(y)=fy* (§ 112) *wnn.t(y)=fy ḥr šms nsw* "he who will see (it) and who will be in the entourage of the king will rejoice."

 *sḏd=i b3.w=k n iti.y* "I will recount your (divine) power to the sovereign."

b. Following the non-enclitic particle *k3* (§ 37):

The king would like to sail over a canal but is unable to do so because there is no water in the canal. The magician Djedi then says:  *k3 rḏi=i ḫpr mw* (§ 75.2) "Then I will let water come into being."

c. In final or consecutive clauses, expressing purpose or consequence:

Following an imperative:  *iri m33=k* "Act, and you will see."

d. In the *in*-Construction (§§ 119–120).

e. In the Old Egyptian negative Future ***n** sḏm(.w)=f / iri.y=f / iri.w* + noun subject. This is the equivalent of the Middle Egyptian *nn sḏm=f* (§ 142 c), which appears mainly in archaising texts, e.g. the Coffin Texts.

f. Following the particle in fulfillable conditions (§ 131.1).

§ 75 **g. SUBJUNCTIVE** *sḏm=f / iri(.y)=f* [1]

Form of the weak stem:

IIae gem.:	*ḳbb*	"to be cool"	*ḳb*
	wnn	"to be"	*wn*
	mꜣꜣ	"to see"	*mꜣn*, *mꜣ*
IIIae inf.:	*iri*	"to do"	*iri.y*, *iri*
	iwi	"to come"	*iwt*
	ini	"to bring"	*int*
	rḏi	"to give"	*ḏi*

Note: [1] Endings often not written. In the course of time, the distinction between the Future *sḏm=f* (§ 74) and the Subjunctive *sḏm=f* was lost.

Usage:

1. In wishes, with or without an introductory particle:

a. without a particle:

iri.y n=k Ḥr.y-ši=f nb Nn-nsw ib=k "May Herishef, the Lord of Heracleopolis, fulfil for you your wish!"

b. with a particle:

kꜣ iri=tw ḫft ir.y "May one act accordingly!"

iḫ mꜣn=k n=k (§ 67b) *iri.tw iḫ.t nb.t mi n.tyt r hp* "May you see (to it) that everything is done like that which is according to the law." (*iri.tw iḫ.t nb.t* is the *tw*-Passive, § 76).

2. In an object clause, ie. as a nominal verb form serving as the object of another verb, in particular *rḏi* and its imperative *imi* "to cause that, to let"; also *ḏd* "say" and *ḫmt* "intend, plan":

 *ḏi=k iwt ꜥḥꜥ.w=i pwy n sbi.t r imꜣḫ* "May you let this my lifetime reach the achieving of veneration."

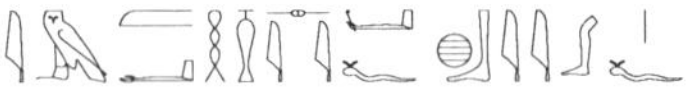 *imi ḥsi.y=f ḫbi.y=f* "Let him sing and dance."

 *ḏd.n=f ꜥḥꜣ=f ḥnꜥ=i* "He said he would fight with me." (see also § 124 example 2)

3. In final or consecutive clauses, expressing purpose or consequence:

 *iḫ iwt n=i rmṯ.w nṯr.w mꜣ=sn wi* "May men and gods come to me so that they may see me!"

 *iyi.n=i mꜣn=i Wsir ꜥnḫ=i r-gs=f* "I have come, that I may see Osiris and live at his side."

4. In the negative equivalent of the Complex Future *iw=f r sḏm* (§ 94): *nn sḏm=f* "he will not hear" (lit.: "that he will hear does not exist", see § 142 c).

5. In the negative verb form *n-sp sḏm=f* "it did not occur, that he heard" (§ 142 a).

6. Following the particle 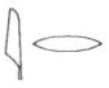 *ir* in fulfillable conditions (§ 131.1).

2. PASSIVE VOICE

a. *tw*-PASSIVE (with the passive element  *tw*) **§ 76**

The passive of the suffix-conjugation is usually formed through affixing the passive element  *tw* (related to the indefinite pronoun *tw* "one", § 27) to the stem or to a modifying element, such as, for example, the tense element *n*:

 (or )	*sḏm.tw=k*	"you are heard"
	*sḏm.ntw=k*	"you were heard", etc.

Usage: The usage of the *tw*-Passive corresponds to that of the active forms, e.g.:

Aorist *sḏm.tw=f* in the Emphatic Construction (§ 70.1):

 *dgg.tw=f mi Rꜥ.w wbn=f* "He (the king) is seen like Re when he rises."

Present Perfect *sḏm.ntw=f* in the Emphatic Construction (§ 71.1):

 *iri.nt(w)=f r ḥwi.t Sṯ.tyw* "That he (the king) was made is in order to smite the Asiatics." (*r* + infinitive §§ 35, 85.2; for , for)

Special Passive Forms:

§ 77 **b.** PERFECTIVE PASSIVE *sḏm(.w/y)=f* / *iri(.w/y)=f*

The -ending occasionally appears with both weak and strong verbs; with weak verbs one also finds the ending . However, as a rule, no ending is written.

Form of the weak stem:

IIIae inf.:	*iri*	"to do":	*iri* , *iri.w*, *iri.y*
	rḏi	"to give":	*rḏi*, *rḏi.w*, *rḏi.y*

Usage:

The Perfective Passive *sḏm(.w/y)=f* appears predominantly in adverbial subordinate clauses with a nominal subject; with a pronominal subject the Old Perfective (§ 81) is used. However, it also occurs in main clauses after particles and in the Emphatic Construction.

In main clauses:

 *m=k wḏ(.w) swꜥb=k* (§74.3) *pꜣ rꜣ-pr.w n.y ꜣbḏ.w rḏi(.w) n=k ḥmw.w r n.t-ꜥ.w=f* "Behold, it has been commanded that you restore (lit.: purify) this temple of Abydos. Craftsmen have been assigned (lit.: given) to you to organise it."

The following sentence contains three examples of this form: the first occurs in an Emphatic Construction in a main clause, the following two in subordinate clauses:

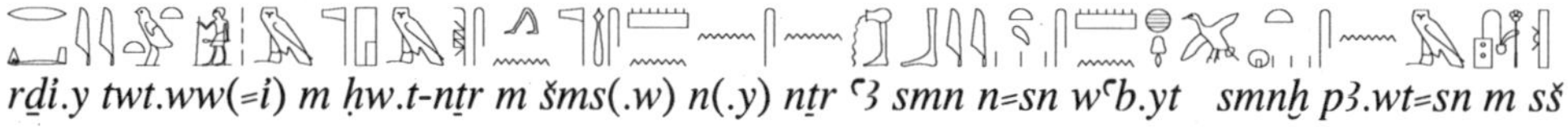
rḏi.y twt.ww(=i) m ḥw.t-nṯr m šms(.w) n(.y) nṯr ꜥꜣ smn n=sn wꜥb.yt smnḫ pꜣ.wt=sn m sš "(My) statues were placed in the temple in the following of the great god, offerings having been established for them, their offering bread having been fixed in writing."

 *msi.y=i m ḥꜣ.t-sp 1 n(.t) sꜣ Rꜥ.w Imn.w-m-ḥꜣ.t* "I was born in year 1 of the Son of Re, Amenemhet." (Emphatic Construction)

In subordinate clauses:

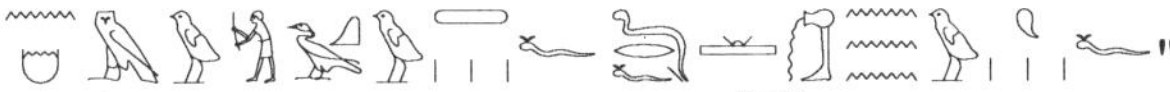 *ỉmỉ ḫsf.tw n=f m ỉꜣw.t ṯf n.t ḥw.t-nṯr m sꜣ n sꜣ iwꜥ n iwꜥ ptḫ(.w)* (§81) *ḥr tꜣ nḥm.w ꜥḳ.w=f ḏrf wꜥb.w=f* "Let that temple office be taken from him from son to son and heir to heir, they (the heirs) being cast to the ground (i.e. deprived of their offices), his income and the title deed of his meat-offering having been confiscated."

Note: 1. The Old Perfective (§ 81) is used where the subject is pronominal.

2. If the logical subject is expressed, it is introduced by 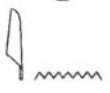 "by" (cp. § 79, last example).

c. PASSIVE *sḏm.t=f* / *ỉrỉ.yt=f* **§ 78**

Form of the weak stem:

IIIae inf.:	*ỉrỉ*	"to do"	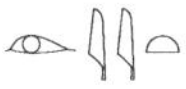	*ỉrỉ.yt*
	msỉ	"to bear"		*msỉ.yt* (also 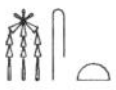)

Usage:

This form is the passive equivalent of the form *sḏm.t=f* (§ 73). The following sentence contains an example of each:

 *ḫpr.n=k n msỉ.yt rmṯ(.t) n ḫpr.t nṯr.w* "You came into being before humankind was born, before the gods came into being."

d. FUTURE PASSIVE *sḏmm=f* / *ỉrỉ.w=f* **§ 79**

This is an Old Egyptian form. It is largely replaced by forms of the *tw*-Passive (§ 76). In Middle Egyptian it is found almost exclusively in archaic or archaising religious texs, in particular the Coffin Texts. It is characterised by the gemination of the last radical of the strong verbs (except for causatives); the form *ỉrỉ.w=f* is found with both weak and causative verbs.

 *Ỉ gr.w ỉpp NN pn ḥr msḫn.t* "O (you) silent ones! This NN will be examined upon the birthing stool."

 *rḏỉ(.w) n=f ꜥḳ.w=s* "Its (the office's) income will be given to him."

Negation with *n*:

n ḫfꜥꜥ=i in Šw n ꜣmm=i in ꜣkr.w "I will not be grasped by Shu, I will not be grasped by the earth-gods."

§ 80 3. THE CONTINGENT TENSES *sḏm.in=f, sḏm.ḫr=f, sḏm.kꜣ=f*

Form:

The element *in*, *ḫr*, or *kꜣ* appears between stem and subject.

Usage:

These verb forms only appear in main clauses. The activity expressed is conditional on a previous action.

a. CONTINGENT PERFECT *sḏm.in=f* "Now/then he heard ..."

Often found in narrative texts:

The eloquent peasant was beaten and began to cry loudly: *ḏd.in Nmt.y-nḫt pn m ḳꜣi ḫrw=k sḫ.ty* "Then this Nemty-nakht said: 'Do not raise your voice, peasant!'"

Nemty-nakht says to the peasant: "Watch out, peasant, lest you tread on my clothing! *ḏd.in sḫ.ty pn iri.y=i ḥsi.t=k* (§ 109) Then this peasant said: 'I will do what you will praise!'"

King Khufu commands that the lector priest Djedi be brought to him and then he himself goes into the audience chamber: *stꜣ.intw n=f Ḏdi* "Then Djedi was ushered in to him ..." (*tw*-Passive)

b. CONTINGENT AORIST *sḏm.ḫr=f* "Then he hears ..."

The person for whom a particular ritual is performed: "he is powerful amongst the gods, *wnn.ḫr=f mi wꜥ im=sn* then he is like one of them."

sḏm.ḫr=f often follows a conditional clause introduced by *ir* (§ 131):

ir swi=f mw stp.ḫr=f "If he drinks water, then he chokes."

The construction *ḫr=f sḏm=f* has the same meaning:

The deceased has successfully passed one of the gates of the netherworld: "Then he reaches another gate. He finds the two sisters standing there.

ḏd.ḫr=sn n=f mi sn=n ṯw ḫr=sn šʿ=sn šr.t ḥnʿ sp.ty n.t ḫm rn.w=sn
Then they say to him, 'Come, that we may kiss you!' Then they cut off the nose and lips of him who does not know their names."

c. CONTINGENT FUTURE *sḏm.k3=f* "Then he will / should hear..."
(expresses consequence):

In a tomb inscription the visitors to the tomb are called on to make an offering to the tomb owner from what they may have with them:

"If you have nothing with you,  *ḏd.k3=ṯn m r3=ṯn* then you should say …"

The deceased says: "If you do not let me escape from my enemies,

pri.k3 Ḥʿpy r p.t ʿnḫ=f m m3ʿ.t
h3i.k3 (i)r=f Rʿ.w r mw ʿnḫ=f m rm.w
then Hapy will go forth to the sky, that he may live off Maat,
then Re will descend to the water, that he may live off fish."

The constructions *k3=f sḏm=f* / *k3 sḏm=f* have the same meaning:

"May you do as I say.  *k3 ḥtp M3ʿ.t r s.t=s* Then Maat will rest in her place."

"Is it a Nubian?  *k3 iri=n mk.t=n* Then we will protect ourselves." ( for , § 37).

OVERVIEW OF FORMS – STEMS OF THE WEAK VERBS (ACTIVE VOICE)

		INDICATIVE				SUB-JUNCTIVE
		Perfect	**Aorist**	**Circumstantial Present**	**Future (Prospective)**	
IIae gem	general	*ḳbb*[1], *ḳb*[2]	*ḳbb*	*ḳbb*	*ḳbb*	*ḳb*
	mꜣꜣ "see"	*mꜣꜣ* *mꜣ*	*mꜣꜣ*	*mꜣꜣ*	*mꜣꜣ*	*mꜣn* *mꜣ*
IIIae inf	general	*iri*	*irr* ,	*iri*	*iri* *iri.y* *hꜣi(w)*[3]	*iri* *iri.y*
	iwi "come"	*iyi* , (*iwi*)	*iww* , (*iw(w)*)	*iwi* (*iyi*)	*iwi*	*iwt*
	ini "bring"	*ini*	---	*ini*	*ini*	*int*
	rḏi "give"	*rḏi*[4] , *ḏi*[5] ,	*ḏd* ,	*ḏi* ,	*ḏi* , , *rḏi*	*ḏi* ,

TABLE 1 – Weak verb: stems of the verb forms (active voice)

Notes

[1] Nominal verb form (§ 71.1).
[2] Verbal verb form (§ 71.2).
[3] Some IIIae inf. verbs have a *-w* ending with a noun subject.
[4] Often nominal verb form (§ 71.1); regularly follows negation *n* (§§ 71.3; 138).
[5] Often verbal verb form of *rḏi* (§ 71.2) and form of *rḏi* in performative statements (§ 71.4).

5) OLD PERFECTIVE (also called "Stative", "Qualitative" or "Pseudo-participle") **§ 81**

Forms and writings of the endings:

	Forms	Writings
sg. 1.c.	*.kw* (older form *.ki*)	
2.c.	*.ti*	
3.m.	*.w*	 (often not written)
3.f.	*.ti*	
pl. 1.c.	*.wyn*	 (both rarely attested)
2.c.	*.twny*	
3.m./c.	*.w* (sometimes *.y*)	
du. 2.c.	*.twny*	
3.m.	*.wy*	
3.f.	*.ty*	

Note: The endings ,  and (for *ti*) are written before the determinative, the others after. The ending cannot be separated from the verb stem by any other element. There is also a rarely-used ending  (*ti*) for the 3rd person pl. fem.

Form of the weak stem:

IIae gem.:	*ḳbb*	"to be cool"		*ḳb.ti*
IIIae inf.:	*h3i*	"to descend"		*h3i.kw*
Irregular:	*iri*	"to do"		*iri.kw*
	iwi	"to come"		*iwi.ti*
				*iyi.kw*
	rḏi	"to give"		*rḏi.kw*
				*ḏi.kw*

Usage:

1. The Old Perfective is partly used as a perfect tense, partly as a Stative (expressing a state).

2. Transitive Verbs:

- In Middle Egyptian the Old Perfective of transitive verbs usually has *passive* meaning: In the instructions to the vizier a messenger is directed to introduce his message as follows:  *hȝb.kw m wpw.t n(.t) sr mn* "I have been sent with a message of the official so-and-so."

- *Active* usage with transitive verbs is rare, only *rẖ* "to learn / know" is regularly used in this way:  *rẖ.kw ȝẖ=s n ỉrr(.w)* (§99) *sy tp tȝ* "I knew that it (justice) is beneficial for the one who does it on earth."

3. Independent Usage:

In a main clause the Old Perfective is used independently, i.e. without a preceding particle, only in the 1st person. This is an Old Egyptian usage in which the Old Perfective functions as an *active* Historic Perfect:

 *rḏi.ki ỉwt* (§75.2) *dȝm.w n(.w) ḥwn.w nfr.w* "I caused that a troop of young men come ..."

Sinuhe recounts: "This ruler conferred with me.  *ḏd.ki* I said ..."

Otherwise, in main clauses it only appears in a Complex Verb Form (§§ 91c, 95.2).

4. In subordinate clauses:

The Old Perfective is mainly used in subordinate clauses.

The shipwrecked sailor relates:  *ỉri.n=ỉ hrw.w 3 wʿỉ.kw* "I spent three days, I being alone." (Stative)

Sinuhe is told: "A funerary procession will be made for you on the day of burial, an inner coffin of gold, (its) head of lapislazuli,  *p.t ḥr=k ḏi.t(ỉ) m mstp.t* the sky/heaven above you, you having been placed on the bier." (Stative)

Ineni addresses the readers of his biography: "May you observe my qualities, do the like thereof; (it) will be beneficial for you,  *wȝḥ ʿnẖ=ṯn tp tȝ wḏȝ.twny* your life will endure on earth, you being prosperous..." (Stative)

𓅮𓃀𓏏𓆑𓅂𓎼𓊖𓏥 *gmi.n=i sw rḫ(.w) st* "I found him, he already knowing it." (Stative)

5. As an adverbial predicate in the Pseudo-verbal Construction (§§ 86–88).

6. In wishes:
In the 2nd and 3rd person the Old Perfective can be used to express a wish:

𓇌𓏭𓏏𓈖𓇋 *iyi.ti n=i* "You are come to me", i.e. "Welcome!"

In the set phrase 𓋹𓍑𓋴 *ꜥnḫ(.w) wḏꜣ(.w) snb(.w)* "May he live, prosper and be healthy!"

Fem.: 𓋹𓍑𓋴 *ꜥnḫ.ti wḏꜣ.ti snb.ti*

6) INFINITIVE   § 82

Forms:

Without ending:

3-radical:	*sḏm*	𓄔𓅓	"to hear"
IIae gem.:	*ḳbb*	𓂝𓃀𓃀𓈖𓈖	"to be cool"
2-radical[1]:	*mn*	𓏠	"to remain"
4-radical:	*wsṯn*	𓅱𓋴𓏏𓈖𓂻	"to stride"
causative 3-radical:	*sꜥnḫ*	𓋴𓋹𓐍	"to vivify"

---

[1] Exception: The 2-radical verb 𓈝𓅓𓂻 *šm* "to go" has the *t*-ending: *šm.t*.

t-ending:

causative 2-radical	*smn.t*	𓋴𓏠𓏏	"to make firm"

t-ending *or* (infrequent) without ending:

IIIae inf.:	*hꜣi.t*	𓉐𓄿𓂻	"to fall" (*t*-ending predominant)
	ḫdi	𓈖𓊝	"to travel downstream" (also *ḥḥy* 𓎛𓎛𓂻 "to seek" and *tni* 𓈖𓏤𓀠 "to become old")
IVae inf.:	*mꜣwy*	𓌳𓄿𓏭	"to be new"
	ḥmsi.t	𓊪𓀉	"to sit"

Irregular:

iri.t		"to do"
rḏi.t		"to give"
iwi.t, iyi.t		"to come"
ini.t		"to bring, fetch"

The infinitive is a nominal form of the verb and as such it shares many of the characteristics of nouns, e.g. it can be followed by a suffix-pronoun to express possession (§ 28.1), it can form part of a direct genitive construction (§ 18) and can serve as the object of certain verbs.

a) SUBJECT AND OBJECT OF THE INFINITIVE

§ 83 **1.** Subject

a. introduced by  *in* "by":

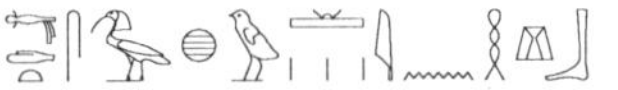 *šdi.t s3ḫ.w in ẖr.y-ḥ3b(.t)* "Reciting of transfigurations by the lector priest."

b. If the subject is pronominal, an independent personal pronoun is used (§ 26):

 ... *ḥnʿ pri.t ntsn m-s3 ḥm-k3=f* "... together with their going forth behind his *ka*-priest."

 *m ḏd st ntf r-gs ir.y-sšm* "through his saying it in the presence of the official" (*st* dependent pronoun object)

c. In the case of *intransitive* verbs, the subject sometimes appears either as a suffix-pronoun:  *m pri.t=f tp.t* "at his first going forth"

or as a noun in a direct genitive construction:  *m pri.t sm* "at the going forth of the sem-priest."

d. With *transitive* verbs, the direct genitive construction is only possible if both subject and object are expressed:

Subject and object both nouns:

 *rḏi.t Mnṯ.w t3.wy* "Month's giving the two lands."

If subject and object are both pronouns, the subject appears as a suffix-pronoun, the object as a dependent personal pronoun:

 *rḏi.t=f sw r ir.y pꜥ.t ḥꜣt.y-ꜥ.w* "His appointing him as Prince and Count."

2. Object § 84

The infinitive is a nominal form of the verb, therefore the object of the verbal content of a transitive verb is attached to the infinitive as a genitive; if the object is pronominal, it usually appears as a suffix-pronoun:  *iyi.n=i ḥr šms=f* "I came following him."

Exception: the dependent personal pronoun  *st* (§ 27) stands for the neutral "it" or the 3rd person plural.

Less frequently, if the subject follows the infinitive as a noun, an independent personal pronoun or a suffix-pronoun, the object can take the form of a noun or dependent personal pronoun (see above § 83 d).

WORD ORDER: suffix-pronoun, dependent pronoun, independent pronoun, noun (§ 117)

b) USAGE OF THE INFINITIVE § 85

1. As the object of certain verbs, such as *wḏ* "to command", *rḏi* "to cause", *mꜣꜣ* "to see", *mri* "to wish", *šꜣ* "determine, command".

 *wḏ ḥm=f sꜥḥꜥ wḏ pn* "His Majesty commanded (§72) the erection of this inscription."

2. Following prepositions, e.g.:

ḥr	+ inf.: Complex Aorist II – accompanying circumstance, "while", § 93
m	+ inf.: Progressive – with verbs of movement in place of *ḥr* + infinitive
r	+ inf.: purpose, future
ḫft	+ inf.: "at the time of, when"
m-ḫt	+ inf.: "after"

3. Following  *nn* "without" (§§ 136c, 143b)

4. In records of expeditions and military campaigns in "telegraph style" to set the scene of an event (see also example 2 in § 138):

"This wonder is what happened for His Majesty: 

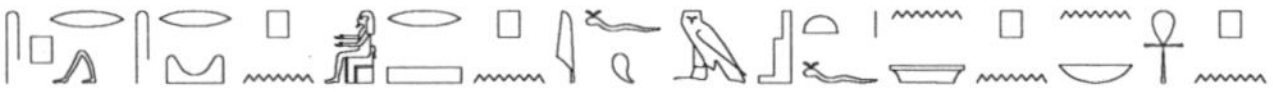

ḫ3i.t n=f in ʿ.wt ḫ3s.wt iwi.t in gḥs.t bk3.t ḥr šm.t ḥr=s r rmṯ.w ḫft ḥr=s iw ir.ty=s ḥr m3 ḥr s3s3 nn ʿn=s ḫ3=s r spr=s r ḏw pn šps r inr pn iw=f m s.t=f n ʿ3 pn n(.y) nb-ʿnḫ pn The descending to him of game of the hill country, the coming of a pregnant gazelle, walking (with) its face towards the people in front of it, its eyes looking straight ahead without its looking behind it until its arrival at this splendid rock, at this stone, it being in its (original) position, (determined) for this lid of this sarcophagus." (The text then continues with the narrative forms § 113 und § 95.3).

m-ḫt nn wḏ3 r Rtnw r iʿi.t ib=f ḫt ḫ3s.wt spr ḥm=f r Nḥrn gmi.t ḥm=f ʿnḫ(.w) wḏ3(.w) snb(.w) ḫr.w pf ṯs=f skw wn.in ḥm=f ḥr iri.t[§96] *ḫ3.t ʿ3.t im=sn* "After this (the Nubian campaign): Departing to Retenu in order to vent his wrath throughout the foreign lands; arrival of his Majesty at Naharin; His Majesty's finding – may he live, be prosperous and healthy – that enemy; his opening battle. Then His Majesty made a great slaughter amongst them." (The account continues in narrative style).

5. As a caption

Accompanying a scene in a tomb:

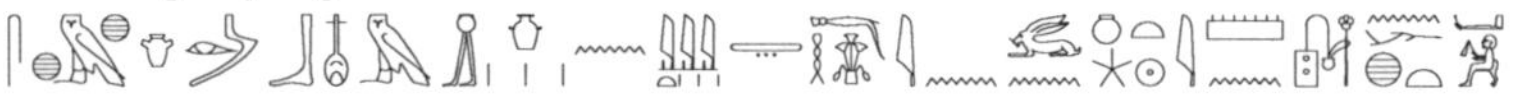

sḫmḫ ib m3 b(w) nfr m in.w n(.w) sḫ.wt t3-mḥ.w in wnw.t(y) Imn.w sš Nḫt "Distracting the heart (i.e. taking recreation), looking at the beauty of the products of the fields of Lower Egypt by the hour watcher of Amun, the scribe Nakht."

In the title of a book:

pri.t m hrw(.w) "Going forth by day" (title of the Book of the Dead).

§ 86 7) THE PSEUDO-VERBAL CONSTRUCTION

Pseudo-verbal Construction is the term used for those sentences which have as predicate either (1) an Old Perfective or (2) an infinitive following the prepositions *ḥr, m* or *r*. From a syntactic point of view, these sentences are Adverbial Sentences of type 2 (§ 44).

They belong to the group of Complex Verb Forms (§ 89ff), and some replace certain other verb forms, e.g.

1. *iw=f ḥr/m sḏm* (= Complex Aorist II / Progressive, § 93) – mainly progressive in meaning; can be used in place of the Complex Aorist I *iw(=f) sḏm=f* (§ 92).
2. *iw=f r sḏm* (= Complex Future, § 94) – the commonly used future; can replace the Future (Prospective) *sḏm=f* (§ 74).

a) PREDICATE **§ 87**

1. Old Perfective:

a. with transitive verbs with passive meaning (exception: *rḫ* "to know", § 81.2)

b. with verbs of movement – focus on resulting situation

c. with adjective-verbs – describes a state or condition (Stative)

2. *ḥr* + infinitive: Complex Aorist II / Progressive § 86 (*m* + inf. § 93, *r* + inf. § 94)

a. with transitive verbs with active meaning

b. with verbs of movement – infrequent, usually expressed by *m* + inf. (§ 93)

c. with adjective-verbs

d. with intransitive verbs which express an action ("to speak" etc.)

Examples:

1.a.  *ḥ3t.t rḏi.t(i) ḥr t3* "The bow-warp has been placed on land."

b. 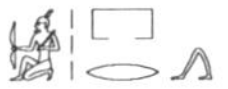 *mšʿ pri(.w)* "The army has gone forth (and is now in the field)."

c.  *ib=f 3wi(.w)* "His heart is wide (i.e. joyful)."

2.a.  *iw mšʿ pn ḥr m33* "This army watched." (Progressive)

 *iw=f ḥr wnm t … ḥnʿ swi* (§35) *ḥnḳ.t* "he ate bread … and drank beer." (Complex Aorist II)

b.  *iw=i ḥr sḫsḫ m-s3=s ḥr rd.wy* "I ran after her (the mare) on foot." (Progressive)

c.  *iḫw ḥr m3wi* "Feebleness is renewed." (Progressive)

d.  *m=k wi ḥr spr n=k* "Look, I appeal to you!" (Progressive)

Note: The infinitive *ḏd* is often not written after *ḥr*:  *ḥr nb ḥr nb=n pw* "Everyone (says), 'He is our lord.'"

§ 88 b) SUBJECT

If the Pseudo-verbal Construction forms an independent main clause, then the pronominal subject must be supported by a particle or an auxiliary verb; these can also be present when the subject is a noun (cp. §§ 43, 44), e.g.:

1. The particle *iw* :

 *iw=i ꜣtp.kw* "I am laden."

 *iw nṯr pn wḏꜣ(.w) m ḥtp* "This god set out in peace."

(In subordinate clauses the particle *iw* is only used with a pronominal subject; § 46b).

2. The particle *m=k* (with a dependent pronoun § 27):

 *m=k wi ḥr spr n=k* "Behold, I appeal to you!"

 *ist* or  *ti* can be used like *m=k* (§ 37).

3. The auxiliary verb *wnn* or *wn.in*:

a. *wnn=f* + Pseudo-verbal Construction – expresses future:

 *wnn=i wḏʿ.kw ḥnʿ=k* "I will be judged with you (i.e. appear before the court)."

b. *wn.in=f* + Pseudo-verbal Construction – marks elements in a sequence of events:

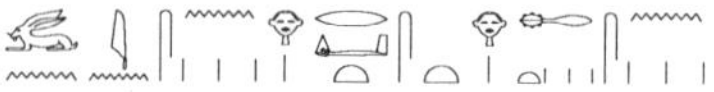 *wn.in=sn ḥr rḏi.t st ḥr ẖ.wt=sn* "Then they threw themselves upon their bellies."

 *wn.in ib n.y ḥm=f ḳb(.w)* "Then the heart of His Majesty became cool (i.e. was joyful)."

§ 89 8) COMPLEX VERB FORMS

Complex Verb Forms are those introduced by particles or auxiliary verbs. They form main clauses that stand at the beginning of a sentence.

§ 90 a) INTRODUCED BY THE PARTICLE  *iw*

iw introduces clauses which contain a statement ("It is the case that ..."). It occurs at the beginning of an account, in contrast to *ʿḥʿ.n*, which introduces a new section of narrative within a longer account (§ 95).

1. PRESENT PERFECT **§ 91**

a. *iw* + *sḏm.n=f* "he (has) heard" – formed predominantly with transitive verbs, never with verbs of movement (in place of which *iw* + Old Perfective – see § 91 c).

In an "ideal autobiography":

 *iw ḏi.n(=i) t n ḥḳr ḥbs.w n ḥ3w.ty* "I have given bread to the hungry and clothing to the naked."

In a sequence of activities of an official at the annual festival of Osiris in Abydos (presumably he regularly took part): 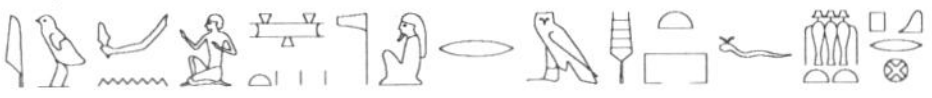

 *iw dsr.n=i w3.wt nṯr r mꜥḥꜥ.t=f ḫnt.(y)t Pḳr iw nḏ.n=i Wnn-nfr hrw.w pf n(.y) ꜥḥ3 ꜥ3* "I cleared the way of the god to his tomb which is in front of Peker. I protected Wennefer (on) that day of the great battle."

The servant Irisu writes to his master Si-ka-iunu: "The overseer Impy said to me:

 *iw rḏi.n=i n=f ḥsb 3* 'I have given him three workers'."

b. *iw* + Passive *sḏm(.w)=f* "he has been heard"

 *iw rḏi.w n=k ṯ3w* "Air has been given to you."

c. *iw* + Old Perfective: *iw=f iyi.w* "he came/has come" – predominantly with intransitive verbs and verbs of movement (see § 91a).

At the start of a biography:

"The treasurer and sole companion, caravan leader and troop commander Intef says:

 NN *iw ḫdi.k(w) ḫnti.k(w) ḥnꜥ NN* 'I travelled downstream and upstream with NN ...' "

2. COMPLEX AORIST I: *iw(=f) sḏm=f* "he can hear/hears" **§ 92**

This form is used for generally accepted statements, e.g. in a proverbial saying:

 *iw r3 n(.y) si nḥm=f sw* "The mouth (i.e. the words) of a man rescue him."

3. COMPLEX AORIST II or PROGRESSIVE: *iw=f ḥr/m sḏm* "he hears/is hearing" **§ 93**

From a formal viewpoint, these constructions belong to the so-called Pseudo-verbal Constructions (§§ 86–88). They are used for incomplete actions or to describe a state or condition.

Note the following distinctions:

a. with transitive verbs: *iw=f ḥr sḏm* "he hears / is hearing"

b. with intransitive verbs of movement: *iw=f m iwi.t* "he comes / is coming"

c. with intransitive adjective-verbs: *iw=f ḥmsi.w* (Old Perfective § 81) "he sits"

Examples:

a. *iw=f* + *ḥr* + infinitive

 *iw=i ḥr rḏi.t p3y=i mty n(.y) s3 n s3=i* "I give my (office of) controller of a (priestly) phyle to my son."

b. *iw=f* + *m* + infinitive (always Progressive)

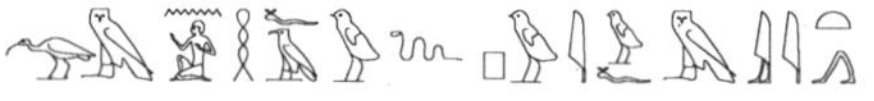 *gmi.n=i ḥf3.w pw iw=f m iyi.t* "I discovered it was a snake coming."

 *gmi.n=f sw m pri.t m sb3 n(.y) pr.w=f* "He found him going out of the door of his house." (Here the form is embedded in a verbal clause whose object *sw*, "him", serves as the subject of the Complex Aorist II, i.e. stands in place of *iw=f*.)

c. *iw=f* + Old Perfective

 *iw=k wr.t(i)* "You are great."

 *iw=s ẖ3ẖ.ti ḥr rd.wy=s* "She (the mare) was swift on her legs."

§ 94 4. COMPLEX FUTURE *iw=f r sḏm* "he will hear"

From a formal point of view, this construction also belongs to the Pseudo-verbal Constructions (§ 86, see also § 85.2).

 *iw dp.t r iyi.t m ẖnw* "A ship will come from the residence."

§ 95 b) INTRODUCED BY THE AUXILIARY VERB 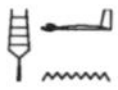 *ꜥḥꜥ.n*

With certain verb forms, *ꜥḥꜥ.n* forms "narrative forms" which mark the beginning of a new section of narrative within a longer passage (§ 90).

1. *ꜥḥꜥ.n* + PERFECT *sḏm.n=f* (§ 71) – predominantly with transitive verbs

"Then Isis said to these gods, 'Why then have we come, if not to do marvels for these children, that we may give an account to their father, who sent us?'

 *ꜥḥꜥ.n msi.n=sn ḫꜥ.w* 3 *n.y nb ꜥnḫ(.w) wḏꜣ(.w) snb(.w)* Then they formed three crowns (lit.: diadems of a lord), may he live, prosper and be healthy!"

2. *ꜥḥꜥ.n* + OLD PERFECTIVE (§ 81) – mostly with intransitive verbs and verbs of movement

The overseer Henu says the king sent him to Punt:

 *ꜥḥꜥ.n pri.kw m Gbtyw* "Then I set out from Coptos."

3. *ꜥḥꜥ.n* + PERFECTIVE PASSIVE *sḏm(.w/y)=f* (§ 77)

While the members of an expedition watch, a gazelle gives birth on a block of stone which the expedition is to quarry.

 *ꜥḥꜥ.n šꜥ.w nḥb.t=s* "Then its throat was cut (and it was sacrificed)."

4. *ꜥḥꜥ.n* + (HISTORIC) PERFECT *sḏm=f* (§ 72)

 *ꜥḥꜥ.n rdi=f wi m rꜣ=f* "Then it (the snake) put me in its mouth."

c) INTRODUCED BY THE AUXILIARY *wn.in* (attested only infrequently) **§ 96**

wn.in(=f) + (HISTORIC?) PERFECT *sḏm=f* has both contingent character (§ 80) and properties of the Aorist (§ 70) and is found in narrative texts; the identity of the *sḏm=f* form is uncertain.

The children of the vizier read his teaching and found that it was good.

 *wn.in ꜥḥꜥ=sn ḥmsi=sn ḫft(.w)* "Then they acted (lit.: stood and sat) accordingly."

The king was told of Sinuhe's situation:

 *wn.in ḥm=f hꜣb=f n=i ḥr ꜣw.t-ꜥ.w* "Then His Majesty sent to me with gifts."

§ 97 9) FINITE VERB FORMS INTRODUCED BY *m=k* AND *ist*

a) *m=k* : THE PRESENTATIVE (§ 37)

m=k attracts the attention of the person addressed and can introduce every verb form:

1. *m=k* + PERFECT *sḏm.n=f* (§ 71)

 *m=k pḥ.n=n ẖn.w* "Behold, we have reached the residence!"

m=k can also precede the negative particle *n* (§§ 37, 133):

 *m=k n wḏ=tw* (§ 138) *iri.t mn.t ir.y* "Behold, one has not commanded to do the like thereof."

2. *m=k* + PERFECTIVE PASSIVE *sḏm(.w/y)=f* (§ 77)

 *m=k msi(.w) n=k ẖrd.w 3* "Behold, three children have been born to you."

b) THE PARTICLE *isṯ* (§ 37) introduces a clause that provides background information about the action expressed in the main clause:

1. *isṯ* + PERFECT *sḏm.n=f* (§ 71)

My Majesty commands the construction of the temple of Ptah, which is in the Temenos of my father Amun…, that he may appear in it … 

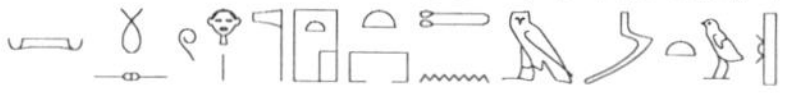 *ist gmi.n ḥm=i ḥw.t-nṯr tn m ḳd m ḏb.t wh3.w sb3.wy=s m ẖt w3i(.w) r w3s{m}i wḏ ḥm=i pḏ šs ḥr ḥw.t-nṯr tn m m3w.t* "Now, my Majesty having found this temple built of bricks, the columns and doors of wood fallen into ruin, my Majesty decrees that the cord be stretched over this temple anew."

2. *isṯ* + PERFECTIVE PASSIVE *sḏm(.w/y)=f* (§ 77)

The king has returned in haste to the residence with his entourage without informing the army.  *ist h3b.w r ms.w nsw* "Meanwhile, the royal children had been sent to, (one of them was called out to as I stood nearby …)."

c) TEXT PASSAGE illustrating §§ 89–97

 *iw rḏi.n Ḥr.w-nḏ-ḥr-it=f* (§91a)

m ḥr=i r ẖnw r ini.t Ḥr.w Nḫn ḥnꜥ mw.t=f ꜣs.t mꜣꜥ.t ḫrw rdi.n=f (§ 71.2c) *wi m ḥr.y im(w) is.t isṯ grt rḫ.n=f* (§ 97 b, § 71.2c) *(w)i m sr mnḫ n.y ḥw.t-nṯr=f rs-tp ḥr swḏ(t).n=f* (§ 107) *ꜥḥꜥ.n=i ḫdi.kw* (§ 95.2) *m mꜣꜥw nfr šdi.n=i* (§ 71.2c) *Ḥr.w Nḫn ḥr ꜥ.wy(=i) ḥnꜥ mw.t=f*

"(The god) Harendotus ordered me to the residence, in order to fetch Horus of Nekhen and his mother Isis, justified. He appointed me (as) commander of a ship and crew, having recognised me as an efficient official of his temple, watchful over that which he commanded. Thereupon I travelled north with a good wind, having taken up Horus of Nekhen and his mother in (my) arms (i.e. having taken charge of them)."

10) PARTICIPLES § 98

a) FORMS:

Like adjectives, participles have **gender** and **number** with corresponding endings.

There are three "tenses":

a. Imperfective: for actions that are in progress, which are repeated or which occur regularly (corresponds to the Aorist).

b. Perfective: for actions where the duration of the action is not of importance, usually in the past but also in the present (e.g. in epithets).

c. Prospective: for possible or expected actions; in passive like Latin gerundive.

There are both active and passive voice.

1. Imperfective Participle § 99

	Active		Passive	
3-radical		*sḏm(.w)*		*sḏm.w*
2-radical		*ḏd(.w)*		*ḏd.w*
IIIae inf.		*hꜣꜣ(.w)*		*mrr.w*
IIae gem.		*ḳbb(.w)*		*mꜣꜣ.w*
iri		*irr(.w)*		*irr.w*
rdi		*ḏd(.w)*		*ḏd.w*
iwi; iyi		*iyi(.w)*	---	---

The singular ending *-w* is seldom written in the active, in the passive occasionally. A full active plural ending *-yw* is sometimes written:  *sḏm.yw*,"those who hear"; otherwise  *mrr.(y)w* "those who love" or only  *wnn.(yw)* "those who exist". In the passive plural only one *w* is written, i.e. the writing of the passive singular and plural is identical. Feminine forms only have the *-t* ending: *prr.t*. ***Note***: gemination of the IIae gem. and IIIae inf. verbs.

§ 100 2. Perfective Participle

	Active		Passive	
3-radical		*sḏm*		*sḏm.w*
2-radical		*ḏd*		*ḏd.w*; *ḏdd.y*
IIIae inf.		*mri*		*mri.y*; *mri.w*
IIae gem.		*m3*	---	---
iri		*iri*		*iri.y*
rḏi		*rḏi*		*rḏi.y*, *rḏi.yt*
iwi; *iyi*		*iwi*; *iyi*	---	---

In the passive, in addition to the form *ḏd.w*, the bi-radical verbs show a further form with gemination: *ḏdd.y* / *ḏdd.w*. In the masculine singular, the IIIae inf. verbs usually have the ending *y*. The plural ending *-w* is sometimes written in the active, seldom in the passive.

§ 101 3. Prospective Participle

		Active		Passive	
3-rad.	m. f.		*sḏm(.y)* *sḏm.ti*		*sḏm(.y)* *sḏm.ti*
2-rad.		---	---		*wn.ti*
IIIae inf.	f.		*msi.t(i)*	---	---
iri	m. f.	---	---		*iri.y* *iri.ti*
rḏi	f.	---	---		*ḏi.ti*

In Middle Egyptian, the active prospective participle is almost completely replaced by the *sḏm.ty=fy*-Form (§ 112).

b) USAGE OF THE PARTICIPLE

1. Nominal usage: **§ 102**

a. As a noun: *sḏm.w* "one who hears/a hearer"; often with a determinative: *ḥmsi.w* "seated ones" (perfective active plural "those who have seated themselves").

Note: Plural strokes are written with feminine collectives (§ 16.5): *ḫpr.t* "that which has happened".

b. As a predicate in a Nominal Sentence with an unstressed subject (§ 50):

ink rḏi pri si 2 ḥtp(.wy)[(§ 81)] "I am one who caused two men to go forth satisfied." (perfective active)

ink ḏd pri.y si 2 ḥtp(.wy) m pri.w n.y rꜣ=f "I am one who causes that two men depart satisfied with what went forth from his mouth." (imperfective active)

2. Adjectival usage: **§ 103**

a. As an attribute, it agrees with the antecedent in gender and number (endings not always written):

m. sg.: *sꜣ sḏm.w* "a son who hears / a hearing son" (imperfective)

wpw.ty ḫdd(.w) ḫnti(.w) r ḫnw "the messenger who (regularly) travels north or south to the Residence". (without grammatical ending, imperfective/gemination)

m. pl.: *nṯr.w wnn.yw m šms.w=f* "the gods who are (regularly) in his following". (imperfective plural)

it.w=i ḫpr(.w) ḫr-ḥꜣ.t "my fathers who existed aforetimes". (without grammatical ending, perfective plural)

f. sg.: *tp.t-rꜣ pri.t m rꜣ* "the utterance which issued forth from the mouth". (perfective fem.)

f. pl.: *gmḥ.wt prr.(w)t n=f* "the wicks which come forth for him". (imperfective/gemination, fem.)

b. As a predicate in an Adjectival Sentence (§ 56) and, like those adjectives, invariable:

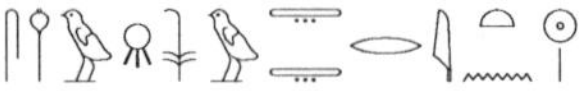 *sḥḏ.w sw tꜣ.wy r itn* "He is one who illumines the Two Lands more than the sun." (i.e. "An illuminator of the Two Lands is he, more than the sun.")

Note: Participles cannot be used adverbially. In Egyptian, in an expression such as "standing, he spoke", "standing" would be an Old Perfective since it expresses a state (§ 81.4).

2. The pronominal object of a participle is expressed by a dependent pronoun:

 *smi nfr n hꜣb sw* "One who reported well for the one who commissioned (sent) him".

§ 104 3. Extended Use of the Passive Participle (Relative Construction without a Subject)

In English, a passive participle can only function as an attributive adjective if the noun being described (in the following example "gold") is the logical *direct* object of the verbal action of the participle (here: "give"): "the given gold".

In Egyptian, the passive participle is also used in this way:  **nbw ḏḏ.w* "the given gold"; here, as in English, the antecedent "gold" is the direct object of the verb of the participle "give".

However, unlike in English, the participle and the antecedent can have a different syntactic relationship. For example, the antecedent can be an *indirect* object (in the following example *nsw* "king"). Within the construction which is dependent upon the passive participle (in the following example the phrase *ḏḏ.w n=f nbw*, "given to him gold"), a resumptive pronoun (*f* in the prepositional phrase *n=f*, "to him") refers back to the antecedent:  **nsw ḏḏ.w n=f nbw* "the king, given to him gold". Such a construction is translated into English as a relative clause: "the king to whom gold is given".

The relationship between the antecedent and the verbal action of the participle can be even looser: 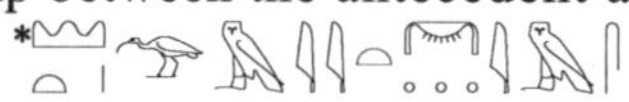 **ḫꜣs.t gmi.yt nbw im=s* "the hill country in which gold is found". Both the resumptive pronoun *s* in the adverbial expression *im=s* "in it" and the participle agree in gender and number with *ḫꜣs.t* . The resumptive pronoun in the above example can be omitted and replaced by an adverb (in the following example *im* "there"): 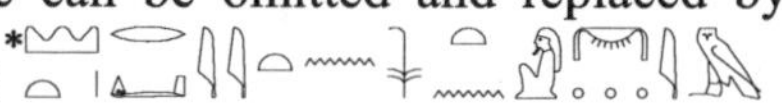 **ḫꜣs.t rḏi.yt n nsw nbw im* "The land where gold was given to the king" (lit.: "The land, given to the king gold there"). Here only the gender and number of the participle reveal the link with the antecedent.

Note: The passive participle can also be formed from intransitive verbs: The king is one  *prr.w hꜣꜣ.w ẖr sḫr=f* "under whose counsel one goes and comes".

11) THE RELATIVE FORM **§ 105**

Participles are *non-finite* nominal forms of the verb, i.e. they do not have a subject. Relative Forms, by contrast, are *finite* nominal verb forms, which have their own subject. Like participles, they are used adjectivally and agree with the antecedent in gender and number:

 *iḫ.t nb.t ḏḏ.t sr nb nḏs nb* (§ 108) *r ḥw.t-nṯr* "everything that any official (or) any citizen gives to the temple".

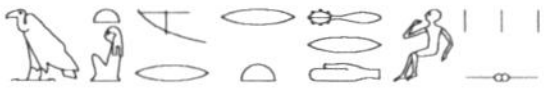 *mw.t mrr.t ẖrd.w=s* "the mother whom her children love".

If, unlike the preceding examples, the antecedent is not the direct object of the action expressed in the Relative Form, a resumptive pronoun must refer back to it:

 *mḫꜣ.t tw n.t Rꜥ.w fꜣꜣ.t=f mꜣꜥ.t im=s* "that balance of Re in which he lifts up Maat". (*mꜣꜥ.t* is the direct, *mḫꜣ.t* the indirect object of *fꜣi* "to lift up"; resumptive pronoun *s*; cp. §104)

The resumptive pronoun is also necessary with the Relative Form of an intransitive verb:

 *wꜣ.t iyi.tn=f ḥr=s* "the road upon which it (the statue) came".

In place of a preposition plus suffix-pronoun expressing location, an adverb can also be used (not, however, in the case of *ḥr* and *ẖr*):

 *bw wrš.w ib=i im=f* "the place in which my heart dwells"

or 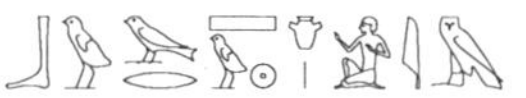 *bw wrš.w ib=i im* "the place where my heart dwells".

a) "TENSES" of the RELATIVE FORM **§ 106**

Corresponding to the Perfect *sḏm.n=f* (§ 71), the Aorist *sḏm=f* / *irr=f* (§ 70) and the Future (Prospective) *sḏm=f* (§ 74), there are three Relative Forms. Like participles and adjectives, they agree with their antecedent in gender and number (fem. *-t,* pl. *-w*).

§ 107 1. Perfective *sḏm.(w)n=f* Relative Form

strong verb		*sḏm.n=f* (m.)	"he, whom he heard"
IIae gem.		*m3.tn=f* (f.)	"she, whom he saw"
IIIae inf.		*iri.n=f* (m.) *gmi.tn=f* (f.)	"he, whom he made" "she, whom he found"
rḏi	 less often	*rḏi.n=i* (m.) *ḏi.n=i* (m.)	"he, whom I gave"
"to come"		*iyi.n=sn* (m.)	"he, (from) whom they came"

§ 108 2. Aorist *sḏm=f* / *irr=f* Relative Form

strong verb		*sḏm(.w)=f* *ḏd.wy=i*	"he, whom he hears" "that which I say"
IIae gem.		*wnn=f*; *wnn.w* + noun subj.	"he, who is"
IIIae inf.		*mrr.w* + noun subject *f33.t=f*	"he, whom NN loves" "she, whom he bears"
rḏi		*ḏd.w=ṯn*	"he, whom you give"

§ 109 3. Prospective *sḏm=f* Relative Form

3-rad., strong vb.		*sḏm(.w)=f* *sḏm.t(i)=f*	"he, whom he will hear" "she, whom he will hear"
2-rad.	without ending, but also 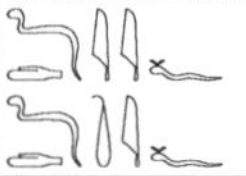	*ḏd.y=f* *ḏd.ti=f*	"that which he will speak"
IIae gem.		*wn=f*	"he, who will be"
IIIae inf.	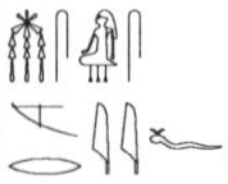 fem. usually with 	*msi=s* *mri.y=f*	"he, whom she will bear" "that which he will wish"
rḏi		*ḏi.t=i*	"that which I will give"
iri		*iri.t=i*	"that which I will make"

b) USAGE OF THE RELATIVE FORM:

The usage of these "tenses" matches that of the corresponding Suffix-Conjugation. Like participles, Relative Forms are used adjectivally and as nouns:

1. Adjectival usage **§ 110**

a. As an attribute, agreeing in gender and number with the antecedent (endings not always written):

 *sr.w mrr(.w)=f* (§ 108) "the officials whom he loves".

 *ḥr.t iri.tn=i* (§ 107) *ḏs=i* "a tomb which I made myself".

As with passive participles (§ 104), Relative Forms are also formed from intransitive verbs:

 *w3.t iyi.tn=f ḥr=s* "the road upon which he came".

b. With a finite verb as object:  *ḏʿm ḏi.n=f int* (§ 75) *ḥm=i m-ḫnt T3-sty* "the gold, which he (Osiris) let My Majesty (Sesostris III) fetch from Nubia".

2. Usage as a noun **§ 111**

The feminine Relative Form, used absolutely, can express an abstract concept.

a. In a direct genitive construction:

 *nb šnn.t itn* "lord of that which / what the sun encircles".

b. As an object:

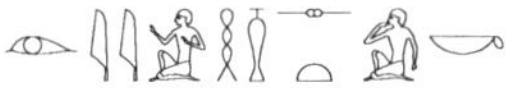 *iri.y=i ḥsi.t=k* "I will do that which you will praise".

c. In a non-verbal sentence (tri-partite *pw*-Sentence § 54):

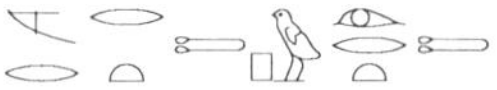 *mrr.t=ṯ pw irr.t=ṯ* "That which you do is that which you wish".

d. As the subject in a *nfr sw* - Sentence (§56):

 *ʿ3 iri.tn=f n=i* "great was that which he did for me".

e. Absolute use as an epithet:

 *mrr.w nw.t=f* "one whom his city loves".

f. With a verb as object:

"I did not neglect 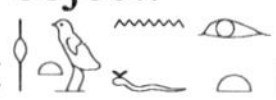 *wḏ.tn=f iri.t* that which he commanded to do."

§ 112 12) FUTURE VERBAL ADJECTIVE *sḏm.t(y)=fy*

Endings:

SINGULAR		PLURAL	
3.m.	*.ty=f(y)*	**3.c.**	*.ty=sn*
3.f.	*.ty=sy*		

Form of the weak stem:

IIae gem.: *wnn* — *wnn.t(y)=fy* "who will be"

IIIae inf.: (occasionally with *w*) — *h3w.t(y)=fy* "who will descend "

Irregular: *rḏi* — *rḏi.t(y)=fy* "who will give"

iwi — *iwi.t(y)=fy* "who will come"

Usage:

The Verbal Adjective is used like the Prospective Participle (§ 101), which it largely replaced. It usually has active, occasionally passive meaning.

a) As an attribute: *ḫ3s.t wnn.ty=sy ḥr mw=f* "the foreign land which will be upon his water (i.e. be loyal to him)".

b) As a noun: *ḫpr.ty=sn* "that which will happen".

§ 113 13) NARRATIVE CONSTRUCTION *iyi.t pw iri.n=f*

This construction indicates the beginning of a new episode in a narrative. It is actually a non-verbal tri-partite *pw*-Sentence (§ 54), with an infinitive as predicate and the (always masculine) Perfective Relative Form of *iri* as subject; it is used almost exclusively with verbs of movement:

nꜥi.t pw iri.n=n m ḫdi "Then we travelled northwards (lit.: That which we did was a travelling northwards)."

For the passive, a Passive Participle replaces the Relative Form (rare):

iwi.t pw iri.y r b3k im "Then one came for this humble servant. (lit.: What was done was a coming, for this humble servant)."

14) THE AUXILIARY VERB  *p3i* § 114

The verb  *p3i*, which can be fully conjugated, has the meaning "to have done in the past". The verb for which it serves as an auxiliary follows as an infinitive.

This verb forms part of a Complex Verb Form following *iw* or the negative particle *n-sp* (§ 131) :

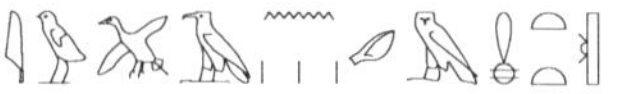 *iw p3i=n sḏm mi.tt* "We have heard the like."

 *n-sp p3i.t(w) iri.t st* "Never has it been done … "

p3i as a Relative Form:

sic

 *n ḫpr mi.tt n b3k.w p3i.n nb=sn ḥsi.t st* "Never did the like happen to servants whom their lord had praised."

J) ADVERBS § 115

1) Egyptian has only few true, i.e. non-derivative adverbs, e.g.:

 *ꜥ3* "here"

 *min* "today"

 *rsy* "completely", after a negative "at all"

 *gr* "also", after negatives "further"

 *ṯn* "where? whence?"

2) There are a number of adverbs which are related to prepositions (§ 35):

 *im* "there"

 *my* "likewise, accordingly"

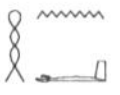 *ḥnꜥ(.y)* "therewith, together with"

 *ḫft.w* "accordingly"

 *ḫnt.w* "before, earlier"

 *ẖr.y* "under"

 *ḏr* "at an end"

3) Other adverbs correspond to compound prepositions (§ 36):

 *m-b3ḥ* local: "in front"
temp.: "before, formerly"

 *m-ḫt* "afterwards"

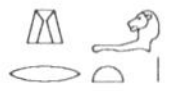 *ẖr-ḥ3.t* "formerly"

 *ḥr-s3* "subsequently, later"

4) Fixed expressions (preposition + noun) that are used as adverbs:

m min (like *min*) "today"

m sf "yesterday"

m dwꜣ(.w) "tomorrow"

m mi.tt "likewise"

n wn mꜣꜥ "in truth"

n sp "at once, together"

r ḥr.w "up"

r ḫnt.w "out"

ḥr ꜥ.wwy "immediately"; also *ḥr ꜥ.w*

ḏr-ꜥ.w "long ago"

5) Fixed expressions (preposition *r* + adjective) that are used as adverbs:

r mnḫ "thoroughly"

r wꜣḏ "vigorously"

r iḳr "exceedingly"

r ꜥꜣ.t "greatly"

6) Adverbs derived from verbal roots, occasionally with *-w* ending (cannot always be clearly distinguished from an Old Perfective) :

ꜥꜣ.w "greatly"

ḫnm.w "cheerfully"

nfr "perfectly, well"

ꜣs "quickly"

wḏf "slowly"

ꜥšꜣ "frequently"

wr "much"; *wr.t* "very"

7) Nouns that are used as adverbs:

ḏ.t "eternally"

rꜥ.w nb "daily"

Usage:

Adverbs follow the expression they qualify.

a) As a predicate in Adverbial Sentences (§ 42 ff)

b) As the attribute of a verb:

… *iyi.n=i min…* "I have come today … "

iw ḥsi.n=f wi ḥr=f r ꜥꜣ.t wr.t "He praised me for it very greatly."

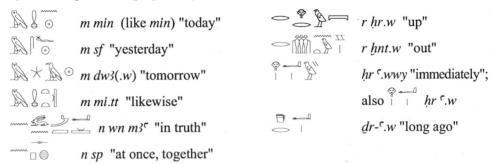

c) As the attribute of a participle:

 *smi nfr n h3b sw* "one who reports/reported perfectly to the one who sent him."

d) As the attribute of an adjective:

 *ink sš ik̇r wr.t* "I am/was a very excellent scribe."

e) Topicalisation of the adverb: adverb in initial position (§ 129)

Note: In certain fixed expressions an adverb can serve as the attribute of a noun:

 *b3k im* "your humble servant (lit.: the servant there)."

K) WORD ORDER

1) For word order in **NON-VERBAL SENTENCES** see §§ 42ff, 48ff, 53–54, 56–57. **§ 116**

2) In **VERBAL SENTENCES** with noun subject and noun object(s) the word order is as a rule: verb – subject – direct object – indirect object – adverb / adverbial expression (for exceptions see §§ 118ff). **§ 117**

Where a sentence contains pronouns the following rules apply:

A pronominal object comes before a noun subject:

* **rḏi.n sw nsw m smr* "The king made him a Companion".

Dative *n* + suffix takes precedence over a noun or pronoun object and also a noun subject:

*	**rḏi.n=f n=i nbw*	"He gave me gold."
*	**rḏi.n n=i nsw nbw*	"The king gave me gold."
*	**rḏi.n n=i st nsw*	"The king gave it to me."

Order of precedence: 1. suffix-pronoun, 2. dependent pronoun, 3. noun.

The word order of a sentence can be modified in order to either emphasise a particular part of the sentence – subject, object, adverbial expression – by contrasting (Focalisation) or in order to mark the theme of a sentence (Topicalisation). This is usually, in the case of Topicalisation regularly, done by placing the relevant part of the sentence at the beginning of the sentence.

§ 118 3) FOCALISATION

Focalisation is achieved by means of cleft sentences:

"It is his daughter who causes that the name of her father lives." (Focus on subject "daughter" in contrast, e.g. to the father himself or a son.)

"It is his field that the father will give his son." (Focus on object: "field" rather than e.g. house.")

"That he will come is today." (Focus on an adverbial expression "today" in contrast to tomorrow.)

Three types of cleft sentences are found in Middle Egyptian:

§ 119 **a)** THE *in*-CONSTRUCTION – FOCUS ON THE SUBJECT

1. The *in*-Construction is used in order to emphasise the subject.

WORD ORDER: Subject – Predicate. The following possibilities and combinations occur:

Subject: a) noun subject, introduced by *in*,

b) pronominal subject: independent personal pronoun in initial position.

Predicate: α) imperfective participle (§ 99) (present)

β) perfective participle (§ 100) (past)

γ) prospective *sḏm=f* (§ 74) (future)

Subject		**Predicate**	
a)		α)	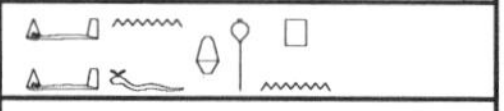
		β)	
b)		γ)	

Every combination of subject and predicate is possible, e.g.:

a) + α) : **in s3=f ḏd(.w) n=f t ḥḏ pn* "It is his son who gives him this white bread."

b) + α) : **ntf ḏd(.w) n=f t ḥḏ pn* "It is he who gives him this white bread."

a) + β) : **in s3=f rḏi n=f t ḥḏ pn* "It is his son who gave him this white bread."

b) + γ) : **ntf ḏi=f n=f t ḥḏ pn* "*He* will give him this white bread."

Note:

In this construction the participle is invariable:

 *in sn.t=f sˁnḫ rn=f* "It is his sister who has caused that his name lives."

The interrogative pronoun *m* "who?" (§ 34) is often used in the *in*-Construction and merges with *in* to form a new word:  >  *in-m* > *nm* (Coptic ⲚⲒⲘ):

 *in-m ir=f ini=f n=i sy* "Who is it, who will bring it (the box) to me?"

2. Negation of the *in*-Construction **§ 120**

a. Negation of the *subject* by ...  *n ... is*

 *n ink is ḏd n=k nw in Gbb ḏd n=k nw ḥnˁ Wsir* "It is not I who said this to you, it is Geb who said this to you, and Osiris."

b. Negation of the *verb* by the Negative Verb  *tm* (§ 132), which is followed by the verb in the form of a Negative Complement:

* *in s3=k tm ini(.w) n=k sy* "It is your son who did not bring it to you." (*tm* – perfective participle § 100)

b) TRI-PARTITE *pw*-SENTENCE: FOCUS ON SUBJECT or OBJECT **§ 121**

In these sentences the third element of the sentence is a participle or a Relative Form; these refer to the subject or the object:

1. Focus on the subject:

NN  *NN pw m3 ms(w).t=ṯn* "It is NN, who saw your birth." (*m3* – perfective participle § 100)

2. Focus on the object:

 *išst pw ir=f iri.t(i)=k n=i m isw ir(.y)* "What is it then, that you will do for me in return for it?" (*iri.ti=k* – prospective Relative Form § 109)

§ 122 **c)** EMPHATIC CONSTRUCTION: FOCUS ON ADVERBIAL EXPRESSION

Focus can be directed upon an adverbial expression by means of the Emphatic Construction:

 *gmi.n sw wpw.tyw ḥr w3.t* "That the messengers found him (was) on the road." (see also §§ 70.1, 71.1, 74.2, 76).

§ 123 4) TOPICALISATION

In the case of topicalisation, those parts of the sentence that indicate the theme stand at the head of the sentence and thereby highlight its theme or *topic*. If it is the subject or object, it re-appears as a pronoun in its regular position, according to § 116 and § 117. The topicalised element can stand without introduction or follow the particle  *ỉr*.

a) Without introduction

§ 124 **1.** Topicalisation of the subject

 *ḫbsw.t=f wr s(y) r mḥ 2* "*His beard, it* was greater than 2 cubits." (Adjectival Sentence § 56)

 *ḥkn.w pf ḏd.n=k ỉnt=k bw pw wr n(.y) ỉw pn* "*That Hekenu oil which you said you would bring, it* is the speciality (lit.: the greatness) of this island." (bi-partite *pw*-Sentence § 53)

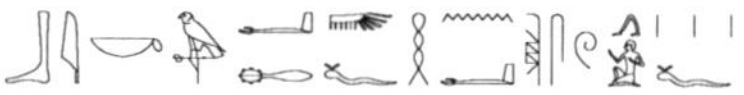 *bỉk ꜥḫ=f ḥnꜥ šms.w=f* "*The falcon* (the king), *he* flew off with his retinue." (Historic Perfect *sḏm=f* § 72)

§ 125 **2.** Topicalisation of the object

 *k3.tn=f*(§ 107) *ỉri.t*(§ 82) *st (ỉ)r=ỉ ỉri.n=ỉ st (ỉ)r=f* "*That which he thought to do against me,* I did *it* against him"

§ 126 **3.** Topicalisation of an adverbial expression

If the main clause is formed with a Complex Verb Form (§§ 89–96), the adverbial expression is topicalised by placing the adverbial subordinate clause at the head of the sentence, e.g.:

- preceding *ꜥḥꜥ.n sḏm.n=f* (§ 95)

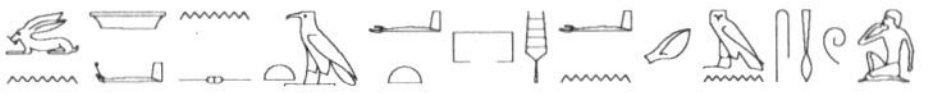 *wn.n=s tꜣ ꜥ.t ꜥḥꜥ.n sḏm.n=s ḫrw* "*After she had opened the chamber*, she heard a sound ..." (adverbial expression: *sḏm.n=f* in a subordinate clause § 71.2)

- preceding *iw* + Passive *sḏm(.w)=f* (§ 91 b)

 *ḥḏ.n (i)r=f tꜣ dwꜣ sp 2 iw iri(.w) mi ḏd=f* "*When the earth had become light, very early*, it was (already) done according to what he said." (adverbial expression: Circumstantial *sḏm.n=f* in a subordinate clause § 71.2)

- preceding a Complex Aorist I (*iw=f sḏm=f*) (§ 92)

 *ꜣsḫ=f iw=i skꜣ=i ꜣsḫ=i* "*As he reaps*, so I plough and I reap." (adverbial expression: Circumstantial Present *sḏm=f* § 69.1)

- preceding the Complex Future *iw=f r sḏm* (§ 94)

 *mri=ṯn ꜥnḫ msḏi=ṯn ḫp.t iw=ṯn r drp n=i* "*As you love life and hate death*, so you will make offering for me." (adverbial expression: Circumstantial Present *sḏm=f* § 69.1)

b) Introduced by  *ir*

1. Topicalisation of the subject **§ 127**

 *ir sf Wsir pw* "*As for yesterday*, it is Osiris."

 *ir šm(.w) grg iw=f tnm=f* "*As for him who follows falsehood*, he goes astray."

Other particles can precede *ir*, e.g. *isṯ*: The text recounts Nemty-nakht's desire to seize the possessions of the peasant and then continues:

 *isṯ (i)r=f*(§ 38) *ir*(§ 125) *pr.w Nm.ty-nḫt pn ḥr smꜣ-tꜣ n(.y) r(ꜣ)-wꜣ(i).t* "Now, as for the house of this Nemty-nakht, (it) lay at the side of the road". The position of the house provided him with the possibility to do so.

2. Topicalisation of the object **§ 128**

 *ir n.t(y)t nb(.t) m sš ḥr šfd.w sḏm st* "*As for everything in writing on the book roll*, obey it!"

§ 129 **3.** Topicalisation of an adverbial expression

 *ir m-ḫt ḥtp(.w) nṯr m iḫ.wt=f ḏd.tw ḥtp-nṯr pn m-bꜣḥ twt.w pn n.y ḥm=i* "*After the god has been satisfied with his things*, this god's offering is placed in front of this statue of my Majesty". (Adverbial expression: *m-ḫt* + Perfective Passive *sḏm(.w/y)=f* § 77)

§ 130 5) CONDITIONAL CLAUSES

Conditional clauses also belong to the category of Focalisation (§§ 118–122). They are either introduced by  *ir* or appear without an introduction.

§ 131 **a)** WITH INTRODUCTORY  *ir*

1. Fulfillable condition:

ir + Future (Prospective) *sḏm=f* (§ 74)

 *ir wdf=k m ḏd n=i ini tw r iw pn rḏi=i rḫ=k tw* "If you hesitate in telling me who brought you to this island, I will cause that you know yourself!"

ir + Subjunctive *sḏm=f* (§ 75)

 *ir iwt=k m ḥfꜣ.(w)t nb(.t) m(w)t.kꜣ Rꜥ.w* "If you should come as any snake, then Re will die."

2. Unfulfillable condition:

This construction is rather uncertain; the only attested (controversial) example:
ir + Perfect *sḏm.n=f* (§ 71) King Amenemhet says:

ir šsp.n=i ꜣs{t} ḫꜥ.w m ḏr.t=i iw ḏi.n=i ḫt ḥm(.w) m-ꜥ(.w) bꜣbꜣ "Had I grasped speed (i.e. hurried), the weapons in my hand, I would have made the cowards retreat with the lance." Another possible interpretation would be to see *ir* as introducing an emphasised adverbial expression (§§ 126, 129) which has been placed at the head of the sentence because the main clause is formed by a Complex Verb Form: "Having grasped speed, the weapons in my hand, I made the cowards retreat with the lance."

§ 132 **b)** WITHOUT INTRODUCTION

Conditions can also be expressed by other sentence types, e.g.

1. by the Balanced Sentence (§§ 49, 70.1b, 71.1d)

2. by an emphasised adverbial expression followed by the Complex Future (§ 126).

L) NEGATION of the VERB

NEGATIVE PARTICLES AND NEGATIVE VERBS

The verb is negated in different ways, depending on the verb form: **§ 133**

a) with the **negative particles** *n* or *nn*;

b) with the construction *n-sp* or

c) with the **negative verbs** *tm* or , *imi.* **§ 134**

Both these verbs are followed by the verb that is negated in a special form, the so-called **Negative Complement**. Its *-w* ending is usually not written. From the New Kingdom onwards, and sometimes earlier, the Negative Complement can be replaced by the infinitive.

tm can be fully conjugated. WORD ORDER: pronominal subject (suffix-pronoun) follows *tm*, nominal subject follows the Negative Complement:

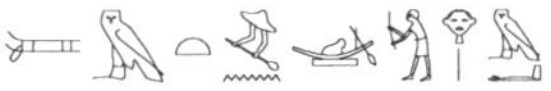 *tm=t ḥn(.w) ḥr m* "*Why* do you not row?" (Aorist *sḏm=f* § 70.1a)

"Do not be strong in your power,  *tm spr(.w) bw ḏw r=k* that evil may not reach you" (Subjunctive *sḏm=f* § 75.3)

The choice of negation depends on the syntactic function and the type of verb form (i.e. nominal vs. verbal form, overview in Table 2 – p. 83).

1) NEGATION of the IMPERATIVE (§ 67) **§ 135**

The imperative is negated by (the imperative of the Negative Verb *tm* § 134), which is followed by the Negative Complement (§ 134).

 *m snḏ(.w)* "Fear not!"

2) NEGATION of the CIRCUMSTANTIAL (PRESENT) *sḏm=f* / *iri=f* (§ 69) **§ 136**

a) *n sḏm.n=f* – identical with the negative Complex Aorist I (§§ 71.3, 92, 142 b).

In adverbial subordinate clauses:

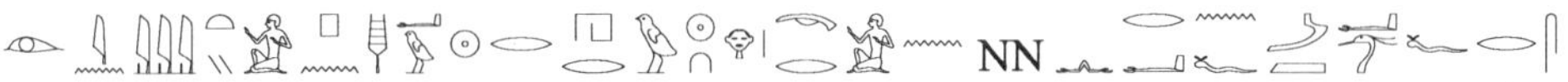

iri.in sḫ.ty pn ꜥḥꜥ.w r hrw.w 10 ḥr spr n NN n rḏi.n=f mꜣꜥ=f (i)r=s "Then this peasant spent a period of up to 10 days petitioning NN, *without him* (NN) *paying attention* (lit.: granting him his temple, i.e. ear)."

iw dbn.n=i ꜥ.t nb.t n.t pr.w nsw ꜥnḫ(.w) wḏꜣ(.w) snb(.w) r ḥḥi n=i s.t-ḳb.t n gmi.n=i sy "I went around every chamber of the palace – may it live, be prosperous and healthy – to find for myself entertainment, *without finding it.*"

b) *nn* + adverbial clause (§ 47.1) (less frequent)

"It (the snake) spoke to me (the shipwrecked sailor),  *nn wi ḥr sḏm st* without me hearing it."

c) *nn* + infinitive (where the identity of the subject is obvious, § 85, 143 b)

"I let his weapons be carried off,  *nn tši.t ḥr ꜥḥꜣ* without desisting from fighting."

Note: If the infinitive is followed by an object that is identical with the subject of the main clause, the construction can best be translated as a passive:

 *pri=k ꜥḳ=k nn ḥnḥn=k* "May you go forth and enter, without being turned back (lit.: your turning back not existing)."

§ 137 3) NEGATION of the AORIST *sḏm=f* / *irr=f* (§ 70)

tm=f sḏm(.w)

a) In the Emphatic Construction (cp. § 70.1):

 *tm=k tr sḏm(.w) ḥr m* "*Why* then do you not listen?"

b) As a nominal verb form:

1. In an object clause (cp. §§ 70.2a):

 *rḫ.n=k tm=sn sfn(.w)* "You know they are not mild."

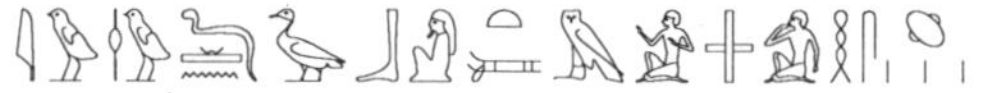 *iw wḏ.n Gbb tm=i wnm(.w) ḥs* "Geb has decreed that I do not eat excrement."

2. As the predicate of a *pw*-Sentence (§ 53):

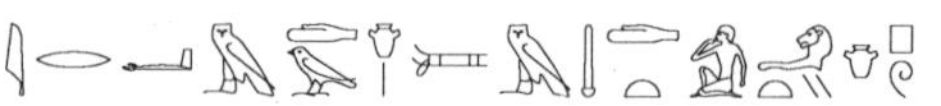 *ir ꜥmd ib tm mdw.t*(inf. § 134) *ḥꜣ.ty pw* "As for slackness of the heart, it is (i.e. signifies) that the heart does not speak."

4) NEGATION of the (PRESENT) PERFECT *sḏm.n=f* (§ 71) **§ 138**

a) Nominal / Emphatic verb form: **tm.n=f sḏm.w* (this form is, however, not attested)

b) Verbal Form: *n sḏm=f* (see § 72.1)

1. In a main clause:

The examples are not unequivocal; *n sḏm=f* negates *sḏm.n=f* in a paratactic main clause (§ 71.2) as well as the Complex Verb Form *iw sḏm.n=f* that introduces an initial main clause. One would expect *n sḏm=f*, like *sḏm.n=f*, to appear in a paratactic main clause, e.g.:

sic!

ink mrr.y h(ꜣ)w=f sdmi n {n} ꜣb.t=f n ḥbs=i ḥr r n.ty m bꜣk.w

"I was one whom his family loves, who was attached to his clan; I did not hide (my) face from him who was in service."

The theme of the negated clause continues that of the *ink*-Sentence; since *h(ꜣ)w*, *ꜣb.t* and *n.ty m bꜣk.w* form a progression from a close circle to a wider circle of people, it is more likely that here *n ḥbs=i* introduces a paratactic main clause, rather than an initial main clause.

2. In a subordinate clause:

iri.t=i (§ 85.4) *šm.t m ḫnty.t n kꜣi=i spr r ẖnw pn ḫmt.n=i* (§ 71.2b) *ḫpr ḥꜣꜥ.yt* (§ 75.2) *n ḏd=i ꜥnḫ r-sꜣ=f* "My going south: I did not intend to reach this residence, having thought that a disturbance would take place and not expecting to live after it (the disturbance)."

The section begins with an infinitive that serves as a heading introducing a new event (§ 85.4); *n kꜣi=i* introduces a main clause (§ 142 a), *ḫmt.n=i* and *n ḏd=i* are in subordinate clauses.

iri.n(=i) ḥsw.t n rmṯ nb rḫ.w mi ḫm.w n sṯni=i "I showed favour to all people, knowledgeable and ignorant alike, without my discriminating."

§ 139 5) NEGATION of the FUTURE (PROSPECTIVE) *sḏm=f* (§ 74)

a) Nominal / Emphatic verb form: *tm(.w)=f sḏm(.w)*

Following  *k3* (§ 37):  *k3 tm(.w)=n rḏi.t* (§ 134) *ib=n m-s3 pḥ n (.y) p3y=n mšʿ* "*For the rear-guard of our army* we will not have concern (lit.: we will not place our heart/thoughts after …)!"

In an object clause:  *iw wḏ.n Gbb it Wsir tm(.w)=i wnm(.w) ḥs* "Geb, the father of Osiris, has commanded that I will not eat excrement."

b) Verbal form: Negative Verb *imi*  (in negative wishes, prohibitions)

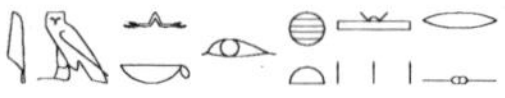 *imi(.w)=k iri(.w) iḫ.t r=s* "You will not do a thing against it."

§ 140 6) NEGATION of the SUBJUNCTIVE *sḏm=f* / *iri(.y)=f* (§ 75)

a) Nominal / Emphatic verb form: *tm=f sḏm(.w)*

In a final clause following  (§ 37):

The eloquent peasant says: "Give me my property,  *iḫ tm=i sbḥ(.w)* that I may not cry out."

b) Verbal form: Negative Verb *imi*  (in negative wishes, prohibitions)

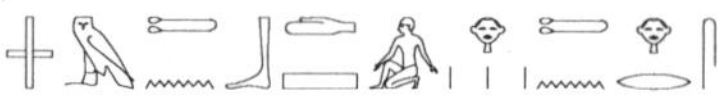 *imi=ṯn bdš(.w) ḥr.w=ṯn ḥr=s* "Let not (may not) your faces be downcast because of it (i.e. don't be depressed)."

 *imi=k wsr(.w) m ẖ.t=s* "May you not be strong in her body."

§ 141 7) NEGATION of the PERFECTIVE PASSIVE *sḏm(.w/y)=f* (§ 77) (Old Egyptian)

a) Nominal / Emphatic verb form: *tm=f sḏm(.w)*

 *m k3i(.w)* (§ 135) *ib=k tm=f dḥi(.w)* "Don't be arrogant (lit.: let not your heart be high), that you (lit.: it/your heart) not be humbled!" (final clause)

"Let him be deprived of his temple office, 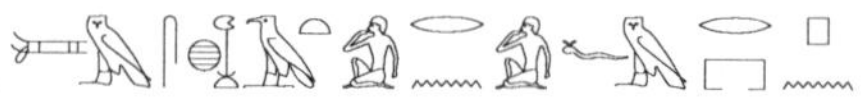 *tm sḫ3.t rn=f m r3-pr.w pn* that his name not be remembered in this temple."

b) Verbal form: *n sḏm=f*

 *iw=f rḏi.w n=i n nḥm=f m-ʿ(.w=i)* "He (the enemy) has been given to me; he was not taken from my hand."

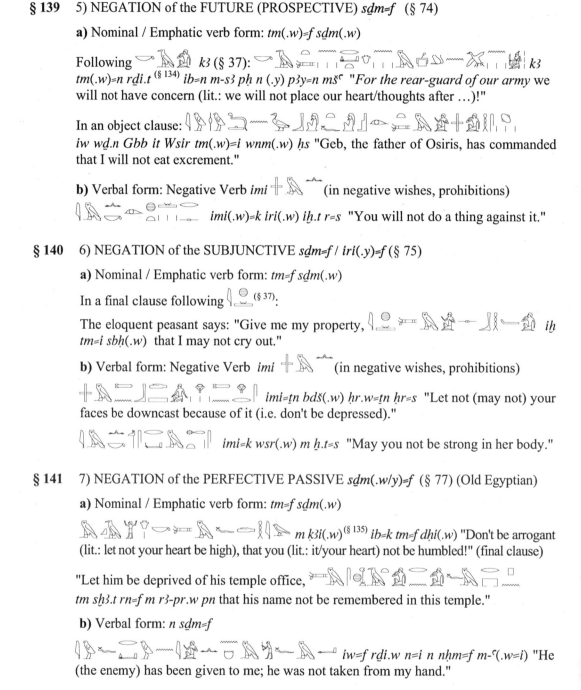

OVERVIEW OF THE SUFFIX CONJUGATION

		Nominal Verb Forms: Emphatic Construction		Verbal Forms: main clauses and subordinate clauses	
		affirmative	negated	affirmative	negated
INDICATIVE					
Aorist	Active	*irr=f*	*tm=f iri(.w)*	---	---
	Passive	*irr.tw=f*	*tm.tw=f iri(.w)*	---	---
Circumst. *sḏm=f* / Old Perf.	Active	---	---	*iri=f* Old Perf.[2] (condition)	*n iri.n=f*[1] *nn sw ḥr sḏm*[2] (*nn* + inf.)[2]
	Passive	---	---	*iri.tw=f*	*n iri.ntw=f*[1]
Perfect	Active	*iri.n=f*	*tm.n=f iri(.w)*	*iri.n=f* (trans.) Old Perf. (intr. movem.)	*n iri=f*[3] (*n iri.t=f*)
	Passive	*iri=f* (OK) *iri.ntw=f*	*tm=f iri(.w)* (OK) *tm.ntw=f iri(.w)*	*iri* + noun Old Perf. (pron. subject)	*n iri=f* (OK) *n iri.tw=f*[3] (*n iri.t=f*)
Future (Prospective)	Active	*iri(.w)=f*	*tm(.w)=f iri(.w)*	*iri(.w)=f*	*imi=f iri(.w)*
	Passive	*iri(.w)tw=f*	*tm(.w)tw=f iri(.w)*	*iri(.w)tw=f*	not attested
SUBJUNCTIVE					
Active		*iri=f*	*tm=f iri(.w)*	*iri=f*	*imi=f iri(.w)*
Passive		*iri.wtw=f*	*tm.tw=f iri(.w)*	*iri.tw=f*	not attested

TABLE 2 – SUFFIX CONJUGATION

Notes:

[1] Also in main clauses, since the negative forms of the Circumstantial (Present) *sḏm=f* and the Complex Aorist I *iw(=f) sḏm=f* are identical (§§ 136, 142, Table 3).

[2] In adverbial subordinate clauses.

[3] Also in main clauses, since the negative forms of the Complex Verb Forms *iw sḏm.n=f* / *iw sḏm.ntw=f* and the verbal *sḏm.n=f* are identical (§§ 138, 142, Table 3).

§ 142 8) NEGATION of the COMPLEX VERB FORMS with *iw* (§§ 90–94)

a) The following negative forms are the negative equivalents of the PRESENT PERFECT FORMS *iw sḏm.n=f* (§ 91 a) and *iw* + Old Perfective (§ 91 c):

- *n sḏm=f* (formally identical with *n sḏm=f* of the Perfect *sḏm.n=f* § 138)

   *n rḏi=i s3=i n ˁ3m* "I did not turn my back to an Asiatic (i.e. did not flee)."

- *n-sp sḏm=f* (*n-sp* § 133 + Subjunctive *sḏm=f* § 75)

   *n-sp iri.y=i msḏd.(w)t nb(.t)* "Never did I do anything hated."

- *n sḏm.t=f* (§ 73.1)

   *ḫpr.n=k ... n ḫpr.t nṯr.w* "That you came into being ... is before the gods came into being."

- *n sḏm=f* (as negative of *iw* + Old Perfective § 81)

  Kheops says to Djedi:  *iw=k rḫ.ti tnw n3-n(.y) ip.wt wn.t Ḏḥw.ty* "You know the number of the naoi of the sanctuary of Thoth." Djedi answers:  *n rḫ=i tnw ir.y* "I do not know the number thereof."

b) *n sḏm.n=f* – negative equivalent of COMPLEX AORIST I *iw(=f) sḏm=f* (§ 92) (identical with *n sḏm.n=f* of the Circumstantial Present *sḏm=f*, § 136).

 *ˁn pw n rḏi.n=f s3=f* "He is one who returns; he does not turn his back."

c) *nn sḏm=f* – negative equivalent of COMPLEX FUTURE *iw=f r sḏm* (§ 94)

 *nn msi=s r nḥḥ* "She will not give birth for eternity."

The following table (Table 3) summarises these constructions:

	affirmative (§§ 90–94)	**negated** (§ 142)
PERFECT *iw sḏm.n=f*	*iw sḏm.n=f* he (has) heard	*n sḏm=f* he has not heard *n-sp* + Subjunctive *sḏm=f* he never heard *n sḏm.t=f* he has not yet heard
iw + **Old Perfective**	*iw=f iyi.w* he has come *iw=f iri.w* he has been made	*n iyi=f* he has not come *n iri.tw=f* he has not been made
COMPLEX AORIST I	*iw(=f) sḏm=f* he hears	*n sḏm.n=f* he does not hear
COMPLEX FUTURE	*iw=f r sḏm* he will hear	*nn sḏm=f* (Middle Egyptian) *n* + Future *sḏm=f* (Old Egypt.) he will not hear

TABLE 3 - COMPLEX VERB FORMS WITH *IW*

9) NEGATION of the INFINITIVE (§§ 82–85) **§ 143**

a) With the Negative Verb  *tm* (§ 132)
tm takes the form of the infinitive; the verb that carries the meaning follows as a Negative Complement. This construction is used when the infinitive either **1.** serves as a noun or **2.** follows a preposition:

1. 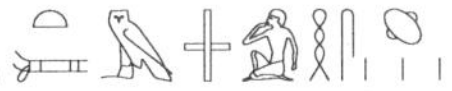 *tm wnm(.w) ḥs* "To not eat excrement." – title of a spell;

2. "The southern boundary made in year 8, …
 *r tm rḏi(.w) sni sw Nḥsy nb* in order not to allow that any Nubian pass it."

b)  *nn* + infinitive "without … ~ing"

In this construction it is not the infinitive as such but rather the whole clause that is negated (cp. §§ 47, 57); primarily used in adverbial subordinate clauses:

"These things are to belong to your son, 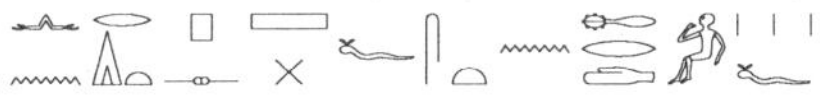
nn rḏi.t psš=f st n ḫrd.w=f without allowing that he divide them for his children."

10) NEGATION of PARTICIPLES, RELATIVE FORMS and the *sḏm.t(y)=f(y)*-FORM **§ 144**

The negative equivalents of the Participles, Relative Forms and the *sḏm.t(y)=f(y)*-Form are expressed with the Negative Verb *tm*. The Negative Verb *tm* takes on the relevant form and the verb that bears the meaning appears as a Negative Complement (or infinitive, § 134).

§ 145 **a)** NEGATION of the PARTICIPLES

1. Active

In the active, the forms of the imperfective and perfective participles of *tm* are the same and they can therefore not be distinguished:

 *in ib sḫpr(.w) nb=f m sḏm(.w) m tm(.w) sḏm(.w)* "It is the heart (i.e. mind) that forms its owner as one who hears or one who does not hear."

It is not always clear whether *tm* in Egyptian is imperfective since, when used in an epithet, the perfective participle can also have present sense.

 *mdw.t m3(w).t tm.t sw3i(.w)* "A new language which has never come to pass (lit.: passed by)."

2. Passive

a. Imperfective participle

 *tm(.w) ḫnn(.w) wḏ.t-mdw=f* "One, whose command is never transgressed."

b. Perfective participle

"All lands  *tmm(.w) ḫnd(.w) st in ky.wy bi.tyw* which have never been trodden by other kings."

Note: *tmm(.w)* is the perfective passive participle of a 2-radical verb with gemination, § 100.

§ 146 **b)** NEGATION of the RELATIVE FORM

 *nn s.t nb.t tm.tn(=i) iri(.w) mn.ww im=s* "There was not any place in which I did not make monuments."

§ 147 **c)** NEGATION of the *sḏm.ty=fy*-FORM

 *ir grt fḫ.t(y)=fy sw tm.t(y)=f(y) ꜥḥ3(.w) ḥr=f* "But as for him who will lose it (the border), who will not fight for it ..."

M) QUESTIONS § 148

Questions are either not specifically marked as such (i.e. they would have been indicated by intonation) or they are introduced by  *in* or the later form  *in-iw* (§ 34).

Word order and syntax are the same as in statements.

 *in-iw ini.n=k mi ḳd* "Have you brought everything?"
Interrogative pronouns and adverbs (§ 34) occupy the same position in a sentence as corresponding parts of speech in statements, e.g. in an Adjectival Sentence (§ 56):

 *pw sw ʿḳ(.w)* "Who is he (lit. he is who), the one who enters?" Here *pw* (for *pw tr* "who?" § 34) takes the place of an adjective, e.g. *nfr* (§ 56).

The enclitic particles  *(i)r=f* or  *tr* (§ 38) often appear in questions of all sorts:

 *išst tr iḫ.t* "What is the thing?"

N) EPEXEGESIS § 149

A pronominal subject can be specified by a name or noun at the end of a sentence:

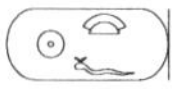 *ḫʿi=f Rʿ.w* "May he rise, (namely) Re." (the name "Khephren", see § 153)

 *msi=s ir=f si nw Rwḏ-ḏd.t* "At what time then will she give birth, (namely) Rudj-djedet?"

O) RELATIVE CLAUSES § 150

Relative Clauses are attribute clauses, i.e. they function like adjectives in that they qualify an antecedent (a preceding noun or pronoun). Like adjectives, they can also be used as nouns. Not only adjectives (§ 24b), participles (§ 103) and Relative Forms (§ 110), but also non-verbal and verbal clauses can serve as attributes. Although Egyptian participles and, in particular, Relative Forms usually have to be translated into English as relative clauses, only non-verbal and verbal clauses which are used as attributes are true Relative Clauses.

The word to which an adjective, participle or Relative Form relates (the antecedent) can be either *determined* or *undetermined.* With Relative Clauses, however, Egyptian distinguishes between these two types of antecedents.

§ 151 **1)** Relative Clause – as attribute of a *determined* antecedent

Here, the antecedent is known and specific – in translation this is indicated by the definite article "the". The Relative Clause is introduced by a Relative Adjective, which agrees in gender and number with the antecedent.

	RELATIVE ADJECTIVE	
	singular	**plural**
masc.	 *n.ty*	 *n.t(y)w*
fem.	 *n.t(y)t*	 *n.t(yw)t*

a) If the antecedent is identical with the subject of the Relative Clause, then the latter is not specifically expressed but is implicit in the Relative Adjective itself:

 *rmṯ Km.t n.t(y)w im ḥnꜥ=f* "the Egyptians who were there with him". (predicate of Relative Clause: adverb)

 *ꜥ.t nb.t n.t si n.t(y)t mr.ti* "each limb of a man which is sick". (predicate of Relative Clause: Old Perfective)

b) If the antecedent is *not* identical with the subject of the Relative Clause, then it is necessary to refer back to the antecedent by means of a resumptive pronoun:

 *wsḫ n.ty sꜣ nsw im=f* "the ship in which the prince was".

 *nṯr pw n.ty ḥr=f m ṯsm* "this god whose face is (that of) a dog".

 *ir.ty=k ipn n.ty mꜣꜣ=k*(§ 70) *im=sn* "these your eyes with which you see." (predicate of Relative Clause: Aorist *sḏm=f*)

c) The resumptive pronoun (*sw* in the following example) is also necessary when the antecedent is the object:  *pꜣ t ḥnk.t ... n.ty rḏi.n=i n=ṯn sw* "The bread and beer ... which I have given to you." (predicate of Relative clause: nominal *sḏm.n=f*)

d) An adverb can take the place of a preposition + resumptive pronoun (cp. §§ 104, 105)

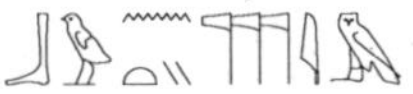 *bw n.ty nṯr.w im* "the place where the gods are".

e) A pronominal subject of a Relative Clause appears as a dependent pronoun and follows the Relative Adjective:

 *sšm pn n.ty wi ḫr=f* "this situation in which I am".

It can also appear as a suffix-pronoun, particularly where the subject is in the 2nd or 3rd person, in which case *n.ty=f* is usually written :

bw n.ty=f im "the place where he is".

Note: *n.ty nb* "everyone who", "whoever"

f) Like an adjective, a Relative Clause can also be used as a noun, i.e. absolutely, without an antecedent:

n.tyw m šms=f "those who are in his following";

n.t(y)t nb.t im=f "everything that/whatever is in him/it".

g) Negative Relative Adjective: , *iw.ty*, f. *iw.tyt*. "one who does not ..."

iw.ty mi.ty=f "one who does not have his equal".

iw.ty n=f "one who has nothing" (cp. §58 b), also *iw.ty sw* "a have-not, a pauper".

Note: *n.tyt iw.tyt* "that which is and which is not" = "everything".

2) Relative Clause – as attribute of an *undetermined* antecedent **§ 152**

A non-verbal or verbal clause whose form is identical to an independent clause can function as a Relative Clause. These "virtual Relative Clauses" follow their antecedent paratactically but are not introduced by a Relative Adjective. Only the context enables one to recognise them as attributes of an antecedent. In these cases, a resumptive pronoun always refers back to the antecedent.

nṯr pw grt nn sn.nw=f "He is indeed a god whose second (equal) does not exist." (Resumptive pronoun *f*. The clause could also be translated paratactically: "He is indeed a god. His equal does not exist".)

mi si wnm.n=f kꜣ.w n.w nh.t "like a man who has eaten the fruit of the sycamore." (Resumptive pronoun *f*; *wnm.n=f* is actually a Perfect *sḏm.n=f* in a subordinate clause [§ 71.2], which could also be translated "like a man, after he has eaten the fruit of the sycamore".)

Adverbial subordinate clauses of time or circumstance with *iw* (§ 46 b) (1) or with an Old Perfective (2) frequently occur as such an attribute of an undetermined antecedent:

(1) *gmi.n=i ḥf3.w pw iw=f m iyi.t* "I discovered it was a snake which was approaching."

(2) *tḫn.wy m ḏʿm bnbn.t=sn 3bḫ.w m ḥr.t* "two obelisks of fine gold whose pyramidions mingle with the sky".

P) APPENDIX

§ 153 1. THE TITULARY AND OTHER DESIGNATIONS OF THE KING

The titulary, *nḫb.t*, of an Egyptian King comprises five titles and names:

1. The Horus name is usually written vertically within the palace-facade upon which the Horus-falcon is perched, sometimes wearing the double-crown. The Horus-falcon on the facade is the writing for the title *Ḥr.w* "Horus". The name can also be written horizontally following the Horus-falcon without the crown and facade (see example below).

2.The "Two Ladies"-name follows the title *nb.ty*, which refers to the two goddesses of the crowns, *Nḫb.t* of Elkab and *W3ḏ.yt* of Buto.

3. The "Golden Horus"-name follows the title *Ḥr.w-nbw,* probably "Horus (made) of gold".

4. The prenomen follows the title *nsw bi.ty*, "King of Upper and Lower Egypt".

The prenomen is usually formed with the name of the sun-god Re ⊙ and is written within a cartouche.

5. The "Son of Re"-name (nomen) follows the title *s3 Rʿ.w*. It is also written within a cartouche. It is the name borne by the king before his accession and conforms to the current dynastic tradition (12th Dynasty: Amenemhet, Sesostris; 18th Dynasty: Amenhotep, Thutmosis; 19th / 20th Dynasties: Seti, Ramesses).

Today, following the ancient Greek tradition, we refer to kings by their "Son of Re" names, whereas the Egyptians of the Old Kingdom used the Horus name, and those of the Middle and New Kingdoms preferred the *nsw bi.ty* name, when referring to the king by only one name.

Example of a complete titulary (Thutmosis III):

Ḥr.w kꜣ nḫt Ḫꜥi-m-Wꜣs.t

Nb.ty Wꜣḥ-nsy.t mi Rꜥ.w m p.t

Ḥr.w-nbw Sḫm-pḥ.ty ḏsr ḫꜥ.w

Nsw bi.ty Mn-ḫpr-Rꜥ.w

Sꜣ Rꜥ.w Ḏḥwty-ms nfr ḫpr(.w)

"Horus: The strong bull who appears in Thebes; Two Ladies: Enduring of kingship like Re in heaven; Golden Horus: Mighty of strength, holy of diadems; King of Upper and Lower Egypt: Menkheperre ('The form of Re endures'(?)); Son of Re: Thutmosis, perfect of forms".

The term "Pharaoh" (< Hebrew <  *pr.w ꜥꜣ* "Great House", i.e. palace) is not used for the ruler until the 18th Dynasty; cp. "Downing Street", "The White House".

2. SYLLABIC- (GROUP-) WRITING **§ 154**

In order to write words such as foreign names, loan words or magical spells in such a way that they might be correctly pronounced, the Egyptian script, which lacked vowels, developed its own distinctive system. Certain groups, generally consisting of at least two Egyptian signs, the last of which is either *w, i* or *ꜣ*, were used to write open syllables (consonant + vowel). Here the (often uncertain) vocalisation of some of these:

	*’a, ’i*		*ra, ri*
	*’u*		*ri*
	*nu*		*ru*
	*‘a*		*ḥa, ḥi, ḥu*
	*ba, bi*		*sa, si*
	*bu*		*su*
	*pa, pi*		*ša, šu*
	*ma, mi, mu*		*ta, ti*
	*na, la*		*ṯa, ṯi, ṯu*
	*ni*		*ḏa, ḏi, ḏu*
	*l* + vowel		

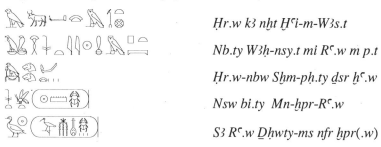

III. Sign List

The numbers following the signs refer to the more extensive list in Gardiner's *Egyptian Grammar*, from which the division into groups with their alphabetic designation has been adopted.

L. = Logogram (also: Ideogram), Ph. = Phonogram, D. = Determinative, Ph.D. = Phonetic Determinative

A. MEN

𓀀	A (1)	Seated man. L. 𓊃𓀀𓏤 *si* "man". D. man, male occupations, male personal names. L. suffix *i* "I" D. in 𓀀𓁐𓏥, people, groups of people.
𓀁	(2)	Seated man with hand to mouth or head. D. eat, be hungry, drink, speak, think, feel.
𓀂	(3)	Man kneeling. D. sit.
𓀃	(4)	Man with raised arms. D. worship; hide.
𓀄	(5)	Man hiding. D. hide.
𓀆	(6)	Man being (ritually) washed. D. pure, purify, purity.
𓀉	(7)	Man sinking to ground. D. be weary, weak.
𓀋	(9)	Man steadying basket on head. D. carry, load, work.
𓀌	(10)	Man with oar. D. in *sḳdw* "sail".
𓀎	(12)	Soldier with bow and quiver. L. 𓀎𓏤 *mšʿ* "army". D. army, enemy.
𓀏	(13)	Man with hands bound. D. enemy, rebel.
𓀐	(14)	Falling man with blood streaming from head. D. die; enemy.
𓀒	(15)	Falling or fallen man. L. 𓀒 *ḫr* "fall". D. fall, enemy.
𓀓	(16)	Man bowing down. D. bend, bow.
𓀔	(17)	Child sitting on lap. L. *ḫrd* "child". D. child; be young.
𓀗	(19)	Bent man leaning on staff. L. 𓀗 *iꜣw* "old", *smsw* "eldest", *wr* "prince". D. old.

A (21) Man standing with staff. L. *sr* "official". D. noble, courtier, friend, statue.

(22) Statue of a man with staff and sceptre. D. in *twt.w* "statue", *iti.y* "sovereign".

(23) King with staff and mace. D. in *iti.y* "sovereign".

(24) Man striking with stick. D. for actions involving effort: strike, rob, teach, be strong.

(25) Man with stick in one hand. L. *ḥwi* "smite".

(26) Man with one arm raised. D. call.

(27) Man hastening with one arm raised. In preposition *in* "by".

(28) Man with raised arms. D. joy, mourning, high. L. *ḳꜣi* "be high, exalted".

(29) Man upside-down. D. *sẖd* "be upside down".

(30) Man with arms in attitude of prayer. D. pray, praise, plead, greet.

(32) Man dancing. D. dance, rejoice.

(33) Man with stick and bundle. D. wander, travel. L. *mniw* "herdsman".

(34) Man pounding, with mortar. D. *ẖwsi* pound, build.

(35) Man building. L. *ḳd* "build". D. build.

(36) Man bending over a vessel. L. D. *ꜥf.ty* "brewer".

(40) Seated god with beard. D. god. L. suffix *i* "I" (when a god speaks).

(41/42) King with beard, uraeus (and flail). D. king. L. suffix *i* "I" (when a king speaks) Variants: (A43), (A44), (A45), (A46).

(47) Seated herdsman with staff and mat. L. *mniw* "herdsman". D. herdsman. L.D. *sꜣw* "to guard; guard". Also for (B8).

(49) Syrian with stick. D. foreigner.

(50) Seated man of rank; can replace A1 or A51. L. suffix *i* "I".

(51) A50 with flail. L. *šps* "noble". Ph. *šps*. D. noble person.

 A (52) Noble squatting with flail. D. noble; also used in place of A51.

 (53) Standing mummy. D. mummy, statue, image, form.

 (54) Recumbent mummy. D. death, coffin.

 (55) Mummy on bed. D. lie, sleep, die; corpse.

B. WOMEN

 B (1) Seated woman. D. woman, female occupations, female personal names. L. suffix *i* "I" (when a woman speaks).

 (2) Pregnant woman. D. *iwr* "conceive", *bkꜣ* "be pregnant".

 (3) Woman giving birth. L. *msi* "give birth". D. give birth.

 (5) Woman suckling child. D. suckle, nurse, care.

 (7) Queen with diadem and flower. D. name of queen.

 (8) (Gardiner A48) Weaver with sticks. L. *iri.t* "weaver". Ph. *iry*.

C. ANTHROPOMORPHIC DEITIES

 C (1) God with human head and sun-disk. L. *Rʿ.w* "Re" (sun-god). D. sun-god.

 (2) God with falcon head, sun-disk and sign of life: like C1.

 (3) God with head of ibis. L. D. *Ḏḥw.ty* "(god) Thoth".

 (4) God with head of ram. L. D. *H̱nm.w* "(god) Khnum".

 (6) God with head of a canine. L. D. *Ỉnp.w* "(god) Anubis".

 (7) God with head of Seth-animal. L. D. "(god) Seth".

 (8) Ithyphallic god with feathers, raised arm and flail. L. D. *Mnw* "(god) Min".

 (9) Goddess with horns and sun-disk. L. D. *Ḥw.t-Ḥr.w* "(goddess) Hathor"

 (10) Goddess with feather on head. L. D. *Mꜣʿ.t* "(goddess) Maat".

 (11) Kneeling god with arms uplifted (supporting the sky), with or without  on his head. L. *Ḥḥ*, "(god) Heh"; *ḥḥ* numeral "million". Ph. *ḥḥ*.

C (12) God with double feather crown. L. D. *Ỉmn.w* "(god) Amun".

(17) God with falcon head and double feather crown. L. D. *Mnṯ.w* "(god) Month".

(18) God with double feather, horns and sun-disk. L. D. (*Tꜣ*)-*Ṯnn* "(god) (Ta)-tenen".

D. PARTS OF THE HUMAN BODY

D (1) Head in profile. L. *tp* "head". D. head, back of head, back; forehead, front. Ph. *tp*.

(2) Face. L. *ḥr* "face". Ph. *ḥr*.

(3) Lock of hair. D. hair, sorrow, widow; bare, empty; colour.

(4) Eye. L. *ir.t* "eye". D. eye, see, blind, cry, wake, watch. Ph. *ir*

(5/6) Eye with eye-paint or eyebrow. D. see, blind, wake.

(9) Eye with tears. L. *rm* "cry". D. cry.

(10) Human eye with markings of falcon's head. L. D. *wḏꜣ.t* "*wedjat*-eye".

(17) Lower part of *wedjat*-eye. L. D. *ti.t* "figure, image"

(18) Ear. L. D. *msḏr* "ear".

(19/20) Nose with eye and cheek. L. *fnḏ* "nose". D. nose, smell, face, joy; be angry. Ph.D. in *ḫnt* (from *ḫnt* "face").

(21) Mouth. L. *rꜣ* "mouth". Ph. *r*.

(24) Upper lip with teeth. L. *sp.t* "edge, border".

(25) Lips. L. *sp.ty* "lips". D. lips.

(26) Lips issuing liquid. D. spit, vomit, bleed.

(27) Breast. L. *mnḏ* "breast". D. breast; suckle, nurse.

(28) Outspread arms. L. *kꜣ* "the *Ka*" (the life-force, a form of the soul). Ph. *kꜣ*.

(29) D28 on standard R12. L. *kꜣ* "the *Ka*" as a divine entity.

D (31) Combination of D32 and U36. L. *ḥm-kꜣ* "*ka*-priest".

(32) Arms in attitude of embrace. D. embrace, open.

(33) Arms engaged in rowing. L. *ẖni* "row". Ph. *ẖn*.

(34) Arms with shield and battle-axe. L. *ꜥḥꜣ* "fight; weapon, fighter".

(35) Arms in attitude of negation. L. *n* and *nn* "not", *iw.ty* "who …. not". D. be ignorant, forget. Ph. *n*.

(36) Forearm. L. "arm", "hand". Ph. ꜥ. Also for ; ; ; (D37, 38, 40, 42), esp. in hieratic texts.

(37) Forearm with -bread. L. in the root *rḏi* "give", also in the imperative *imi* "give". Ph. *ḏ, d* and *m*.

(38) Forearm with round bread. D. in *imi* "give". Ph. *mi* and *m*.

(39) Forearm with spherical vessel. D. offer, present, sacrifice.

(40) Forearm with stick in hand; used in place of A24.

(41) Forearm, palm facing downwards, upper arm bent. D. arm, shoulder; bend, sing, cease, pause, refuse.

(42) Like D41 but with upper arm straight. L. *mḥ* "cubit". D. cubit.

(43) Forearm with flail. L. *ẖwi* "protect". Ph. *ẖw*.

(44) Arm with *ꜥbꜣ*-sceptre. L. D. *ẖrp* "control, guide, lead".

(45) Arm with a *nḥb.t*-sceptre. L. D. *ḏsr* "splendid, holy".

(46) Hand. L. *ḏr.t*. Ph. *d*.

(47) Hand with curved palm. D. *ḏr.t* "hand".

(49) Fist. D. grab, conquer.

(50) Finger. L. *ḏbꜥ* "finger". D. finger. Ph. *ḏbꜥ* in numeral 10,000.

(50A) Two fingers. D. straight, exact.

(51) Horizontal finger. L. *ꜥn.t* "nail, claw". D. nail, claw, measure, take.

(52) Phallus. D. male. Ph. *mt*. Ph. and D. *kꜣ*.

(53) Phallus with fluid issuing from it. D. urinate; poison; husband, L. in *m-bꜣḥ* "in front of".

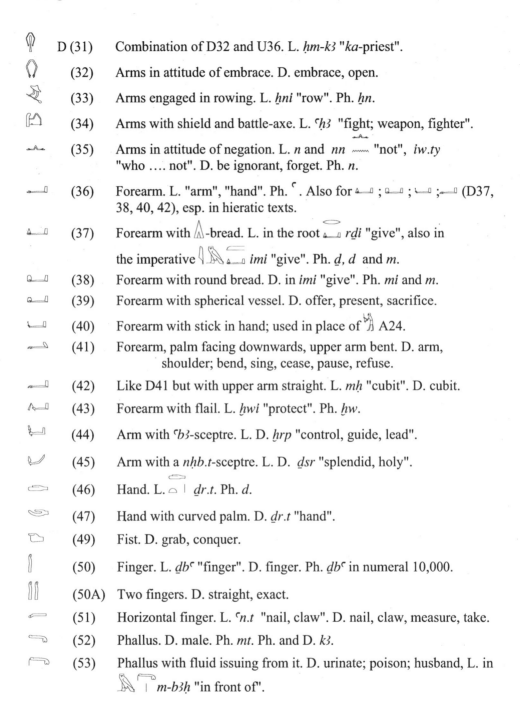

D (54) Legs walking. L.  [sign] *ỉwi* "come". D. walk, approach, hurry, halt, hesitate. L. *nmt.t* "step, movement".

(55) Legs walking backwards. D. backwards, turn about; again.

(56) Leg. L. *rd* "foot". D. leg, foot, thigh. Ph. (1) *pd*, (2) *wꜥr*, (3) *sbḳ*, (4) *gḥ* or *gḥs*.

(58) Leg. Ph. *b*.

(60) D58 combined with a vessel from which water flows. L. *wꜥb* "pure".

(61) Toes. L. *sꜣḥ* "toe". D. toe. Ph. *sꜣḥ*.

E. MAMMALS

E (1) Bull. L. *kꜣ* "bull, ox". D. cattle, herd.

(2) Aggressive bull. L. in [sign] *kꜣ nḫt* "strong bull" (epithet of the king).

(3) Calf. D. Calf, cattle.

(6) Horse. L. *ssm.t* "horse". D. horse, team.

(7) Donkey. L. D. *ꜥꜣ* "donkey".

(8) Kid. D. small cattle. Ph.D. and Ph. *ib*.

(9) New-born antelope. Ph. *iw*.

(10) Ram. D. ram, sheep. D. *H̱nm.w* "(god) Khnum".

(12) Pig. D. *rri* "pig".

(13) Cat. D. *miw* "cat".

(14) Dog (slughi). D. dog.

(15) Recumbent jackal or dog. L. *Ỉnp.w* "(god) Anubis". D. Anubis.

(16) E15 on a shrine; like E15. L. *ḥr.y sštꜣ* "he who is over the secrets".

(17) Jackal. L. D. *sꜣb* "jackal, judge".

E (18)	Wolf (? a canine) on a standard. L. or D. *Wpi-w3.wt* "the opener of the ways", "(god) Wepwawet".
(20)	The Seth-animal. L. *Stẖ, Swty*, "(god) Seth". D. Seth, turmoil, storm, thunder.
(21)	E20 recumbent. D. turmoil, storm.
(22)	Lion. L. *m3i* "lion". D. lion.
(23)	Recumbent lion. L. *rw* "lion". Ph. *rw*, *šnʿ*.
(24)	Panther. L. D. *3by* "panther".
(26)	Elephant. D. *3bw* "elephant". Ph.D. *3bw* "Elephantine".
(27)	Giraffe. D. *sr* "foretell", *mmy* "giraffe".
(31)	Goat with cylinder-seal hung about its neck. L. D. *sʿḥ* "rank, honour".
(34)	Desert hare. Ph. *wn*.

F. PARTS OF MAMMALS

F (1)	Head of ox. Replaces E1 *k3* "ox" in offering formula.
(3)	Head of hippopotamus. Ph.D. *3.t* "strength". Ph. *3t*.
(4)	Forepart of a lion. L. *ḥ3.t* "beginning, front", *ḥ3.ty* "heart".
(5)	Head of antelope. Ph. *šs3*. Inaccurately Ph.D. in *sš3*.
(6)	Forepart of antelope. Like F5.
(7)	Head of ram. D. in *šf.t* "ram, head of ram" and *šf.yt* "majesty, honour, worth, dignity".
(8)	Forepart of ram. Like F7.
(9)	Head of leopard. Written twice: L. D. *pḥ.ty* "strength".
(10)	Head and neck of an animal. D. throat; swallow.
(11)	Form of F10 in the Old Kingdom.
(12)	Head and neck of a canine. Ph. *wsr*.
(13)	Horns of ox. L. *wp.t* "crown of head, horns". Ph. *wp*.

F (16) Horn. L. *db* "horn". D. horn. Ph. *ꜥb*.

(17) F16 and a vessel from which liquid issues. L. D. *ꜥbw* "purification".

(18) Elephant tusk. D. tooth; bite, laugh. Ph. *bḥ*, *ḥw*.

(20) Tongue. L. *ns* "tongue"; *ỉm.y-rꜣ* "overseer". D. tongue; taste. Ph. *ns*.

(21) Ear of ox. L. *msḏr* "ear". D. ear; hear, be deaf. Ph. *sḏm, ỉdn*.

(22) Hind part of a lion. L. *pḥ.wy* "hind quarters". Ph. or Ph.D. *pḥ, kfꜣ*.

(23) Foreleg of an ox. L. *ḫpš* "foreleg, arm". D. foreleg, arm, strength.

(25) Leg of an ox. L. *wḥm.t* "hoof". Ph. *wḥm*.

(26) Skin of goat. L. *ḫn.t* "hide, skin". Ph. *ḫn*.

(27) Hide of ox. D. hide, leather, mammal.

(28) Variant of F27. L. *sꜣb* "dappled, variagated" in *sꜣb šw.ty* "variagated of feathers" (epithet of god Horus).

(29) Hide of ox pierced by arrow. L. D. *sti* "shoot". Ph. *st*.

(30) Water-skin. Ph. *šd*.

(31) Three fox skins tied together. Ph. *ms*.

(32) Belly of animal with teats and tail. L. *ẖ.t* "torso, body". Ph. *ẖ*.

(33) Tail. D. *sd* "tail". Ph.D. *sd*.

(34) Heart. L. *ỉb* (occasionally also *ḥꜣ.ty*) "heart". D. heart.

(35) Heart and windpipe. Ph. *nfr*.

(36) Lung with windpipe. Ph. *smꜣ*.

(37) Backbone with ribs. L. D. *ỉꜣ.t* "back".

(39) Backbone with marrow issuing from it. Ph. *ỉmꜣḫ*.

(40) Backbone with marrow issuing from both ends. Ph. *ꜣw*.

(41) Backbone with vertebrae. D. *psḏ* "back", *šꜥ.t* "slaughter".

(42) Rib. L. *spr* "rib". Ph. *spr*. Confusion with N11.

(44) Leg bone of ox with meat attached. Originally two signs (seldom

F (44) distinguished) for:
(a) D. in *iwꜥ* "thigh of ox". Ph. and Ph.D. *iwꜥ*.
(b) D. in *sw.t* "leg of beef". Ph. *isw*.

(46/47) Intestines. D. intestines. Ph. *ḳꜣb, pẖr, dbn.* D. turn around.

(51) Piece of meat. D. meat, bodily part.

(52) Excrement. D. *ḥs* "excrement".

G. BIRDS

G (1) Egyptian vulture. Ph. *ꜣ*

(4) Long-legged buzzard. Ph. *tw*

(5) Falcon. L. *Ḥr.w* "(god) Horus". D. in *bik* "falcon".

(7) Falcon on a standard. D. god; in hieratic texts regularly used in place of A40.

(7A) Falcon in boat. L. *Nm.ty* "(god) Nemty".

(8) Falcon on S12. L. *Ḥr.w-nbw* "Horus of Gold" (title of king, §153).

(9) Falcon with sun-disk. L. *Rꜥ.w-Ḥr.w-ꜣḫ.ty* "(god) Re-Harakhte".

(10) Sokar-barque. D. in *Skr* "(god) Sokar"; *ḥnw* "*Henu*-Barque" of Sokar.

(11) Image of falcon. D. in *ꜥšm* (*ꜥḫm, ꜥẖm*) "divine image".

(14) Vulture. D. vulture. Ph. *nrw, mw.t, mt.*

(15) Vulture with flail. L. *Mw.t* "(goddess) Mut".

(16) The vulture-goddess Nekhbet and the snake-goddess Uto on baskets. L. *Nb.ty* "the Two Ladies" (title of king, § 153).

(17) Owl. Ph. *m*.

(21) Sennâr guinea-fowl. L. *nḥ* "*neh*-bird". Ph. *nḥ*.

(22) Hoopoe. Ph. *ḏb*.

(23) Lapwing. L. *rḫy.t* "subjects, commoners". Ph.D. in the same word.

(24) Lapwing with twisted wings. Like G23.

G (25) Crested ibis. L. *ꜣḫ* "*akh*-spirit" (the transfigured deceased). Ph. *ꜣḫ*.

(26) Ibis on a standard. D. in *Ḏḥw.ty* "(the god) Thoth".

(27) Flamingo. D. flamingo. Ph. *dšr*.

(28) Black ibis. Ph. *gm*.

(29) Stork. L. *bꜣ* "*ba*-spirit" (the empowered spirit of the deceased). Ph. *bꜣ*.

(30) Three storks. L. *bꜣ.w* "souls, power".

(31) Heron. D. *bnw* "phoenix".

(32) Heron on a perch. L. D. *bꜥḥ* "be inundated".

(33) Egret (?). L. *sdꜣ* "*seda*-bird". Ph.D. *sdꜣ* "tremble".

(35) Cormorant. Ph. *ꜥḳ*.

(36) Swallow. Ph. *wr*.

(37) Sparrow. D. small, evil, incomplete, empty, sick.

(38) Goose or duck (not always distinguished from G39). L. *ꜣpd* "bird". D. goose, bird, flying animals (e.g. grasshopper). Ph. *gb* in *Gbb* "(god of earth) Geb".

(39) Pintail duck. Ph. *sꜣ*.

(40) Flying duck. L. *pꜣ* "fly". Ph. *pꜣ*.

(41) Duck alighting. D. alight, bird. Ph.D. *ḫn*. Appears as D. for no apparent reason in various words; also in place of G40.

(42) Duck. L. *wšꜣ* "fatten". D. in *ḏfꜣ* "provisions".

(43) Quail chick. Ph. *w*.

(47) Duckling. L. *ṯꜣ* "duckling". Ph. *ṯꜣ*.

(48) Three ducklings in nest. D. *šs* "nest".

(49) Three ducks' heads protruding from water. L. D. *sš* "bird-pool", "nest".

(51) Egret (?) catching fish. D. to fish.

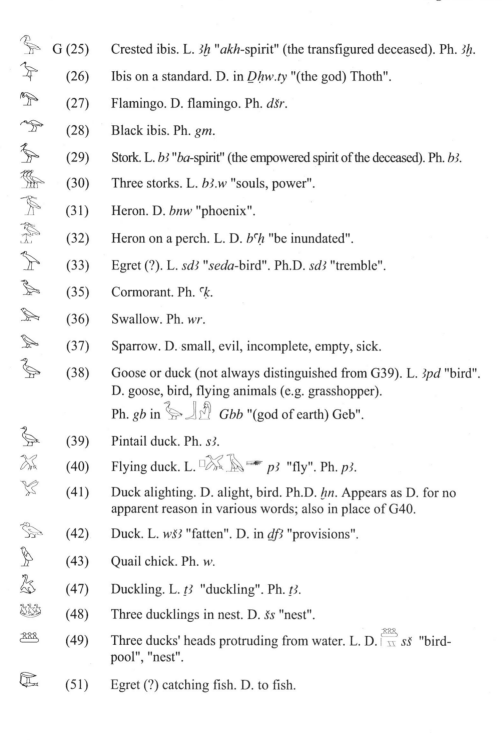

G (52) Goose picking up grain. D. in *snm* "feed (transitive)".

(53) Bird with human head. L. *bꜣ* "*Ba*-spirit".

(54) Trussed goose or duck. D. bird; offer. Ph. *snḏ*.

H. PARTS OF BIRDS

H (1) Head of pintail duck. For G38. L. *ꜣpd* "bird". D. *wšn* "wring neck (of a bird)".

(2) Head of a bird with a crest. Ph.D. *mꜣꜥ, wšm*.

(3) Head of a spoonbill. Ph.D. *pꜣḳ*.

(4) Head of vulture. Ph.D. *nr* in *nr.w* "terror". In a writing of *rmṯ* "people".

(5) Wings. D. wings; fly.

(6) Feather. L. *šw.t* "feather". Ph. *šw, mꜣꜥ.t*.

(8) Egg. D. egg; goddess. L. *sꜣ* "son".

I. AMPHIBIOUS ANIMALS AND REPTILES

I (1) Lizard (*Tarentola mauritanica*). D. lizard. Ph. *ꜥšꜣ*.

(3) Crocodile. L. *msḥ* "crocodile". D. crocodile; be greedy, aggressive, angry. Two crocodiles: Ph. *iti.y* "sovereign".

(5) Crocodile, tail curved inward. Ph.D. *sꜣḳ* "collect (oneself)".

(6) Crocodile tail with scales. Ph. *km*.

(7) Frog. D. *ḳrr* "frog"; *Ḥḳ.t* "(goddess) Hekat".

(8) Tadpole. Ph. *ḥfn*; numeral 100,000.

(9) Horned viper (*Cerastes cerastes*). D. father. Ph. *f, it*.

(10) Cobra. Ph. *ḏ*.

(12) Cobra in position of attack. D. uraeus, goddess.

(13) Cobra on basket. D. *Wꜣḏ.yt* "(goddess) Wadjet" of Buto.

I (14) Snake. L. *ḥf3.w* "snake". D. snake, worm.

K. FISHES

K (1) Bulti-fish (*Tilapia nilotica*). D. fish. Ph. *in*.

(2) A fish (*Barbus bynni*). Ph.D. in *bw.t* "abomination, taboo".

(3) A fish (*Mugil cephalus*). Ph. *ꜥḏ* in title *ꜥḏ mr* "administrator of a district".

(4) Oxyrhynchus fish (*Mormyrus kannume*). Ph. *ḫ3*.

(5) A fish (*Petrocephalus bane*). D. *rm.w* "fish". Ph. *bs*.

L. INSECTS AND SMALL ANIMALS

L (1) Dung beetle (*Scarabaeus sacer*). L. *ḫpr* "dung beetle". Ph. *ḫpr*.

(2) Bee. L. *bi.t* "bee". Ph. *bit*.

(6) Bivalve shell. Ph. *ḫ3* in *ḫ3w.t* "offering table".

(7) Scorpion. L. *Srk.t* "(Scorpion-goddess) Selkis".

M. TREES AND PLANTS

M (1) Tree. D. tree. Ph. *i3m, im*.

(2) Herb. D. plant, flower. Ph. *ḥn, is*; rare: for suffix-pronoun 1st person singular. *=i* "I".

(3) Branch. L. *ḫt* "wood, tree". D. wood, object of wood. Ph. *ḫt*.

(4) Palm rib. D. be young. Ph. *rnp*. In the group *rnp.t sp* (alternative reading *ḥ3.t-sp*) "regnal year". Ph.D. in *tr* "time"; often combined with other signs: (M5), (M6) or (M7). Also in *T3-mri* "Egypt".

(8) Pool with lotus flowers. L. *š3* "lotus pool, meadow". Ph. *š3*; *3ḫ* in the group *3ḫ.t* "inundation (season)".

M (11) Flower on long twisting stalk. L. D. *wdn* "offer".

(12) Lotus flower. Ph. *ḫꜣ*; numeral 1,000.

(13) Papyrus stalk. L. *wꜣḏ* "papyrus plant, papyrus column". Ph. *wꜣḏ*, *wḏ*.

(15) Clump of papyrus with buds hanging down. D. papyrus, watery terrain, swamp, Lower Egypt. Ph. *ꜣḫ, mḥ*.

(16) Clump of papyrus. Ph. *ḥꜣ*, also *mḥ* (like M15).

(17) Reed. Ph. *i*.

(18) Reed combined with D54. In *iyi* "come".

(19) Conical loaves between a slice of bread and a vessel. L. D. in *ʿꜣb.t* "offering".

(20) Three reeds and three shoots. L. and D *sḫ.t* "marsh land, flat land, field". Ph. *sm*, in place of M21.

(21) Like previous sign with a loop at side. L. *sm* "herb, plant". Ph. *sm*.

(22) Rush with shoots. Two signs: Ph. *nn*.

(23) Plant. L. "*sw.t*-plant". Ph. *sw*.

(24) M23 combined with D21. Ph. *rs*.

(26) Plant, perhaps flowering form of M23. L. *šmʿ* "Upper Egypt". Ph. *šmʿ*.

(29) Pod containing sweet fruit. Ph. *nḏm*.

(30) Sweet root (?). L. D. in *bnr* "sweet".

(31/32) Root of the lotus plant. D. grow. Ph.D. *rd*.

(33) Three grains. L. *it* "barley". D. corn, grain.

(34) Ear of emmer. L. D. in *bd.t*, var. *bd.t* "emmer".

(35) Heap of grain. D. *ʿḥʿ.w* "heaps, piles".

(36) Sheaf of flax. Ph. *ḏr*.

(40) Bundle of reeds. Ph. *is*.

(42) Blossom (?). Ph. *wn* (often replaced by Z11).

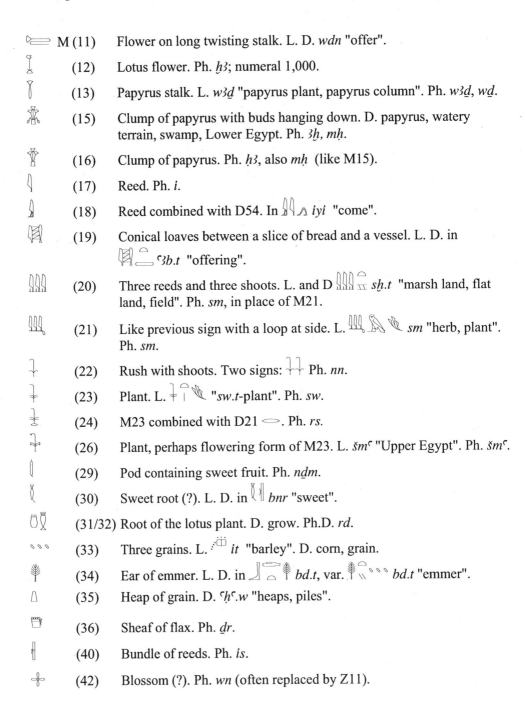

M (43) Vine trellis on prop. D. wine, garden, figs.

(44) Thorn. D. thorn, sharp. Ph. *spd*.

N. SKY, EARTH, WATER

N (1) Sky. L. D. *p.t* "sky". L. *ḥr.y.* "upper, chief".

(2) Sky with something suspended from it. L. *grḥ* "night". D. night, darkness.

(4) Water falling from sky. L. *iꜣd.t* "dew". D. dew, rain.

(5) Sun. L. *rꜥ.w* "sun, day"; *hrw.w* "day"; in dates is read *sw*. D. sun, rise, yesterday, tomorrow, period of time.

(6) Sun with uraeus. L. D. *Rꜥ.w* "(sungod) Re".

(7) Sun on the sign T28. Abbreviation for *ẖr.t-hrw.w* "what belongs to the day".

(8) Sun with rays. D. sunshine, rays; rise. Ph. *wbn, ḥnmm.t*.

(9) Moon with lower half obscured. L. *psḏn.tyw* "New-moon festival"; Abbr. *psḏ* in *psḏ.t* "Ennead (nine primaeval gods; assembly of gods)".

(10) Moon partially obscured. Like N9.

(11) Crescent moon. L. *iꜥḥ* "moon". In dates: *ꜣbd* "month"; otherwise usually written or . D. moon. Sometimes confused with F42.

(12) Like N11. Also (17th / early 18th Dyn.).

(14) Star. L. *sbꜣ* "star". D. star, constellation, period (time). Ph. *sbꜣ, d(w)ꜣ* in *dwꜣ.t* "netherworld".

(15) Star in circle. L. *dwꜣ.t* (*dꜣ.t*) "netherworld".

(16) Flat land with grains of sand (also without these). L. *tꜣ* "land, earth". Ph. *tꜣ*. D. land, earth, estate (*ḏ.t*), thus also in *ḏ.t* "eternity".

(17) Like N16.

(18) Sandy tract. L. or *iw* "island". D. desert, foreign land.

(20) Tongue of land. D. sandbank, shore. Ph. *wḏb*.

N (21) Tongue of land. L. , *i͗db* "shore" (dual *i͗db.wy* "the two banks", "Egypt"). D. earth, land, geographic terms.

(23) Irrigation canal. D. irrigated land, also for N21.

(23A) (Gardiner Aa11). Mound of earth, pedestal. Ph. *mꜣꜥ*.

(24) Plot of land with irrigation canals. L. *spꜣ.t* "district, nome". D. district, nome (province), names of nomes, garden.

(25) Desert land. L. *ḫꜣs.t.* "desert, foreign land". D. desert, mountains, foreign land, cemetery.

(26) Sand-covered mountain. L. *ḏw* "mountain". Ph. *ḏw*.

(27) Sun rising over mountain. L. *ꜣḫ.t* "place of sunrise / sunset, horizon".

(28) Sun rising over a hill. L. *ḫꜥ* "hill of the sunrise". Ph. *ḫꜥ*.

(29) Sandy hill-slope. Ph. *ḳ* (also transliterated *q*).

(30) Mound of earth with bushes. L. D. *i͗ꜣ.t* "mound".

(31) Road with bushes. L. *wꜣ.t* "road". D. road, ascend, general expression of location (e.g. "here"), distance. Ph. *ḥr, wꜣ*.

(33) Grain of sand. D. sand, granular substances, metal, minerals, medicines.

(34) Now U30A.

(35) Ripple of water. Ph. *n*. Three ripples of water L. *mw* "water". D. water, liquid; drink, wash. Ph. *mw*.

(36) Canal with water. L. *mr* "canal". D. river, lake, sea (often together with). Ph. *mr, mi*.

(37) Pool. L. *š* (*ši*) "pool". Ph. *š*. Variants N38 , N39 .

(40) Combination of N37 and D54 in *šm* "go".

(41/42) Well filled with water. D. well, pool. Ph. *ḥm, bi͗ꜣ, pḥ*.

O. BUILDINGS AND PARTS OF BUILDINGS

O (1) House. L. *pr.w* "house". D. house, building, place. Ph. *pr*.

O (2) O1 and T3 combined. In *pr.w ḥḏ* "treasury", lit.: "house of silver".

(3) Combination of O1, P8, X3 and W22. In *pr.t-ḫrw* "funerary offering".

(4) Shelter of matting in field. Ph. *h*.

(6) Plan view of rectangular enclosure. L. *ḥw.t* "large building, temple, tomb."

(9) Basket (V30) on top of house (O6). *Nb.t-ḥw.t* "(goddess) Nephthys".

(10) Falcon (G5) in house (O6). *Ḥw.t-Ḥr.w* "(goddess) Hathor".

(11) Palace. L. *ꜥḥ* "palace".

(16) Gate surmounted by uraei. L. in *tꜣy.ty* "vizier".

(22) Open hut with central post. L. *sḥ* "hut, hall". D. hut, hall. Ph. *sḥ*.

(23) Thrones with canopy used in the Sed-festival. L. in and D. in *ḥꜣb-sd* "Sed-festival".

(24) Pyramid. L. *mr* "pyramid". D. in names of pyramid complexes.

(25) Obelisk. L. D. *tḫn* "obelisk".

(26) Stele. L. D. *wḏ* "stele".

(28) Column with tenon at top. L. *iwn* "column, pillar". Ph. *iwn*.

(29) Tent-pole. Ph. *ꜥꜣ*.

(31) Door leaf. L. *ꜥꜣ* "door". D. door, open.

(32) Gateway. D. door, gateway. L. *sbꜣ* "door".

(34) Bolt. L. *s* "bolt". Ph. *s*, also for R22.

(35) Combination of O34 and D54. Ph.D. in words implying movement beginning or ending with *s*: *sbi* "go, send", *si* "perish"; also in *ms* "bring, offer".

(36) Wall. L. *inb* "wall". D. wall, bulwark, fort.

(38) Corner of wall. D. corner, angle, council of officials (L. *ḳnb.t*), gate, street.

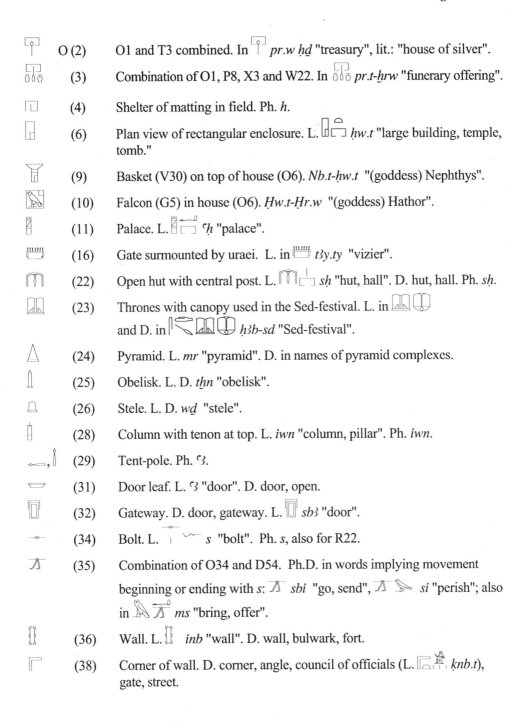

O (39) Block of stone. D. *i͗nr* "stone"; weight, brick.

(40) Stairway. D. L. stairway, e.g. , var. *r(w)d* "stairway"; , var. *ḫtyw* "terrace, terraced hill".

(42) Fence. Ph. *šsp*.

(44) Emblem of god Min. L. in and D. in *i͗ꜣw.t* "office, rank".

(45) Vault. L. in and D. in *i͗p.t* "private apartments harim".

(49) Town plan with crossroads. L. *nw.t* (*niw.t*) "town". D. village, town, city, Egypt, nome, estate.

(50) Threshing-floor with grain. D. threshing-floor. Ph. *sp*.

P. SHIPS AND PARTS OF SHIPS

P (1) Boat on water. D. ship, boat, barque; travel downstream/north.

(1A) P1 upside down. D. capsize, overturn, upset.

(2) Sailing boat. D. sail upstream, travel south.

(3) Sacred barque. L. *wiꜣ* "sacred barque". D. in the names of various sacred barques.

(4) Fishing boat with net. L. *wḥꜥ* "fisherman".

(5) Mast (P6) with sail. L. *ṯꜣw* "wind, air, breath". D. wind, storm, sail.

(6) Mast. Ph. *ꜥḥꜥ*.

(8) Oar (also written horizontally, e.g. in *mꜣꜥ ḫrw*). D. oar, rudder. Ph. *ḫrw*.

(11) Mooring post. D. mooring post; to land. Also for Aa28 (*ḳd*).

Q. DOMESTIC AND FUNERARY FURNITURE

Q (1) Seat. L. in *s.t* "seat, place". Ph. *st*; *s* in *Wsir* (or *ꜣsir*) "(god) Osiris"; *ḥtm*.

(2) Portable seat. Ph. *s* in *Wsir* (or *ꜣsir*) "(god) Osiris".

(3) Stool of reed matting. Ph. *p*.

Q (6) Coffin. L. D. *ḳrs.t* "coffin, burial".

(7) Brazier with flame . D. fire, flame; cook, be hot; torch, wick.

R. TEMPLE FURNITURE AND SACRED SYMBOLS

R (4) Bread offering on mat. L. *ḥtp* "altar, offering, be pleased". Ph. *ḥtp*.

(5) Censer. L. *k3p* "fumigate". Ph. *k3p, kp*.

(7) Bowl for incense with smoke rising from it. L. *snṯr* "incense". Also in or *b3* "*ba*-spirit".

(8) Pole wrapped in cloth with end of cloth as pennant; old sign for a numen. L. *nṯr* "god". Ph. *nṯr*.

(10) Combination of R8, T28 and part of N25. L. *ḫr.t -nṯr* "necropolis".

(11) Column of stalks or ears of corn bundled together. L. *ḏd* "djed-pillar". Ph. *ḏd*.

(12) Standard upon which religious symbols are borne. D. standard. Combined with numerous signs for deities (e.g. G26).

(13) Falcon on a standard, in front of him (H6). L. *imn.t* "west".

(14) Feather on a standard. L. *imn.t* "west", *wnm.y* "right".

(15) Spear-standard. L. *i3b.t* "east", *i3b.y* "left". From the 18th Dynasty onwards Ph. *3b* through confusion with *3b* (U23).

(19) Sceptre S40 with feather. L. *W3s.t* "Thebes".

(22) Two belemnites? L. *Mnw* "(god) Min (of Coptos)"; *Ḫm* the city Letopolis in the Delta. Ph. *ḫm*.

(24) Two bows in a sheath. L. or D. *N(i).t*. "(goddess) Neith".

S. CROWNS, DRESS, STAVES

, S (1/2) White crown of Upper Egypt. L. *ḥḏ.t* "the White Crown". D. White Crown.

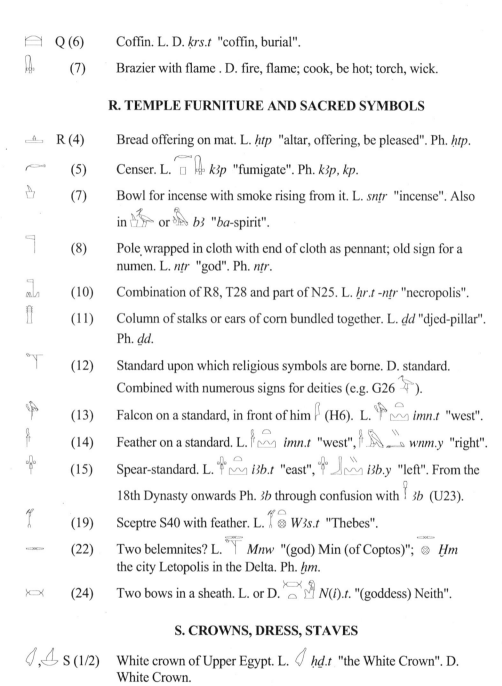

S (3/4) Red crown of Lower Egypt. L. *dšr.t* "the Red Crown". D. Red Crown. Ph. *n*.

(5/6) Double crown. L. *sḫm.ty* "the two mighty ones (i.e. crowns)". D. double crown.

(7) The blue crown. L. *ḫprš* "the blue crown". D. blue crown.

(8) The *Atef*-crown. L. *ꜣtf* "the *Atef*-crown". D. *Atef*-crown.

(9) Two feathers. L. *šw.ty* "double feather". D. double feather.

(10) Hair band with tied bow. L. *wꜣḥ.w* "wreath"; *mḏḥ* "to bind, hew". Ph. *mḏḥ*.

(11) Ornamental broad collar. L. *wsḫ* "broad collar". Ph. *wsḫ*.

(12) Collar of beads. L. *nbw* "gold". D. gold, precious metals.

(15) Pectoral of faience. L. *ṯḥn.t* "faience, glass". D. faience, glass, gleam, dazzle.

(18) Counterpoise for ornamental collar. L. D. *mni.t* "counterpoise, *Menit*".

(19) Cylinder-seal attached to necklace. L. in *ḫtm.w* (also read *sḏꜣ.wty*) "Seal-bearer, treasurer".

(20) Cylinder-seal attached to necklace seen from front. L. *ḫtm* "seal"; D. in *ḫtm.w* (also read *sḏꜣ.wty*) "seal-bearer, treasurer"; *šʿ.ty* a unit of value. D. seal, seal-ring; to seal. Ph. *ḫtm*.

(22) Shoulder-knot. Ph. *sṯ*.

(23) Knotted strips of cloth. L. D. *dmḏ* "unite".

(24) Girdle knot. L. *ṯs.t* "knot, vertebra". Ph. *ṯs*.

(27) Strip of cloth with two strands of a fringe. L. D. *mnḫ.t* "clothing".

(28) Piece of cloth with selvedge. D. clothing; clothe, be naked, cover, uncover, hide.

(29) Folded cloth. Ph. *s*. Abbr. for *snb* in the formula *ʿnḫ(.w) wḏꜣ(.w) snb(.w)* "may he live, be prosperous and healthy".

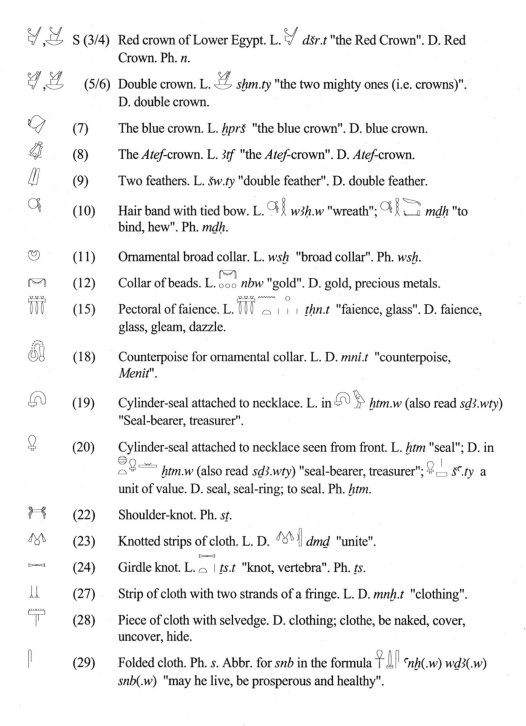

S (32) Piece of cloth with fringed edge. L. D. *siꜣ.t* "piece of cloth". Ph. *siꜣ*.

(33) Sandal. L. *ṯb.t* "foot, sandal". Ph. *ṯb*.

(34) Sandal strap (or phallus sheath ?). Ph. *ꜥnḫ*.

(35) (also) sun shade made of ostrich feathers. L. *šw.t* "shade, fan". D. shade, fan, standard.

(37) Fan. L. D. *ḫw* "fan".

(38) Shepherd's crook. L. *ḥḳꜣ.t* "sceptre". Ph. *ḥḳꜣ*. Also used for S39.

(39) Peasant's crook. Ph. *ꜥw.t*.

(40) Sceptre with forked base and head of Seth-animal. L. *wꜣs* "*Was*-sceptre". Ph. *wꜣs*. Often used in place of S41.

(41) U41 with spiral shaft. Ph. *ḏꜥm*. Also replaced by S40.

(42) Sceptre of authority. L. D. (1) *ꜥbꜣ* "*aba*-sceptre", (2) *sḫm* (a) "*sekhem*-sceptre", (b) sistrum, (3) *ḫrp* "to lead, guide". Ph. *ꜥbꜣ, sḫm, ḫrp*.

(43) Walking stick. L. *mdw* "stick, staff". Ph. *md*.

T. WARFARE, HUNTING , BUTCHERY

T (1) Prehistoric mace with dish-shaped head. Ph. *mn*. *mn* in *m n=k* "take for yourself!"

(3) Mace with pear-shaped head. L. *ḥḏ* "mace". Ph. *ḥḏ* (confused with V24).

(8) Dagger. Ph. *tp*.

(9) Composite bow of horn. L. D. *pḏ.t* "bow". Ph. *pḏ*.

(10) Composite bow with string. Like T9.

(10A) (Gardiner Aa32) Archaic bow. L. in *Tꜣ-Sty* "Nubia".

(11) Arrow. D. arrow. Ph. *sin, swn*.

(12) Bow-string. L. D. *rwḏ* "bow-string". Ph. *rwḏ, ꜣr, ꜣi*. Also in (abbrev.) *dꜣr* "subdue".

(13) Pieces of wood bound at joint. Ph. *rs*.

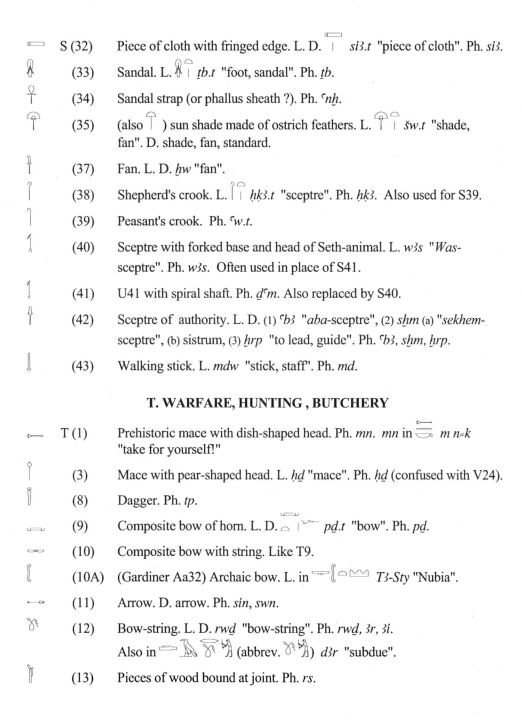

T (14) Throwing-stick and club (foreign weapon). D. *ḳmꜣ* "throw-stick, throw, create". D. foreign peoples. Ph. *ʿꜣm, ʿwt*. Also for D50.

(17) Chariot. L. D. *wrr.yt* "chariot".

(18) Crook (S39) with package and knife; equipment of prehistoric chieftain (?). L. *šms* "following (n.); follow".

(19) Harpoon of bone. D. bone, harpoon. Ph. *ḳs, gn*.

(21) Harpoon with a barb. L. *wʿ* "one".

(22) Spear-head or arrow-head with two barbs. L. *sn.nw* "two". Ph. *sn*.

(24) Fishing net. D. net. Ph. *ʿḥ, iḥ*.

(25) Float of reeds. Ph. *ḏbꜣ*.

(28) Butcher's block. Ph. *ẖr*.

(30) Knife. D. knife, sharp; cut, slaughter.

(31) Knife-sharpener. Ph. *sšm*.

(32) Combination of T31 and D54. Ph. *sšm*.

(34) Butcher's knife. Ph. *nm*.

U. AGRICULTURE, CRAFTS

U (1) Sickle. Ph. *mꜣ*.

(6) Hoe. D. hoe (n.), cultivate. Ph. *mr*.

(9) Corn-measure with grains pouring from it. L. *iti* "barley". D. grain, measure of grain.

(13) Plough. D. plough. Ph. *hb, šnʿ*.

(15) Sledge. Ph. *tm*.

(17) Pick excavating a pool. L. *grg* "found, establish". Ph. *grg*.

(19) Carpenter's adze. Ph. *nw*.

(21) U19 on a block of wood. L. *stp* "cut up". Ph. *stp*.

(22) Chisel, graver. Ph. *mnḫ*.

U (23) Chisel (?). Ph. *mr*, *ꜣb*.

(24) Drill used to hollow out stone vessels. L. *ḥm.t* "craft, art".

(26) Drill used to bore holes in beads. L. *wbꜣ* "open".

(28) Fire-drill. Ph. *ḏꜣ*. Abbreviation for *wḏꜣ* in the formula *ꜥnḫ*(*.w*) *wḏꜣ*(*.w*) *snb*(*.w*) "May he live, prosper and be healthy".

(30) Potter's kiln. Ph. *tꜣ*.

(30A) (Gardiner N34) Crucible. L. *biꜣ* (?), *ḥm.t* (?) "copper". D. copper or bronze.

(32) Pestle and mortar. D. weight; press down, be heavy. Ph. *smn*. Abbreviation in *ḥsmn* "natron", *ḥsmn* "bronze".

(33) Pestle. Ph. *ti*, *t*.

(34) Spindle. Ph. *ḥsf*.

(35) U34 combined with I9. Like U34.

(Aa23) Warp stretched between two uprights. D. in *mḏd* "hit (a mark)", "adhere to (a path)".

(Aa24) Old Egyptian form of Aa23.

(36) Club used by fullers in washing. Ph. *ḥm*.

(38) Balance. L. D. *mḫꜣ.t* "balance".

(39/40) Post of balance. D. balance; lift up, carry. Ph.D. *wṯs* "lift up, raise".

V. ROPE, BASKETS, BAGS ETC.

V (1) Rope. D. rope, bow warp of ship; drag, pull, bind, surround. Ph. *šn*; *št* in numeral 100.

(2) Bolt (O34) with cord to draw it. L. *sṯꜣ* "drag, pull". Ph. *sṯꜣ*, *ꜣs*.

(4) Lasso. Ph. *wꜣ*.

(6) Cord. Ph. *šs*.

(7) V6 with ends downward. Ph. *šn*.

V (10)	Oval cartouche. D. circuit, name. Surrounds the 4th and 5th names of a king, see § 153.
(12)	Band. D. band, garland, roll of papyrus; loosen. Ph. *ʿrḳ*.
(13)	Tether. Ph. *ṯ*. Var. (V14).
(15)	V13 combined with D54. L. *iṯi* "to take, seize".
(16)	Hobble. Ph. *sꜣ*.
(17)	Life preserver. L. , var. *sꜣ* "protection".
(19)	Hobble for tethering animals. L. D. *mḏ.t* "(cattle-)stall" D. mat, sack, shrine. Ph. *tmꜣ, ẖꜣr*.
(20)	V19 without cross-bar. Ph. *mḏ* in numeral 10.
(22)	Whip. Ph. *mḥ*.
(24/25)	Cord wound on stick. Ph. *wḏ*. Can be confused with T3.
(26)	Netting needle. Ph. *ʿḏ, ʿnḏ*.
(28)	Wick of twisted flax. Ph. *ḥ*.
(29)	Swab of tufts of fibre. Ph. *sk, wꜣḥ*.
(30)	Wickerwork basket. L. *nb.t* "basket". Ph. *nb*.
(31)	Basket with handle. Ph. *k*.
(33)	Bag of linen. L. *sšr* "linen, cloth". D. cloth, perfume; tie up. Ph. *sšr*, infrequently *g*.
(36)	Container. Ph. *ḥn*.
(37)	Bandage? D. in *idr* "bandage". Ph.D. in *idr* "herd".

W. VESSELS OF STONE AND EARTHENWARE

W (1)	Sealed unguent vessel. D. *mrḥ.t, mḏ.t* "ointment, unguent".
(2)	Sealed vessel of alabaster (calcite). Ph. *bꜣs*.
(3)	Alabaster (calcite) bowl. D. festival. Ph. *ḥb*.
(4)	W3 combined with (O 22). D. festival (cf. O23).

W (5) T28 and W3 combined. L. D. *ḥꜣb* "festival".

(7) Granite bowl. D. granite, Elephantine. Ph. *mꜣṯ, ꜣb.*

(9) Jug with handle. Ph. *ẖnm.*

(10) Cup or basket. D. cup, bowl. Ph. *iꜥb, wsḫ, ḥnt.*

(11) Ring stand for pottery vessels. Old form W12 L. D. *ns.t* "throne". Ph. *g*.

(14) Water pot. Ph. *ḥs.*

(15) W14 with water pouring from it. D. be cool, libate.

(17/18) Three or four water pots in a stand. Ph. *ḫnt.*

(19) Milk jug in a net. Ph. *mr, mi.*

(20) Milk jug. D. *irṯ.t* "milk".

(21) Wine jars. D. *irp* "wine".

(22) Beer jug. L. *ḥnk.t* "beer". D. beer, dry measure, tribute. In *wdp.w* "butler".

(23) Used as a determinative like W22; also for *wdp.w* "butler".

(24) Spherical vessel. Ph. *nw*; *n* in *ink* "I" § 26. Appears in place of in *ḏꜣḏꜣ.t* "council", *ḳd* "build" (phonetic determinative § 11); archaic phonogram *n* used as phonetic complement in *nḏ* "protect".

(25) W24 combined with D54. In *ini* "bring".

X. LOAVES AND CAKES

X (1) Bread. L. *t* "bread". Ph. *t*.

(2/3) Bread. D. bread.

(4) Loaf of bread. D. bread, food, offerings. Ph. *sn.*

(6) Loaf of bread with mark of baker's finger. D. in *pꜣ.t* "loaf". Ph.D. in *pꜣ.t* "primeval time".

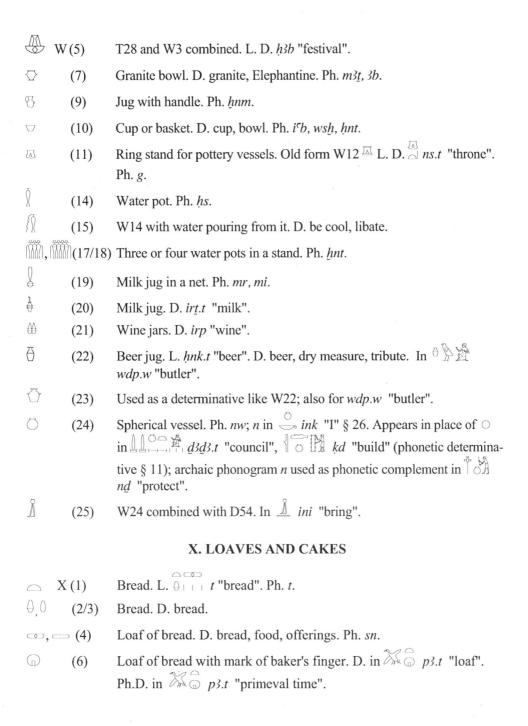

𓏐	X (7)	Half-loaf of bread. D. *gs.w* "half-loaves"; *sn.w* "food offering"; 𓏐𓏐 abbrev. for *wnm* "eat".
𓏙	(8)	Conical loaf. L. 𓂋𓏙 *rḏi* and 𓏙 *ḏi* "give".

Y. GAMES, INSTRUMENTS FOR WRITING AND MUSIC

𓏛, 𓏛	Y (1)	Roll of papyrus tied with string and sealed. L. 𓏛𓏏𓏥 *mḏ3.t* "roll of papyrus, book". D. in words that cannot be pictured but only written: abstract nouns, adjectives, etc.; abbrev. for 𓏛 *dmḏ* "total".
𓏜	(2)	Older form of Y1 without string; after 11th Dyn. gradually replaced by Y1.
𓏞	(3)	Writing equipment: palette, bag for powdered pigments and reed pen. L. 𓏞𓏛 *sš* (*sš3*, older *sẖ3*) "to write, writing", with D. 𓀀 "scribe". Ph. *sš* (*sš3*, older *sẖ3*), *nꜥꜥ*.
𓏠	(5)	Game board with pieces. Ph. *mn*.
𓏡	(6)	Game piece. L. D. *ib3* "game piece"; abbrev. *ib3* "dancer". Ph.D. *ib3*.
𓏣	(8)	Sistrum. L. D. *sšš.t* "sistrum". D. in same word.

Z. STROKES, GEOMETRIC FIGURES, SIGNS ADOPTED FROM HIERATIC

𓏤	Z (1)	Stroke. L. D. 𓌡𓂝𓏤 *wꜥ* "one"; sign in numerals 𓏤 "one". (§ 39).
𓏥; 𓏥; 𓏥	(2/3)	Three strokes. D. plural. Ph. *w* (as ending).
𓏭	(4)	Two oblique strokes. D. dual. Ph. *y* (as ending).
𓏮	(5)	Diagonal stroke, curved. See §10 b.
𓏯	(6)	Hieratic sign for A14.
𓏲	(7)	Ph. *w* derived from hieratic sign for 𓅱 G43.
𓏶	(8)	Oval. D. *šnw* "oval, circle, circuit".
𓏴	(9)	Two crossed sticks. D. break, cross, reckon. Ph. *sw3*, *sḏ*, *ḥsb*, *šbn*, *wp*, *wr*.

Z (11) Two crossed planks. Ph. *ỉm, w(n)m*. Sometimes in place of M42.

Aa. UNCLASSIFIED

Aa (1) Basket, seen from above. Ph. *ḫ*.

(2) Pustule (?) gland (?) bandage (?) L. D. *wt* "embalm"; *wḥꜣ.t* "cauldron." D. wound (n.), sickness; suffer, be swollen, fat, reckon, embalm, stink, be narrow. Ph. *wḥꜣ, gꜣ*.

(5) Part of ship's stearing gear? L. *ḥp.t* "the *hepet*-implement". Ph. *ḥp*.

(6) An implement. D. in *ṯmꜣ* "mat". Ph.D. *tmꜣ, ṯmꜣ*.

(7) Doubtful. D. or Ph.D. or *sḳr* "smite".

(8) Canal (?) L. *ḏꜣt.t* "estate". Ph. *ḳn*. Ph.D. *ḏꜣḏꜣ.t* "council". Wrongly replaces N24, V26, O34.

(11) See N23A

(13) Doubtful. Older form Aa14. L. *gs* "side". Ph. *gs, ỉm, m*.

(17/18) Lid of quiver. Ph. *sꜣ*.

(19) Doubtful. Ph.D. *ḥr*.

(20) Tassel (?) Ph. *ꜥpr*.

(21) Carpenter's tool (?) L. or D. , *wḏꜥ* "to judge".

(23/24) See after U35.

(25) L. (?) *smꜣ* "stolist" (priestly title).

(26) Ph.D. *sbỉ* (often replaced by T14).

(27) Doubtful. Ph. *nḏ*.

(28) Brick-maker's striker. Older form Aa29. Ph. *ḳd*. Confused with P11.

(30) Ornamental frieze at upper edge of walls, originally the bound ends of reeds that were used to reinforce mud walls and which protruded from the top of the wall. L. or D. *ẖkr* "ornament".

(32) See T10A.

IV. EXERCISES

SCRIPT

§ 5 

§§ 5 & 9 (1) 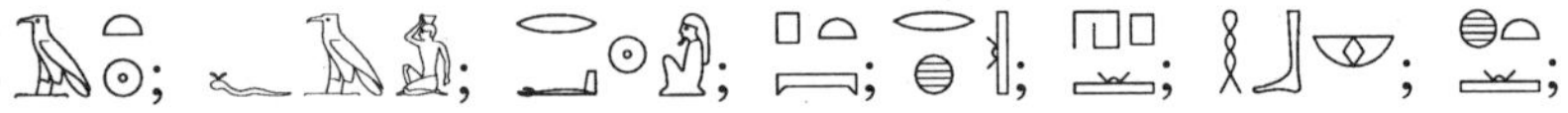

(2) 

(3) 

(4) 

§§ 6 & 9 (1) 

(2) 

(3) 

(4) 

(5) 

(6) 

(7) 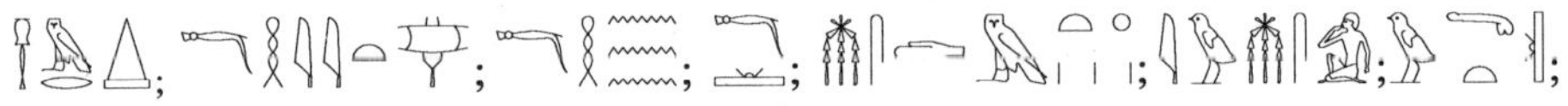

(8) 

(9) 

(10) 

(11) 

(12) 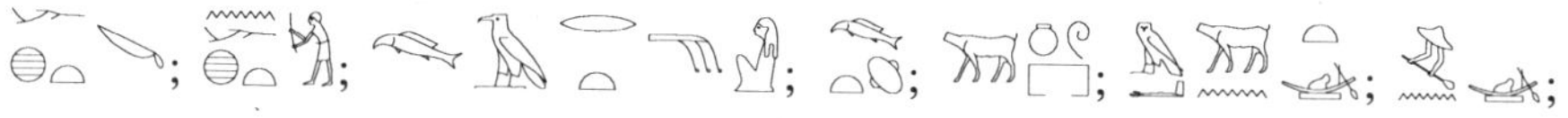

(13) 

(14) 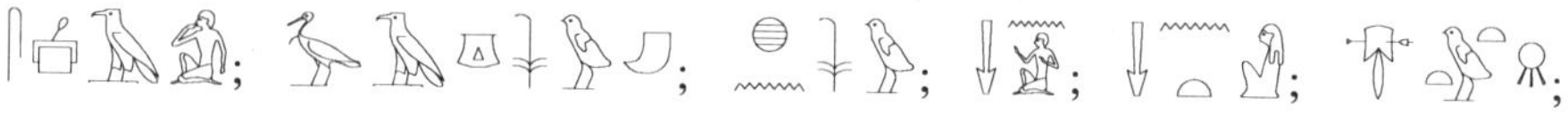

(15) 

(16) 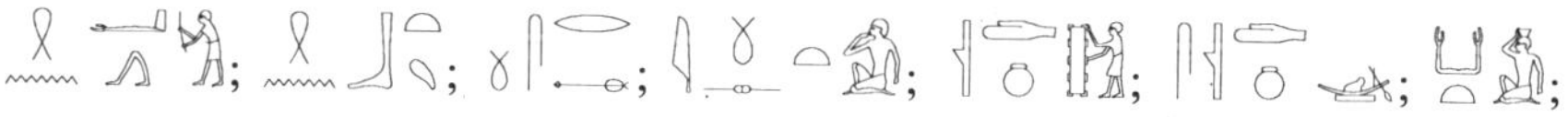

(17) 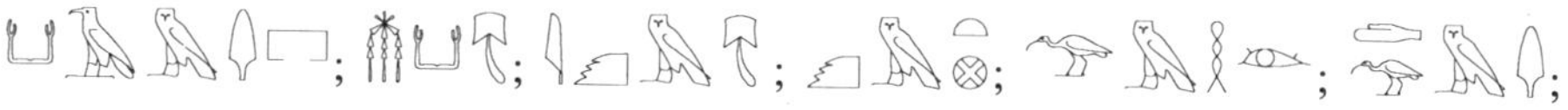

(18) 

(19) 

(20) 

§§ 7, 9 & 11 

§ 8 

§ 10 a) (1) 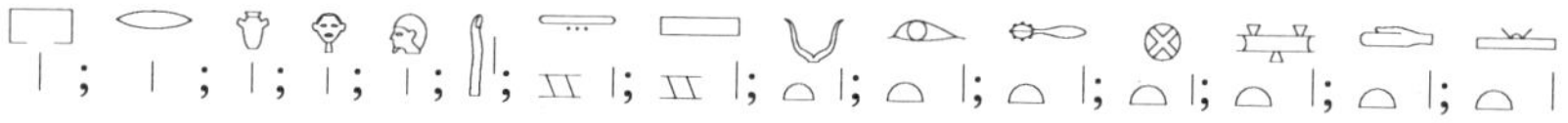

(2) 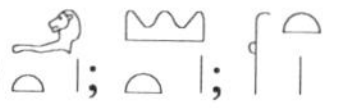

§ 10 c) 1. 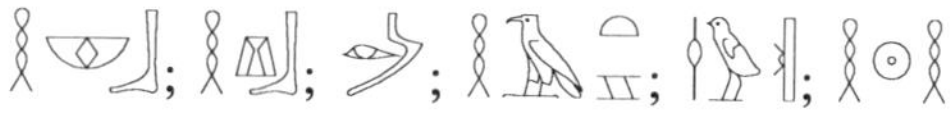

§ 10 c) 2. 

§ 10 c) 3. a. 

§ 10 c) 3. b.## ACCIDENCE AND SYNTAX

§§ 18 & 19 Genitive

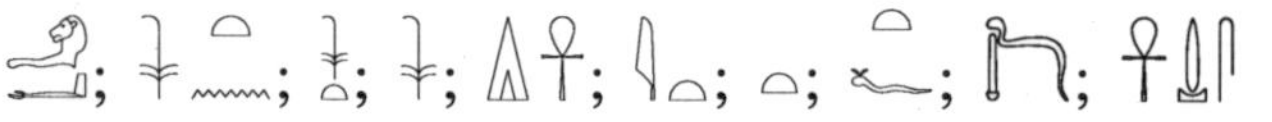

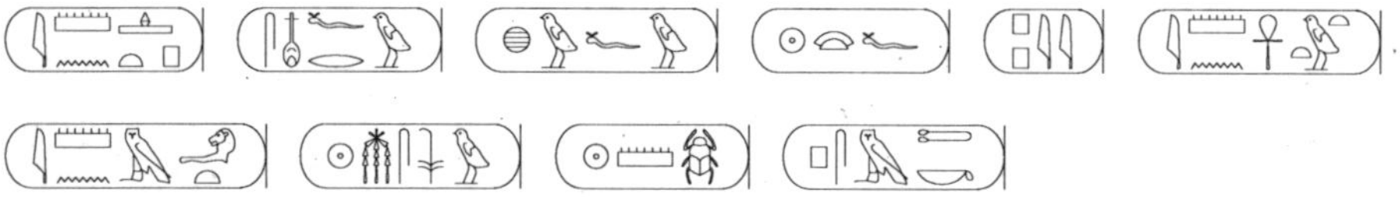

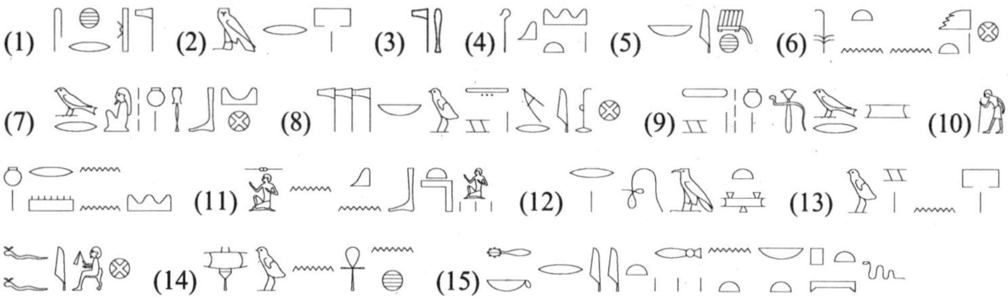

(1) (2) (3) (4) (5) (6)

(7) (8) (9) (10)

 (11) (12) (13)

 (14) (15)

§§ 22–25 Adjectives

(1) (2) (3) (4) (5)

 (6) (7) (8)

 (9) (10) (11) (12)

(13) (14)

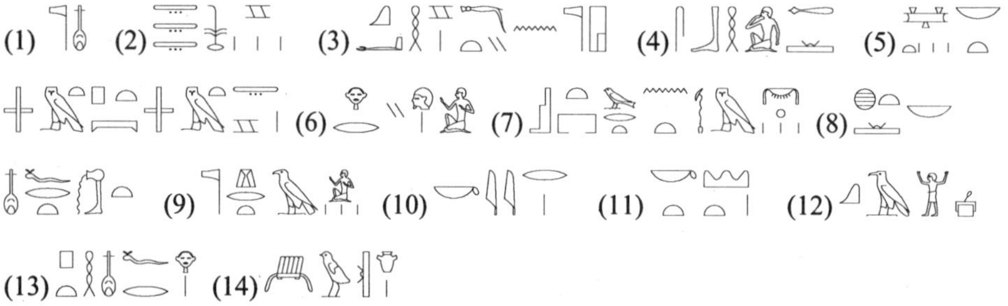

§ 28 Suffix Pronouns

(1) (2) (3) (4) (5)

(6) (7)

§§ 29–33 Demonstrative Pronouns

(1) (2) (3) (4)

(5) [hieroglyphs] (6) [hieroglyphs]

§§ 42–47 Adverbial Sentences

(1) [hieroglyphs] (2) [hieroglyphs] (3) [hieroglyphs]

[hieroglyphs] (4) He subdued the foreign lands, [hieroglyphs]

[hieroglyphs] (5) [hieroglyphs] (6) They besieged the city, [hieroglyphs]

[hieroglyphs] (7) [hieroglyphs]

[hieroglyphs] (8) [hieroglyphs] (9) [hieroglyphs]

[hieroglyphs] (10) [hieroglyphs] (11) I grew up in Elkab,

[hieroglyphs] (12) [hieroglyphs]

[hieroglyphs]

§ 48–52 Nominal Sentences

(1) [hieroglyphs] (2) [hieroglyphs] (3) [hieroglyphs]

[hieroglyphs] (4) [hieroglyphs] (5) [hieroglyphs] (6) [hieroglyphs]

(7) [hieroglyphs] (8) [hieroglyphs] (9) [hieroglyphs]

[hieroglyphs] (in place of *is*) [hieroglyphs]

§§ 53–55 *pw*-Sentence

(1) [hieroglyphs] (2) [hieroglyphs] (3) [hieroglyphs]

(4) [hieroglyphs] (5) [hieroglyphs]

(6) [hieroglyphs] (7) [hieroglyphs] (8) [hieroglyphs] (9) [hieroglyphs]

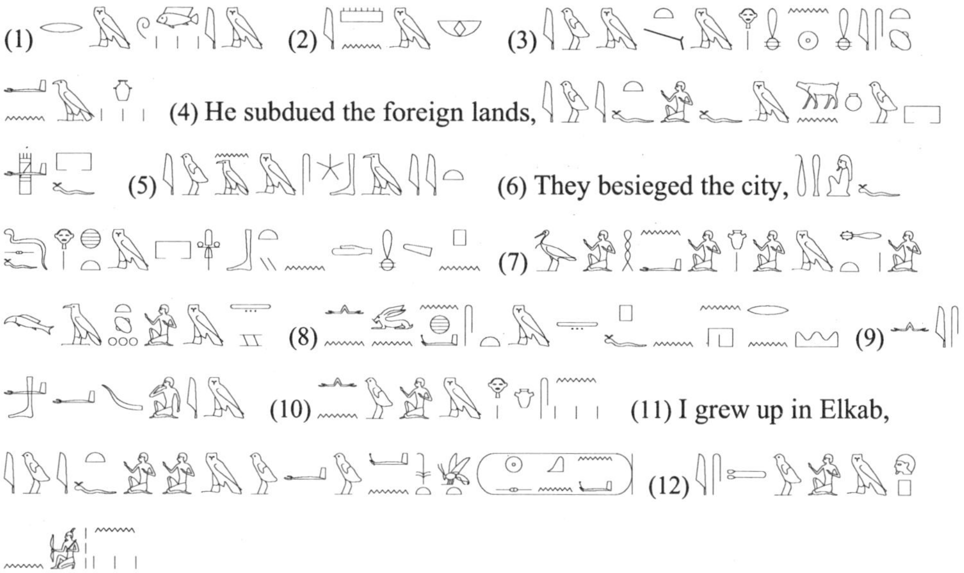

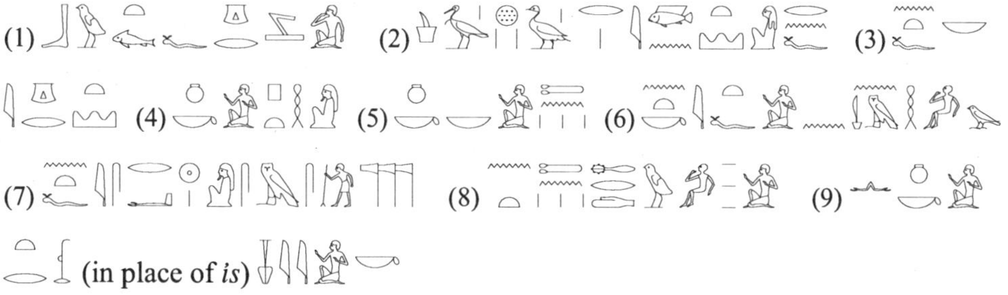

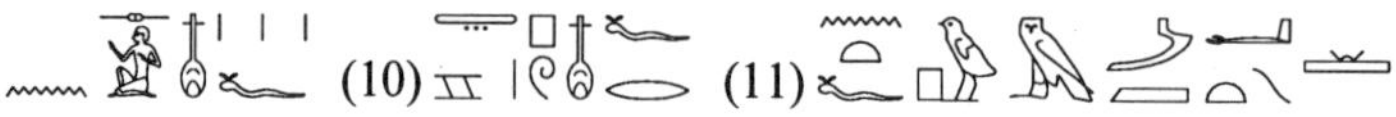

§ 56 Adjectival Sentences

(1) ⸻ (2) ⸻ (3) ⸻

(4) ⸻ (5) ⸻ (6) ⸻

⸻ (7) ⸻ (*n=s* prep. + suffix: "her",. § 35) (8) ⸻

(9) ⸻

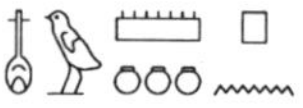

§ 58 Expressions of Possession

(1) ⸻ (2) ⸻ (3) ⸻ (4) ⸻

(5) ⸻ (6) ⸻ (7) ⸻ (8) ⸻

⸻ (9) ⸻

THE VERB

§ 67 Imperative

(1) ⸻ (2) ⸻ (3) ⸻

(4) ⸻ (5) ⸻

⸻

⸻

⸻

⸻

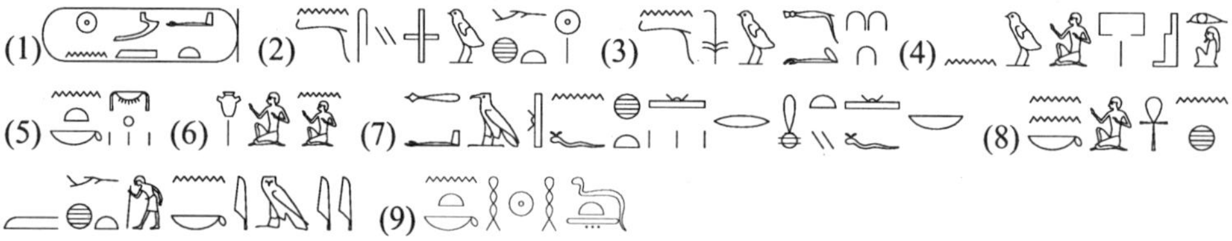

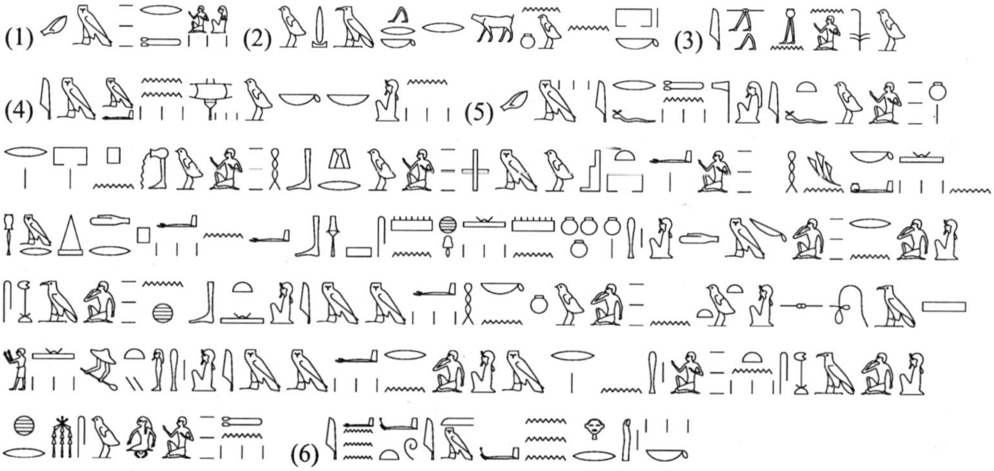

§§ 69–70 Circumstantial *sḏm=f* and Aorist *sḏm=f* / *ỉrr=f*

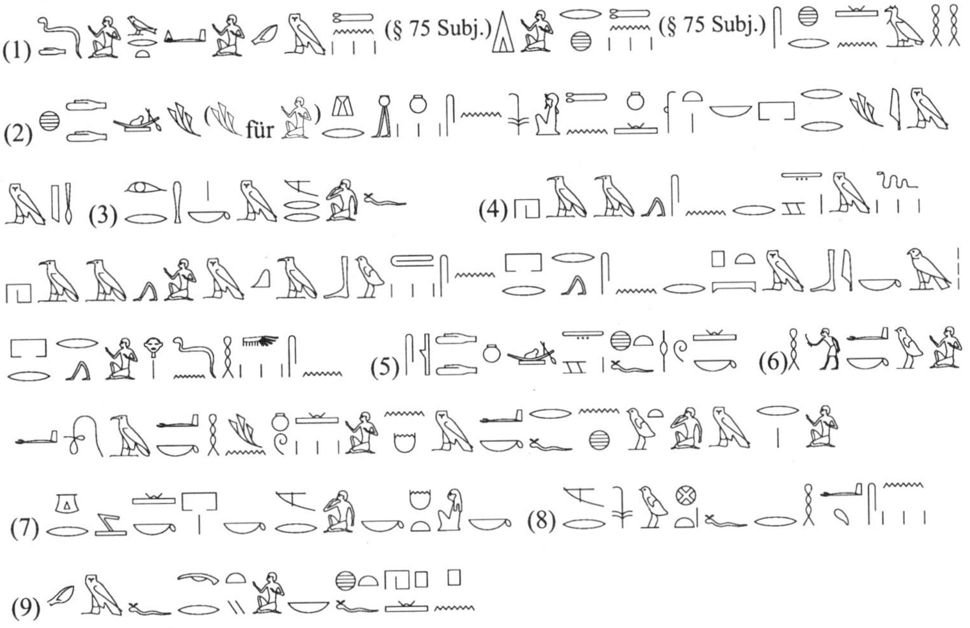

§ 71 (Present) Perfect *sḏm.n=f*

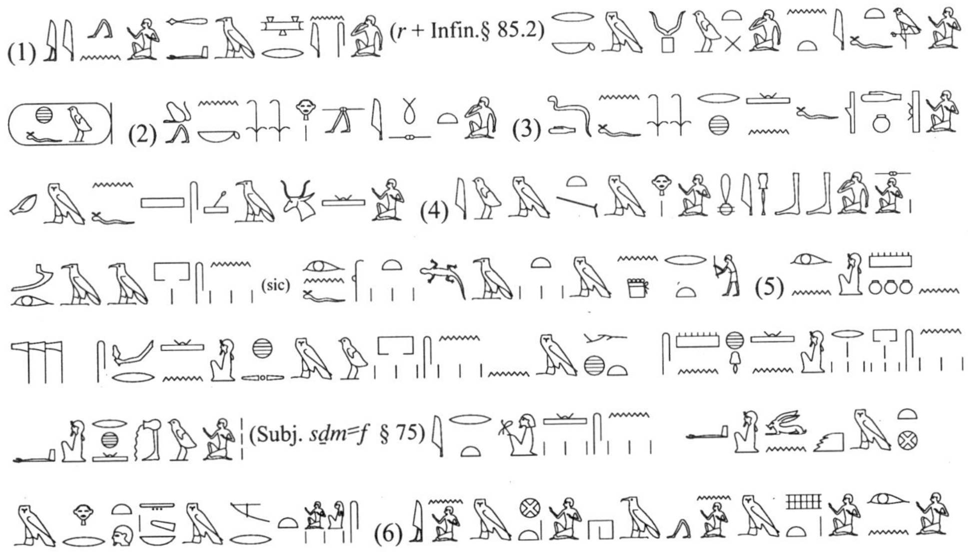

(*mrr.t=f* "that which he loves" Relative Form § 108) (7) (8) (9) (10) (§91) (11)

§ 72 Historic Perfect *sḏm=f* / *iri=f*

(1) (2)

(3) (*sḏm.in=f* § 80 a)

(*sḏm.tw=f* Passive § 76)

§ 73 The Form *sḏm.t=f*

(1) (2)

(3)

§ 74 Future (Prospective) *sḏm=f* / *iri(.y/w)=f*

(1) (2)

(3) (4)

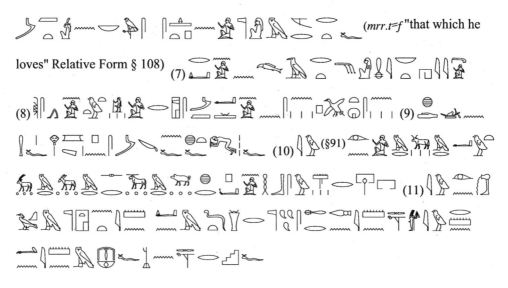

(5) 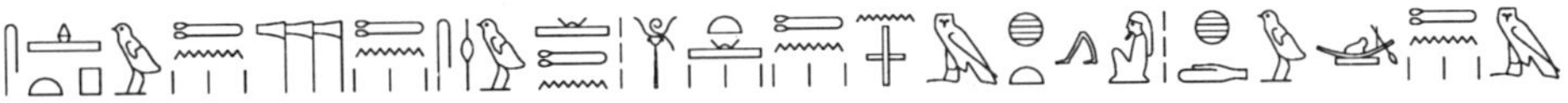
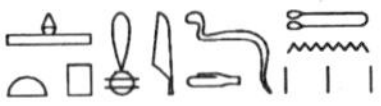

§ 75 Subjunctive *sḏm=f / iri(.y)=f*

(1) 

(2)  (3) 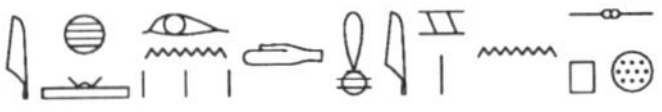

(4)  (5) 
 (6) 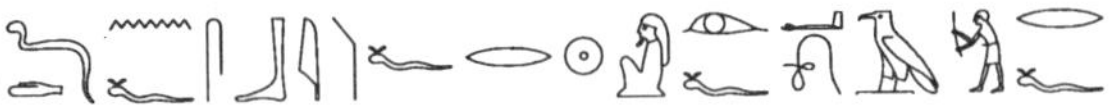 (7) 
 (8) 
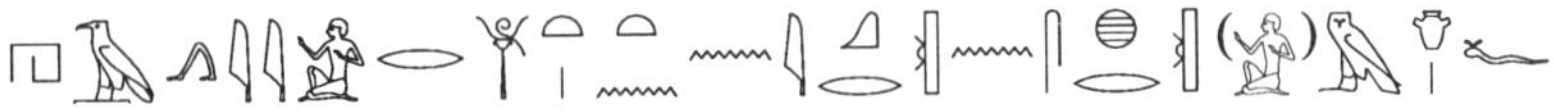 (9) 
 (10)  (i.e. Osiris) 
 (11) 

(12) 

§ 76 *tw* Passive

(1) The eloquent peasant says of the chief steward: 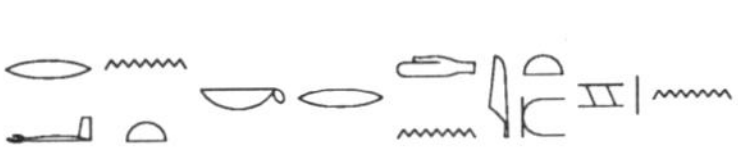
 (here, as in other texts written in hieratic script,  is written for ) (2) 

(3) Sinuhe says regarding the letter of the king brought to him: 

 (4) Sinuhe describes the king:  (§ 85.2)

 (5) 

§ 77 Perfective Passive *sḏm(.w/y)=f*

(1)  (§ 97a)  (2) 

(3) 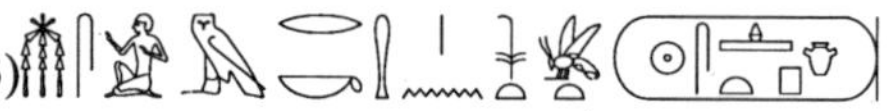 (4)  (§ 91) 

 (5)  (§ 97 b) 

(6)  (§ 91)  (7) 

 (8) 

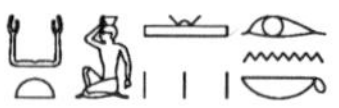 (*iri.n=k* Perfective Relative Form § 107 "which you have done")

§ 80 Contingent Tenses

(1)  (2) 

 (3) If you see someone suffering from *st.t* in the belly which has no exit,

 (4) One who does X, 

 (5) Should X happen, 

§ 81 Old Perfective

(1) 

(2)  (3) 

(5) (6)

(7)

§§ 82–85 Infinitive

(1) (2) (3)

(4)

(5) (6)

(7)

(8) (9)

(10)

§ 86–88 Pseudo-verbal Construction

(1) (Var.:

§§ 92–93) (2) (3)

(4)

(5) (6)

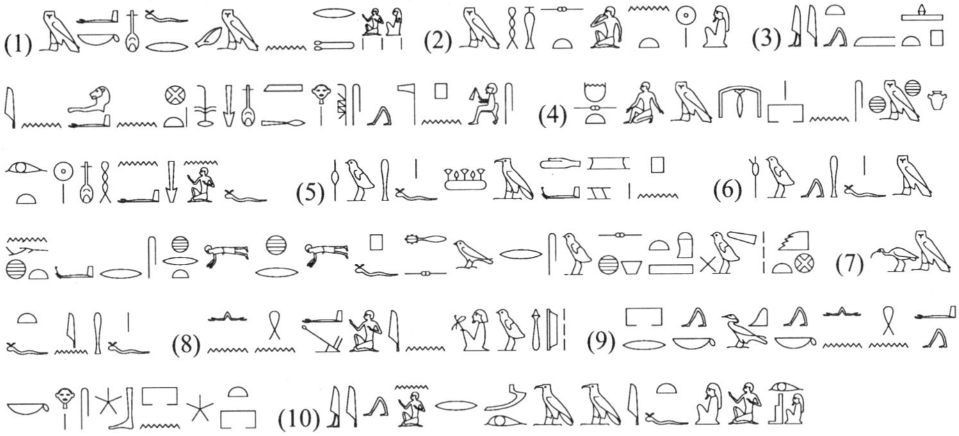

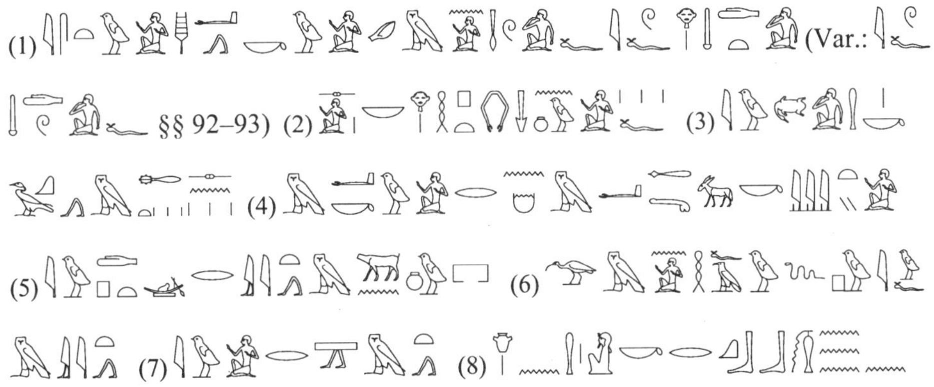

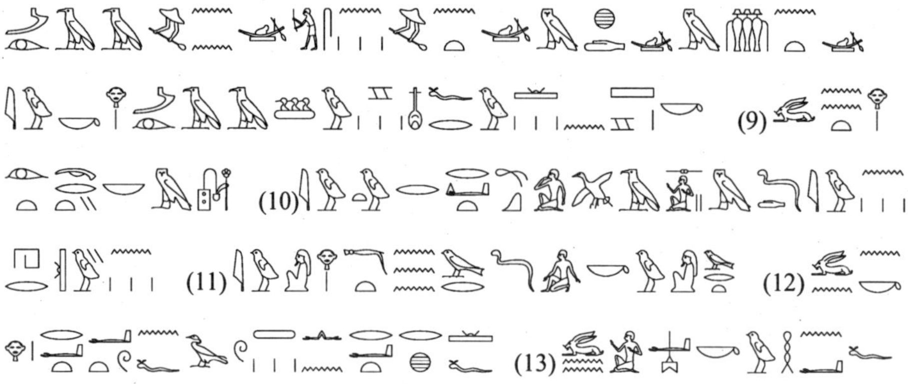

§§ 89–97 Complex Verb Forms

§ 91 Present Perfect with *iw*

§ 91 a. (1) 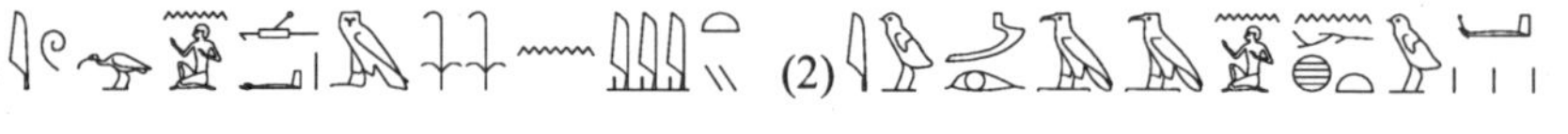

§ 91 b. (1) 

§ 91 c. (1)  (*sḏm.t* §§ 98, 102 "that, which is heard")

§ 92 Complex Aorist I

 (5) 

§ 94 Complex Future *iw=f r sḏm*

(1) All who read it, 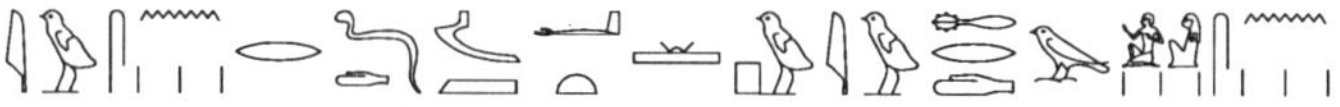

 (2) 

§ 95 Introduced by *ꜥḥꜥ*

(1)  (2) 

(3)  (4) 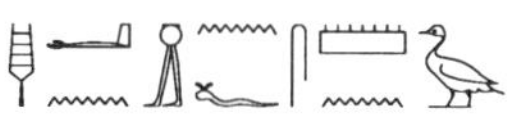

(5)  (6) 

 (7)  (8) 

§ 96 Introduced by *wn.in*

(1)  (2) 

(3) 

§ 97 Finite Verb Forms introduced by *m=k* or. *isṯ*

(1)  (2) 

 ...  (3) Statement regarding fields taken at

the battle of Megiddo (follows list of booty): 

(4) NN 

§§ 89–97 Text Passage

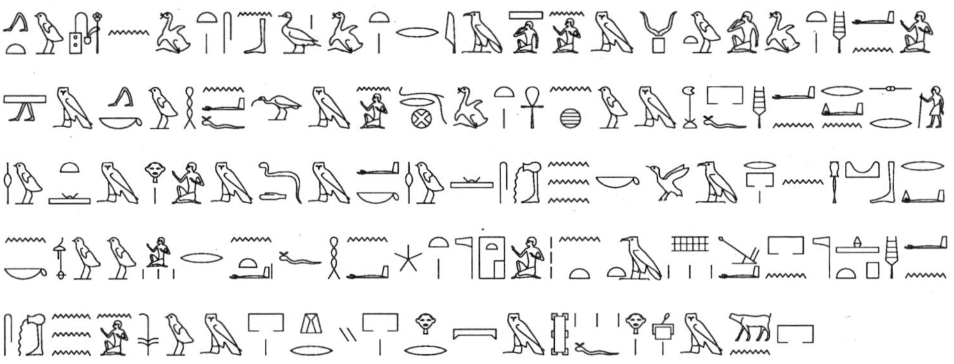

§ 98–104 Participles

(1) 

(2)  (3) 

(4)  (5) 

 (6)  (7)  (PN)

 (PN) (8) 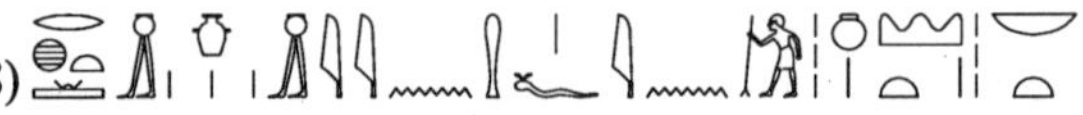

(9)  (10) 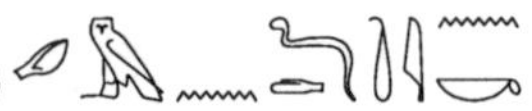

(11) 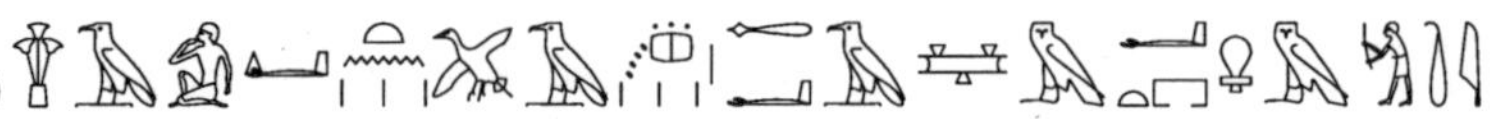 (12) 

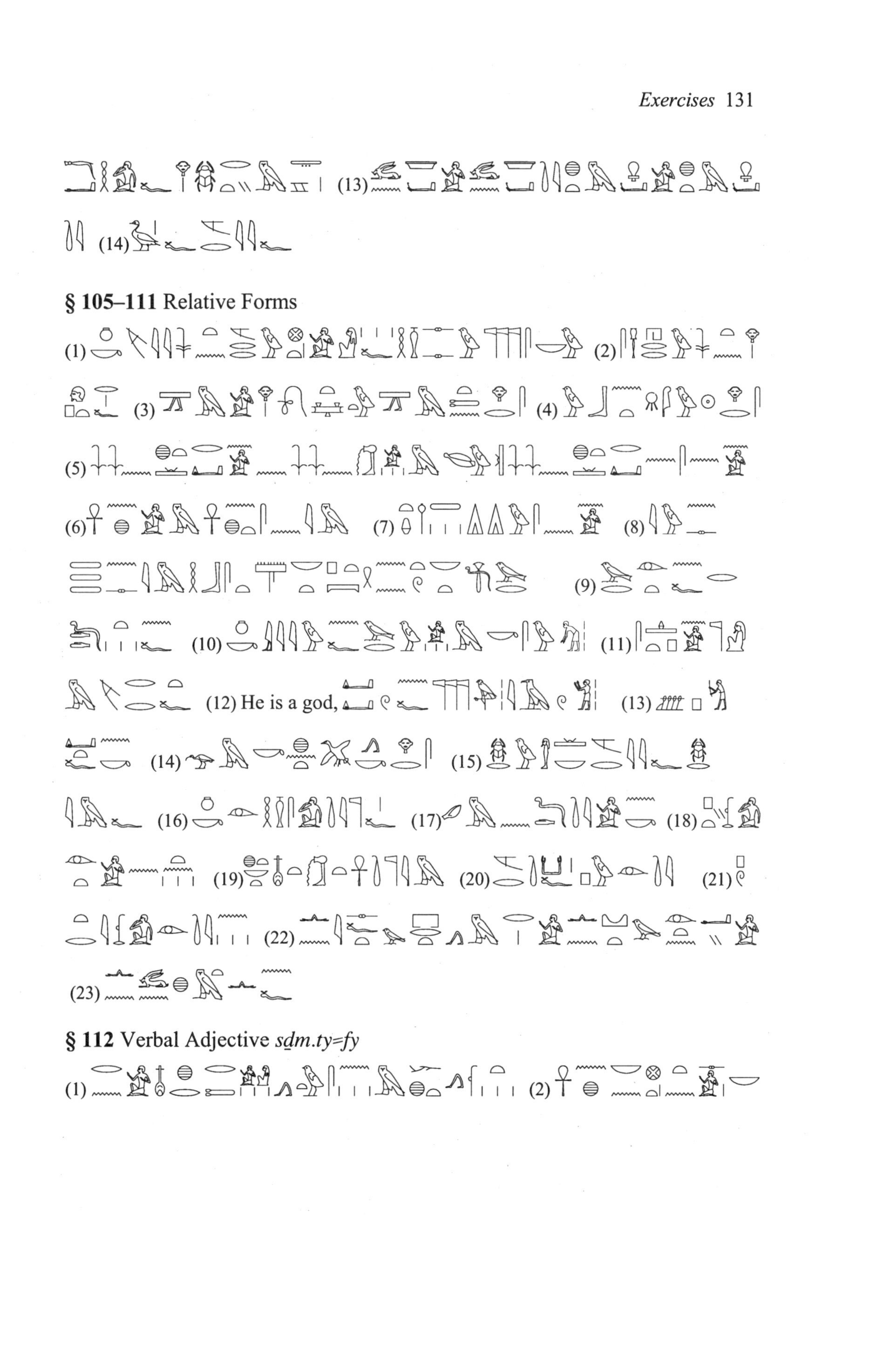

(13) (14)

§ 105–111 Relative Forms

(1) (2) (3) (4) (5) (6) (7) (8) (9) (10) (11) (12) He is a god, (13) (14) (15) (16) (17) (18) (19) (20) (21) (22) (23)

§ 112 Verbal Adjective *sḏm.ty=fy*

(1) (2)

§ 113 Narrative Construction *iyi.t pw iri.n=f*

§ 114 Modal Verb *p3i*

Word Order

§§ 119–120 The *in*-Construction

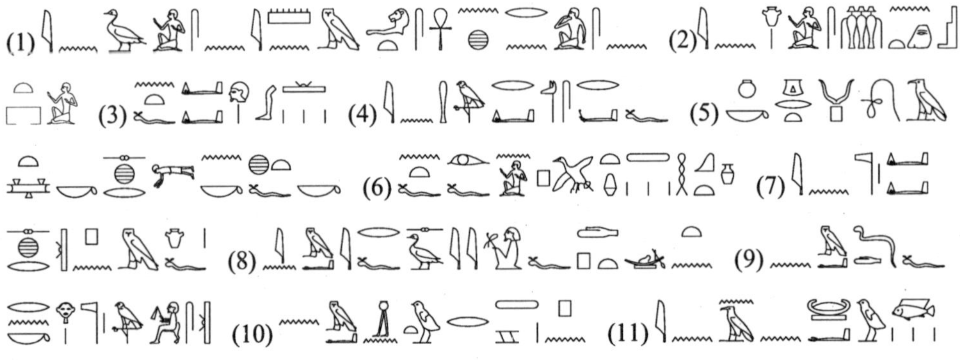

§§ 123–126 Topicalisation without introduction

§§ 127–129 Topicalisation introduced by *ir*

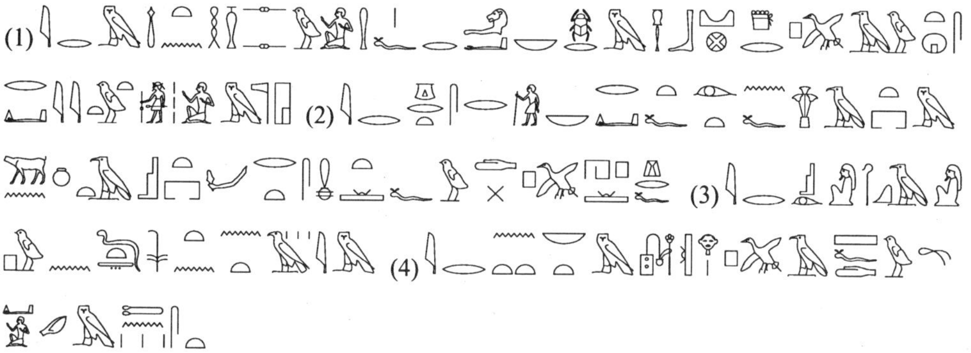

§§ 130–132 Conditional Sentences

§ 131 Following *ir*

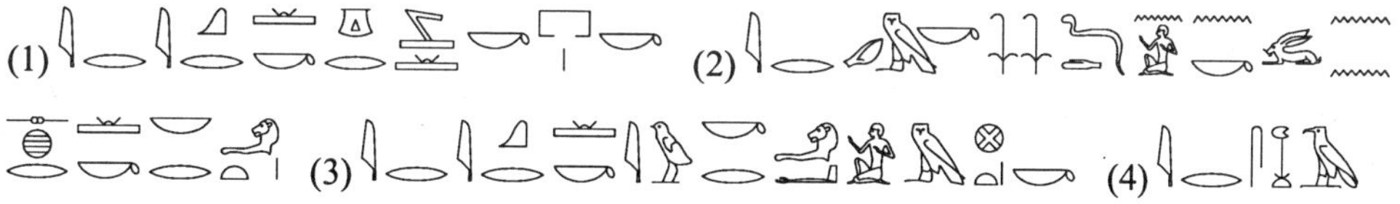

[hieroglyphs] (5) [hieroglyphs] ...

[hieroglyphs] ...

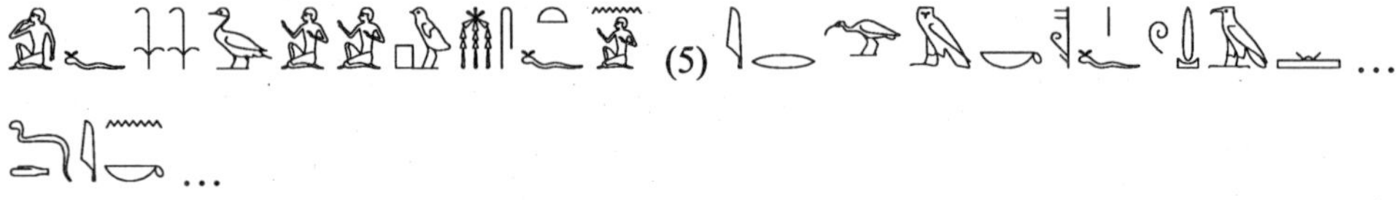

§ 133 Without introduction or condition expressed by other sentence types

(1) [hieroglyphs] ... [hieroglyphs] ... (2) [hieroglyphs]

[hieroglyphs] ... (3) [hieroglyphs] (4) [hieroglyphs]

[hieroglyphs]

[hieroglyphs]

[hieroglyphs] ...

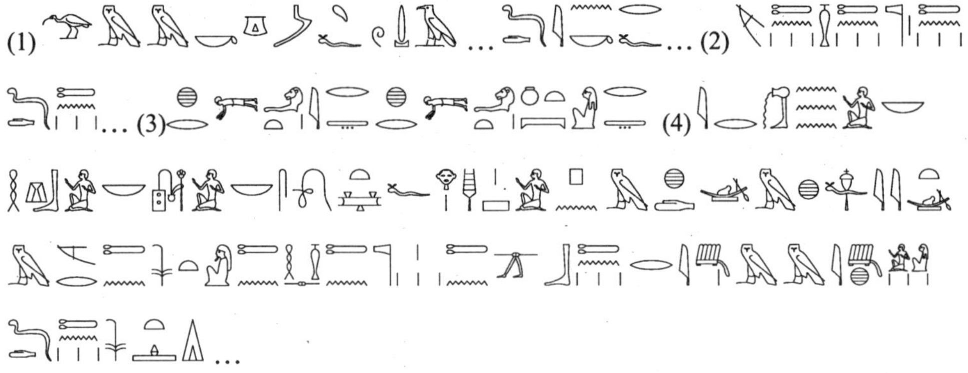

§ 133–147 Negation of the verb

§ 135 Negation of the imperative

(1) [hieroglyphs] (2) [hieroglyphs]

§ 136 Negation of Circumstantial *sḏm=f* (or Aorist I *iw=f sḏm=f*)

(1) [hieroglyphs] (2) [hieroglyphs]

[hieroglyphs]

[hieroglyphs]

§ 137 Negation of Aorist *sḏm=f*

(1) [hieroglyphs]

[hieroglyphs]

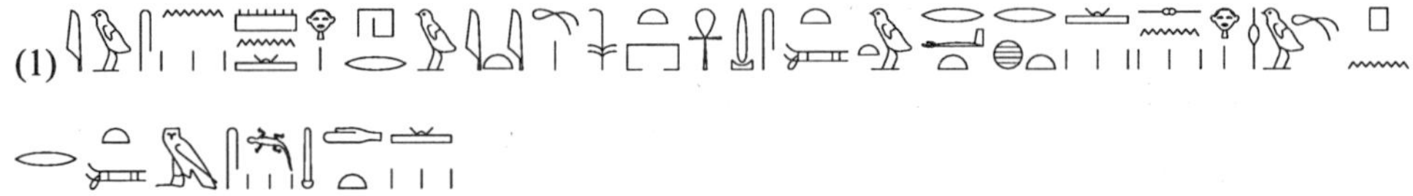

§ 138 Negation of (Present) Perfect *sḏm.n=f*

1. Paratactic main clause

(1) This example is preceded by example (2) of § 138.2 (see below) : 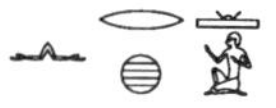

 (Note: the suffix.1st pers. sg. subject is generally not written.)

2. In subordinate clauses

(1) 

(2) Sinuhe says: 

§ 139 Negation of Future *sḏm(.y)=f*

(1) 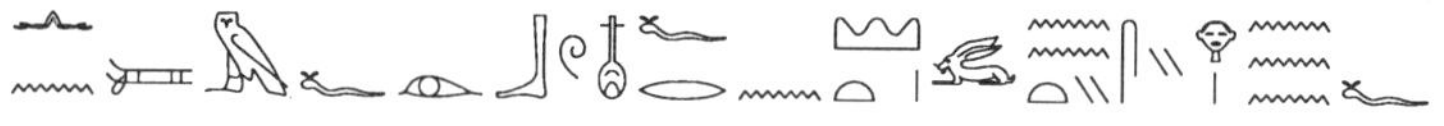 (2) 

§ 140 Negation of Subjunctive *sḏm=f*

(1)  (2) 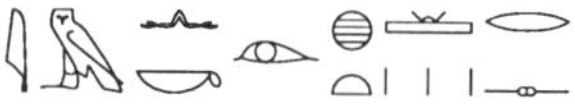 (could also be Future)

§ 142 Negation of Complex Verb Forms with *ỉw*

a) (1) 

 (2) 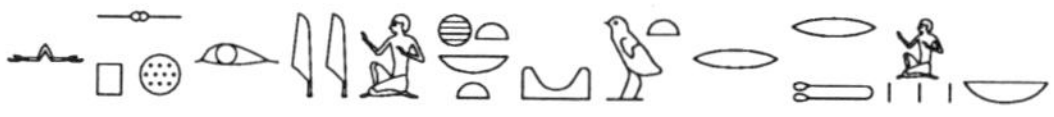 (3) 

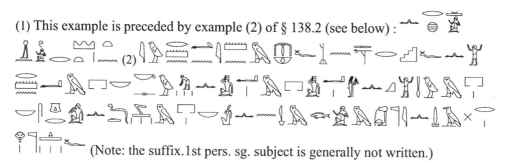

b) (1) 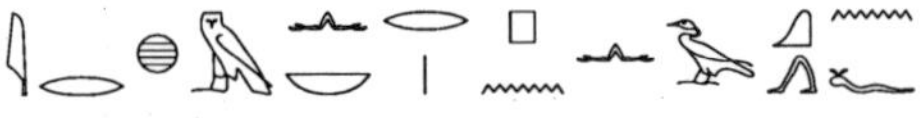 (2) 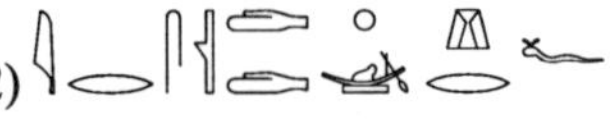 (i.e. truth) 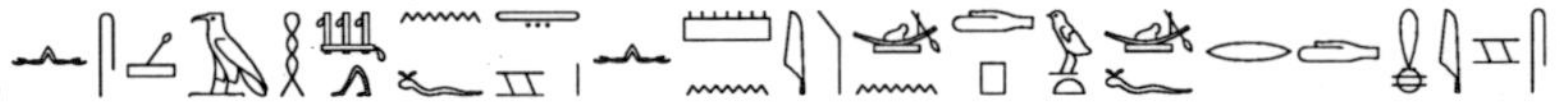

(3) 

c) (1) 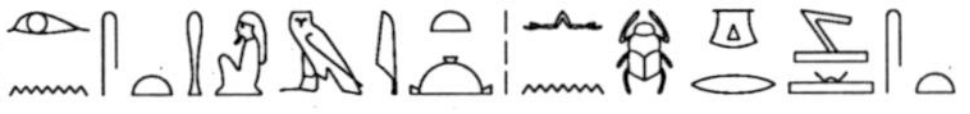 (2) The guardian says:  

§ 143 Negation of infinitive

(1) 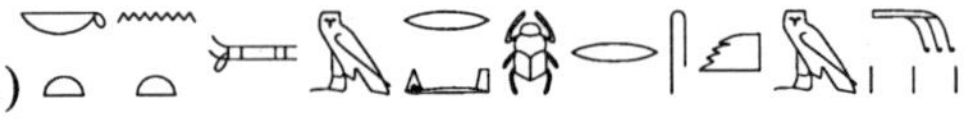 (2) 

(3)  (4) Khufu asks: What is it, Djedi,   (5) Nubians who are on legitimate business may pass the border,  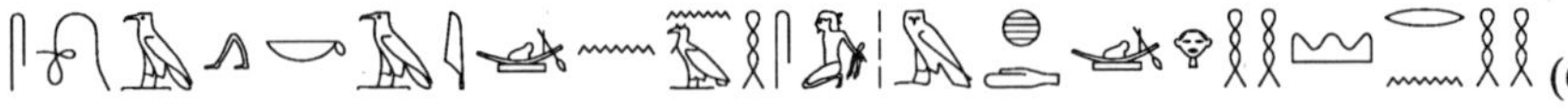 (6)   (§ 37) 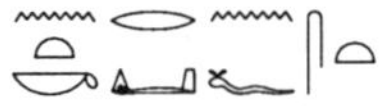

§§ 144–145 Negation of participles

(1)  (2)   (3) 

§ 146 Negation of Relative Forms

(1) Amun is an efficacious god, 

§ 147 Negation of the *sḏm.ty=fy* - Form

(1) May they who transgress my command be cut off from this god, [hieroglyphs]

§ 148 Questions

(1) [hieroglyphs]   (2) [hieroglyphs]

(3) [hieroglyphs]   (4) [hieroglyphs]

§ 149 Relative Clauses

(1) [hieroglyphs]

[hieroglyphs] (2) [hieroglyphs]

[hieroglyphs] (3) [hieroglyphs]

[hieroglyphs] (4) [hieroglyphs] (5) [hieroglyphs]

(6) [hieroglyphs] (7) [hieroglyphs]

[hieroglyphs] (8) Osiris, [hieroglyphs] (9) [hieroglyphs]

(10) [hieroglyphs] (11) [hieroglyphs]

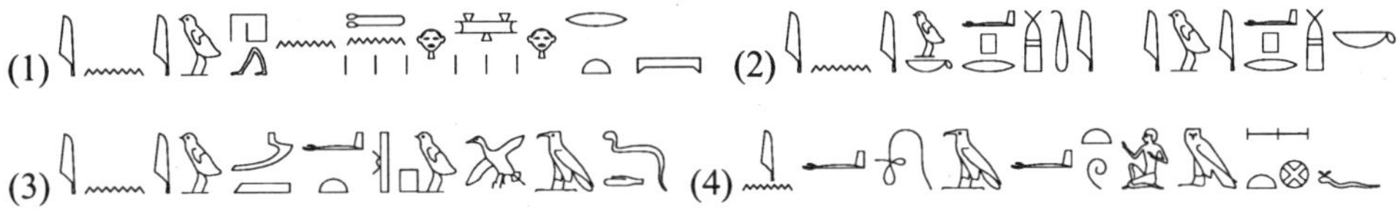

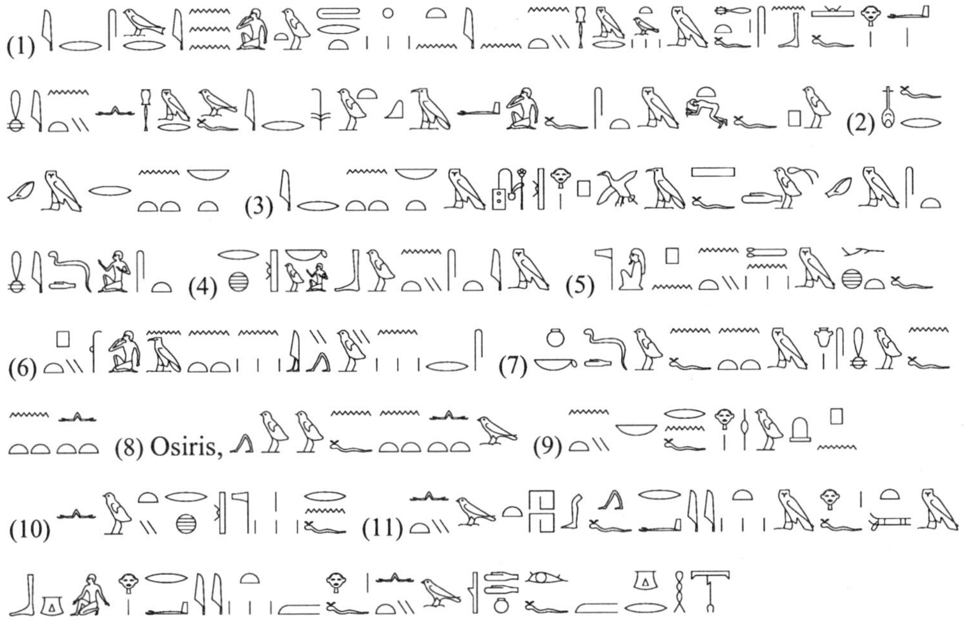

V. Reading Exercises

1. Queen Tiy (Scarab of Amenhotep III)

2. From the Autobiography of  (Time of Thutmosis IV)

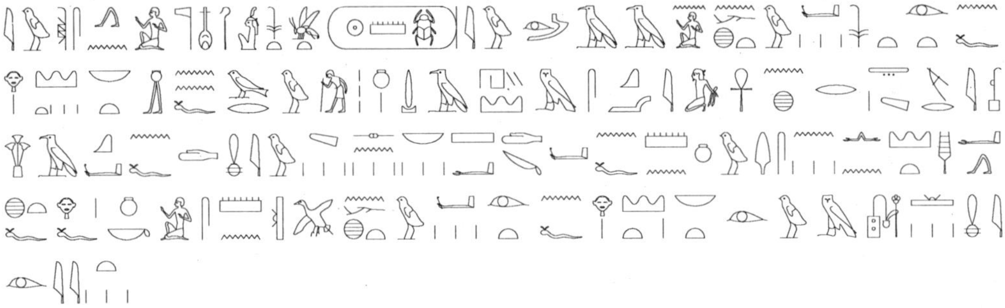

3. From the Amada-Stele of Amenhotep II

4. Two Royal Inscriptions from Sehel

a.

b.

5. From the Biography of  (Time of Sesostris I)

6. The Story of the Shipwrecked Sailor

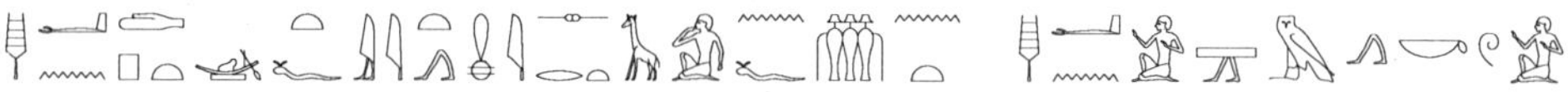

7. From the Gebel Barkal Stele of Thutmosis III

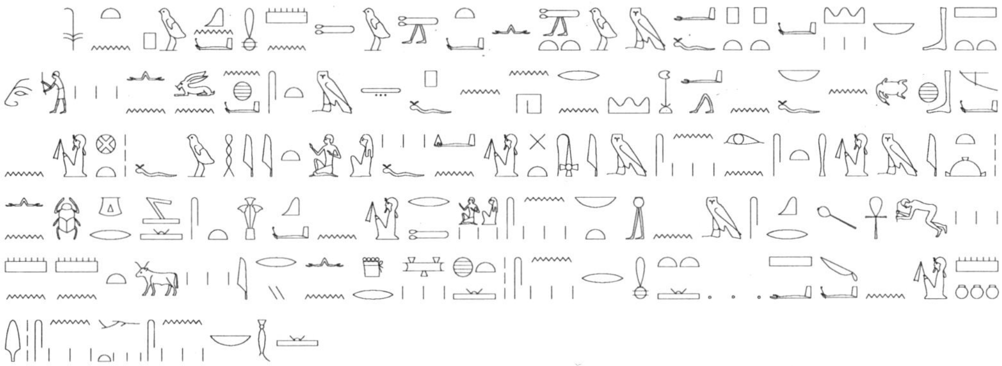

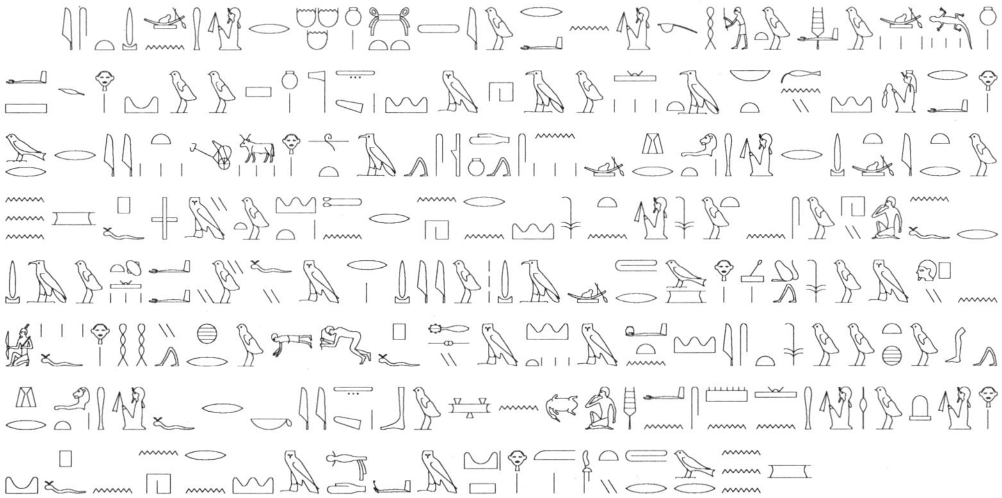

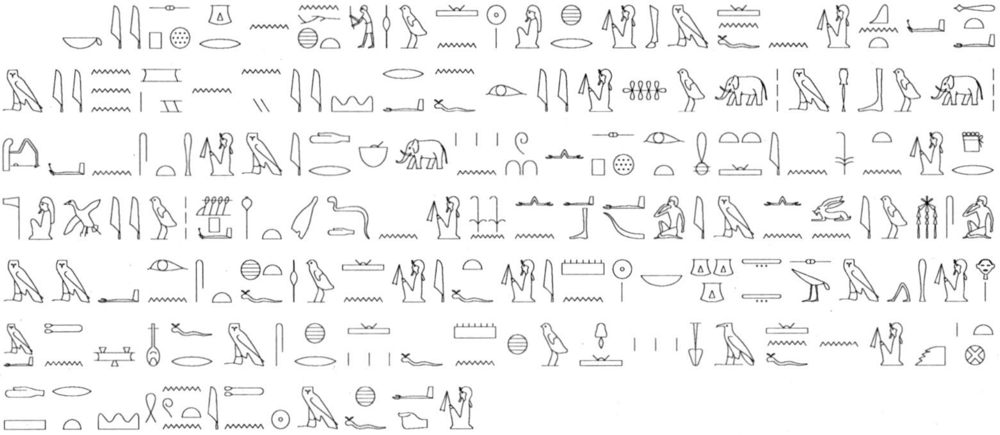

8. From the Autobiography of  (Time Amenhotep II)

9. From the Prophecy of 

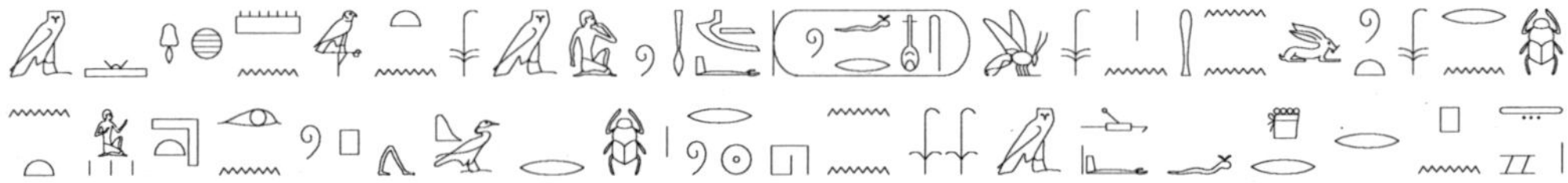

VI. VOCABULARY

All nouns ending with *.t* are feminine. This *.t* ending and the *.w* ending of some masculine words are not taken into consideration in the alphabetical sequence of the words (e.g. *ỉn.t* precedes *ỉnỉ*). This also applies to the weak radical *ỉ* of the IIIae and IVae infirmae verbs; such words follow corresponding bi-radical words (*wḏỉ* appears directly after *wḏ* ahead of *wḏꜣ*). Since adjectives are usually identical with participles of adjective-verbs, only the verbal stems are listed, occasionally the adjective itself.

Not all words that are mentioned in the grammar are included here. For the interrogative pronouns and adverbs, as well as prepositions and particles the student is referred to §§ 34–38, for adverbs to § 115.

Abbreviations: acc. (accusative / direct object), adv. (adverb), caus. (causative), det. (determinative), f. (feminine), GN (geographic name), n. (noun), m. (masculine), part. (particle), PN (personal name), prep. (preposition), √ root.

ꜣ

ꜣ encl. part. following *ḥwỉ*

ꜣ.t moment, instant, time

ꜣwỉ be long, wide; length

ꜣbỉ to wish, desire

ꜣbỉ to cease, tarry, stay,

ꜣb elephant

ꜣbw GN Elephantine

ꜣbd ; month

ꜣbḏw GN Abydos

ꜣpd bird

ꜣḥ.t field

ꜣḫ spirit, deceased

ꜣḫ be useful, beneficial

ꜣḫ.t inundation (season)

ꜣs.t (goddess) Isis

ꜣsḫ to reap

ꜣtp to load

ỉ

ỉ interjection: "oh!"; to say

ỉꜣ.t mound, ruin

ỉꜣw praise

ỉꜣwỉ be old, aged

ỉꜣw.t office

ỉꜣb.t east

ỉꜣm.t see *ỉmꜣ.t*

ỉꜣrr.t grapes

ỉꜣš see *ʿš*

ỉꜣḳ.t leeks, vegetables

iꜣd.t net

iyi to come

iʿi to wash

iw non-encl. part. § 37

iw island

iwi to come, + *m* come from, come out of; *iwi iḫ.t* something occurs, happens

Ꞽw-snb PN m. Iuseneb

Ywiꜣ PN m. Yuia

iwms lie (n.)

iwn colour, character

Ꞽwnw GN Heliopolis

iwḥ to water (a field)

iwsw balance (n.)

iwd to separate (+ *r* from)

iwdnb incense

ib to think, suppose

ib to thirst

ib heart, wish

ibi unguent, ladanum (?)

ibd (*ꜣbd*) month

Ꞽpt PN f. Ipet

ip.t grain measure

im adv. from *m*: there, therein, therewith (§ 115)

im.y see § 23 and § 35

im.y-rꜣ , , overseer

im.y-rꜣ nw.t overseer of the city

im.y-rꜣ kꜣ.t overseer of work

im.y-ẖt in the following of, follower;

im.yw-ẖt posterity

im.y-s.t-ʿ.w acolyte

im.ytw between (also + *r*)

ym sea, lake, pool

imi to mourn

imi "give!" (imperative of *rḏi*)

imi neg.verb see § 132

imꜣ > *iꜣm* be pleasing, gracious

imꜣ.t , grace, χαρις

imꜣḫ honour, veneration

Ꞽmn.y PN m. Ameni

Ꞽmn.w (god) Amun

Ỉmn.w-ꜥꜣ PN m.
Amen-aa

Ỉmn.w-m-ḥꜣ.t PN m.
Amenemhet (king, 12th Dyn.)

Ỉmn.w-m-ḥꜣb PN m.
Amenemheb

Ỉmn.w-ḥtp.w PN m.
Amenhotep (king, 18th Dyn.)

imn.t , *imn.tt* west

in , §§ 77, 83, 119

in eyebrow

in-iw §§ 34, 148

in.t valley

ini to bring, fetch

in.w gift, produce

inb wall

Ỉnp.w (god) Anubis

inr stone

Ỉntf (*Ỉni-it=f*) PN m. Intef

ir regarding, if (§§ 35, 127–131)

ir.y belonging to (§ 25)

ir.y-pꜥ.t "prince" (a title of rank)

ir.y sšm
(official) departmental head

iri.t duty, task

iri to do; exercise (an office); pass (time)

ir.t eye

irw form, shape (n.)

irp wine

iḥ ox; *iḥ.w* oxen

iḥw weakness

iḫ.t thing, something (§§ 17.2; 25b)

is enclit. part. (§ 38)

is tomb; chamber

is.t crew

isi "go!" (imperative)

isw , reward, exchange (n.)

isf.t sin, disorder

isṯ non-encl. part. (§ 37)

išs.t what? (§ 34)

iḳr be successful, excellent; *n iḳr n* on account of the excellence of; *r iḳr* see § 115.

ikm shield

igr.t (√*gr* be silent) cemetery, realm of the dead

it , father

it-nṯr "god's father" (priestly title)

iti.y sovereign

iti barley, grain

(I)tm(.w) , (god) Atum

itn sun disk

itrw river, Nile

iṯi to seize, rob, take; + *m* take possession of

idr bandage; det. herd

idḥ.y marsh dweller

ʿ

ʿ.w arm

m-ʿ.w with, by (§ 36)

n.t-ʿ.w custom, habit

ḥr-ʿ.wwy , *ḥr-ʿ.w* immediately (§ 115)

ẖr.t-ʿ.w tool, utensil

tp-ʿ.w before

ʿ.t bodily part

ʿ.t chamber

ʿ3i be great; great

ʿ3.t a great thing; *m/n ʿ3.t n.t* because of the greatness of; inasmuch as

ʿ3 donkey

ʿ3 here, hence (§ 115)

ʿ3 door

ir.y-ʿ3 , doorkeeper

ʿ3m Asiatic

ʿ3g.t hoof

ʿw.t , small cattle

ʿw3i to steal, rob

ʿwn be greedy

ʿb3 offering slab, altar, stele

ʿbʿ to boast; boasting (n.)

ʿpr equip

ʿm swallow; to know

ʿmd be weary

ʿnn to turn away

ʿnḫ to live, + *m* live off; life

ʿnḫ.w living (person); (pl.) people

ʿnḫ.w PN m. Ankhu

ʿntyw myrrh

ꜥnd be few

ꜥrr.yt gate; guard
n.tyw r ꜥrr.yt those of the guard

ꜥrḳ , to swear

ꜥrḳ to know, perceive

ꜥḥ palace

ꜥḥ.t farm-land

ꜥḥꜣ to fight

ꜥḥꜣ.w weapons, arrows

ꜥḥꜥ to stand, wait, stand up; auxiliary verb § 95

ꜥḥꜥ.w life, lifetime

ꜥḥꜥ.w ship

ꜥḥꜥ.w pile, heap, treasures

ꜥḥꜥ.w tomb

ꜥẖi to fly

ꜥẖnw.ty "cabinet" (room in the palace)

ꜥš to call

ꜥš , cedar

ꜥšꜣ be plentiful, rich; much, often (adv. § 115)

ꜥḳ to enter

ꜥḳ.w provisions

ꜥḏ be safe

ꜥḏꜣ guilt; be guilty; injustice

w

w district, region

wꜣi be far

wꜣ.t road, way

wꜣw wave

wꜣḥ set down, to lie, lay down; endure

Wꜣs.t GN Thebes

wꜣḏ be green, fresh, young; green semi-precious stone

wꜣḏ-wr sea (lit: the "great green")

wꜥi be alone

wꜥ one, only

wꜥw soldier

wꜥb be pure; det. priest

wꜥb.yt , meat offering

wbꜣ open, open up (a path)

wbn to rise (sun), overflow

wp.t crown (of head)

wpi to open

Wpi-wꜣ.wt (god) Wepwawet

wp.wt message

wmt be thick

wn to open

wnw.t hour

wnw.t priesthood

wnm , to eat

wnn to exist; see §§ 44 b, 96.

wr to be great, great

wr prince, great one

wr.t very (adv. § 115)

wrr.yt chariot, wagon

wrš spend the day

wrḏ be/become tired

whi to fail

wḥy.t settlement;
det. tribe

wḥꜥ fisherman

wḥm to repeat;
m wḥm, *m wḥm ꜥ.w* again

wḥm.w herald (n.)

Wsir (*ꜣsir*) (god) Osiris

wsr be strong

wsr oar

wsḫ be wide, broad;
wsḫ.w width

wsḫ.t barge

wsṯn to move freely, stride

wš be empty

wšb answer (vb. & n.)

wšn to (ritually) offer (birds)

wšd , to greet

wtḫ to flee

wṯs to lift, raise

wdi to place, put, throw, send forth, apply

wdp.w butler

wdf to delay, be sluggish

wḏ to command; decree (n.)

wḏ stele (also with)

wḏi to depart (for war)

wḏꜣ be hale, uninjured

wḏꜣ to go, set out

wḏꜥ to judge, judge between

wḏꜥ(y).t shell (for ink) (?)

b

b3 *ba*-soul

b3.w (sg.) renown, power

b3ḥ phallus; front

m-b3ḥ , *m-b3ḥ-ʿ.w* prep.: in front of, before (§ 36)

B3st.t (goddess) Bastet

b3k to work; work (n.), (pl.) taxes
+ *m* work with, inlay with

b3k servant

b3gi be tired, weary

b3gsw dagger

bi.ty King of Lower Egypt

bi3 mine

bin evil, bad

bik falcon

bw 1. place
2. to form abstract notions:
bw w3i distance
bw wr much
bw nfr good

bw.t abomination

bnw.t mill stone

bnr be sweet

bḥs calf

Bḥd.t GN Edfu

bs to introduce

bšṯ to rebel

bgi see *b3gi*

bdš be tired, weary

p

p.t sky, heaven

p3i see § 114

p3w.t primeval time

p3.t (offering) loaf

p3s scribe's water pot

pw § 29; §§ 53–54, as copula § 54

Pwn.t GN Punt

Ppy PN Pepi (king, 6th Dyn.)

pr.w house

pr.w-ʿ3 palace, pharaoh (§ 153)

pr.w nsw palace

pr.w-ḥḏ treasury

pri to go, come out

pr.t winter

pḥ to reach; attack

pḥ.wy , hindquarter, pelvic region; end

pḥ.ww marshlands; furthest north

pḥrr to run

pẖr to turn, turn around

pẖr.t prescription, remedy

Pẖr-wr (river) Euphrates

Psmtk PN m. Psammeticus (king, 26th Dyn.)

psḏ to shine

Pḳr GN Umm el-Qab (near Abydos)

ptpt to tread, trample

Ptn GN Peten (region near the Bitter Lakes)

ptr to see

Ptḥ (god) Ptah

f

f3i ; to carry

Ffi PN m. Fefi

fḫ to loosen, release, leave

fd.t sweat

m

m prep.: in (§ 35)

m-ʿ.w prep.: with (§ 36)

m-ḫt prep.: after, behind (§ 36); future (n.)

m , encl. part. (§ 38); following an imperative: "do …"

m imperative: "take!" (§ 67)

m3wy be new

m3(w) new

m3w.t , a new thing, novelty

m m3w.t anew, newly (§ 115)

m3i , , lion

m33 , to see

m3ʿ true, real, rightly, just

m3ʿ-ḫrw be justified, triumphant ("true of voice")

m3ʿ.t , , divine order, justice, truth

m3ʿ.tyw the just

m3ʿ to offer, present

m3r pauper, wretched person

m3ẖ to burn

mꜣs.t knee

mi prep.: like (§ 35)

mi.ty equal (n.)

mi imperative of *iwi* "come!"

miw cat

min today (§ 115)

mꜥḥꜥ.t (√*ꜥḥꜥ*) , tomb

mw water
ḥr mw=f to be "in his wake", to be loyal

mw pẖr-wr GN Euphrates

mw.t mother

m(w)t , to die, death

mmy giraffe

mn to remain, endure, stay

mn.w monument

Mn-ḫpr-Rꜥ.w Menkheperre: Thutmosis III (king, 18th Dyn.)

mn "so-and-so" (in place of a name)

Mn.w (god) Min

mn.t the like; manner, mode
mn.t ir.y such a thing

mni to land (trans./intrans.); to die

mnw , trees

mnmn to quake

mnmn.t cattle

mnḫ potent, effective, excellent; excellence

Mnṯ.w (god of war) Month

mr be sick, ill; suffer

mr.t sickness, disease

mr canal

mr.yt riverbank, shore

mr pyramid

mr.t serfs

mri to love, desire

mr.wt love

Mrw PN m. Meru

mrr.yt lumps

mḥ cubit (approx. 52 cm)

mḥ to fill (+ *m* with)

mḥ-ib trust (n.), confidant

mḥi be concerned

mḥi to swim

ȝ *i* ꜥ *w b p f m n r h ḥ ḫ ẖ s š ḳ k g t ṯ d ḏ*

mḥ.t/*mḥ.tt* north

mḥ.yt north wind

mḥ.ty northern

mḥ.tyw Northerners

mḫꜣ.t (√*ḫꜣi*) balance

mḫn.t (√*ḫni*) , ferry (n.)

mẖr (√*ẖr*) pasture, meadow

mẖr (√*ẖr*) store room

mẖr.w (√*ẖr*) requirements

ms to bring, present

msi , to bear, give birth; create (of god)

ms , pl. child

mskꜣ skin

mstp.t portable shrine

msdm.t (√*sdm*) black eye-paint

msḏi to hate, detest

msḏr (√*sḏr* sleep) ear

mšꜥ army

mšrw evening

mk.t protection

mkꜣ be brave, determined

mkḥꜣ back of head and neck; to neglect

mt see *m*(*w*)*t*

mty n.y sꜣ controller of a (priestly) phyle

Mṯn GN Mitanni

mṯn path, road

mdwi to speak;

mdw word, speech

md(*w*)*.t* word, speech

mḏ be deep

mḏw.t depth

mḏꜣ.t bookroll, book

mḏḥ to hew (timber)

n

N.y-Mꜣꜥ.t-Rꜥ.w PN Ni-Maat-Re: Amenemhet III (king, 12th Dyn.)

Ny GN Ny (region around the Orontes river)

nis to call

nꜥi to travel (by ship), traverse, cross

nw (point in) time

Nw.t (goddess of sky) Nut

nw.t (*niw.t*) city

nw.tyw citizens

nwy water, flood

nwḥ rope

nb every, all (§§ 25 b, 58 e, 151)

nb lord (also det. , ,)

nb.t mistress

nbi to swim

nbw gold

nbw "the Golden One" (Hathor)

nf be foolish

nfr be perfect, beautiful

nfr.w , perfection

Nfr.ty PN m. Neferty

nm transgress (+ *m* against)

nm.w (pl.) (wine) vats

nm.t executioner's block

nmḥ orphan; deprive (+*m* of)

nms.t jar

nmt.t stride (n.), journey

Nn-nsw GN Heracleopolis

nni be tired, weary

nr.t vulture

nh.t sycamore

nhy a bit, a little

nhw loss

nhmhm to roar, shout

Nhrn , GN Naharin (Mitanni)

nḥb.t neck

nḥm to steal, take away; to rescue

nḥḥ eternity

Nḥsy Nubian

nḫ to protect; protection

nḫw.t complaint, lament

nḫb.t royal titulary (§153)

nḫn child

nḫt strength, might

nḫt.w victory; hostage

ns tongue

nsw , , king

n.t-ꜥ.w organise, establish

nṯr god

nṯr.t goddess

nṯr.y divine (§ 23)

nḏ ask, inquire
nḏ ḫr.t inquire the health of, greet

nḏm be sweet, pleasant

nḏr.t imprisonment

nḏḥ.t tooth, tusk

nḏs be small

r

r3 mouth, speech

r3 pw or (§ 21)

r3-pr.w temple (precinct)

r3-w3.t path, way

r3-ḏ3y.w battle

rw to remove

rwḏ be firm, strong; to prosper

Rwḏ-ḏd.t PN f. Rudj-djedet

(i)r=f encl. part. (§ 38)

rm.w fish (pl.)

rmi to cry, lament

rmn shoulder

rmni carry

Rmnn GN Lebanon

rmṯ person

rmṯ.t humankind, people

rn name

rnpi become young

rnp.t year

rnp.t sp year (in dates)

Rnsi PN m. Rensi

rri pig

rhn to lean (*ḥr* upon)

rḫ.w comrades (pl.)

rḫ , to learn, know

rḫ.t list (n.)

rḫ.yt subjects commoners

rs-tp be watchful

rsy south, southern

ršw to rejoice

rk , time

rḳ.y enemy

Rṯnw GN Retenu (Syria-Palestine)

rd leg

rdw , stairway

rḏi , to give, + *r* appoint,
+ *sḏm=f* to cause,
m ḥr to command, commission

h

h3i , to descend (+ *r* to)

h(3)y husband

h3w vicinity

h3b to send; write (to)

hbny ,
ebony

hp law

hnw , box, chest

hnw jar, measure (ca. 0.48 l)

hrw be satisfied

hrw.w day

hrw.yt journal

ḥ

ḥ3 non-encl. part. (§ 37)

ḥ3.t tomb

ḥ3.t front, beginning;
face, forehead, brow

im.y-ḥ3.t ancestor

ẖr-ḥ3.t §§ 36, 115

ḥ3.t -ˁ.w beginning (of text)

ḥ3.t sp see *rnp.t sp*

ḥ3.ty-ˁ.w count (title); NK mayor

ḥ3.ty heart, chest; mind

ḥ3t.t bow warp

ḥ3y be naked

ḥ3w.ty naked man

ḥ3w increase, excess (n.)

ḥ3b (*ḥb*) festival

ẖr.y-ḥ3b(.t) lector priest

ḥ3p to hide

ḥ3ḳ to plunder, capture

ḥy.t rain

ḥˁw ship

ḥˁw body, self, body surface, skin

ḥwi to beat, strike, smite

Ḥw.t-wˁr.t GN Avaris

ḥw.t-nṯr temple

ḥw3 to rot

ḥwy non-encl. part. (§ 37)

ḥwr.w pauper

ḥbs to hide; dress, clothing

ḥpt to embrace

ḥfꜣ.w snake

ḥm majesty

ḥm servant

ḥm.t female servant

ḥm-nṯr "servant of god", priest

ḥm.t wife, woman

ḥmꜣ.t natron

ḥmw oar

ḥmw.w craftsman

ḥmsỉ to sit

ḥn provide, equip; + *n* commend s'one to

ḥn.t greed

ḥnꜥ with (§ 35), and (§ 20)

ḥnw jar, chattel, possession

ḥnḥn to hinder

ḥnk.t lock of hair

ḥnḳ.t beer

ḥnk to present, make an offering

ḥntꜣsw lizard

ḥr face; prep.: upon (§ 35)

ḥr-ꜥ.w immediately (§ 115)

ḥr nb everyone

ḥr-sꜣ outside

ḥr.y-ib middle, midst

ḥr.y-tp chief

ḥrw upper part, top
r-ḥrw upwards

ḥr.t tomb, necropolis;
det. heaven; what is above

ḥrỉ be far, distant

Ḥr.w , (god) Horus

Ḥr.w-ꜣḫ.ty (god) Harakhte

Ḥr.y-šỉ=f (god) Herishef

ḥrr.t flower

Ḥḥ GN Heh (near Mirgissa in Nubia)

ḥḥỉ to seek, search

ḥsỉ to sing, praise

ḥs.t favour

ḥs excrement

ḥḳ.t = *ḥnḳ.t* beer

ḥḳꜣ ruler

Ḥḳꜣ-ib PN m. Hekaib

ḥḳr be hungry

ḥkn.w praise; det. incense

ḥtp to be peaceful, gracious, satisfied; peace, grace

ḥtp.t offering

ḥtp.w peace

ḥtp nṯr god's offering

ḥtp-di-nsw funerary offering formula: "offering which the king gives"

ḥḏ be white, bright

ḥḏ silver

ḥḏ.t the white crown of Upper Egypt

ḥḏi to injure, damage

ḫ

ḫ.t see *iḫ.t*

ḫ.t fire (n.)

ḫꜣ office (building)

ḫꜣi to measure, weigh

ḫꜣw.t offering table

ḫꜣꜥ to leave, abandon, throw

ḫꜣm to bow, bend

ḫꜣs.t desert, hill country, foreign land

ḫꜥi to appear

Ḫꜥi=f-Rꜥ.w PN m. Khephren (king, 4th Dyn.)

*Ḫꜥi-kꜣ.w-Rꜥ.*w PN m. Sesostris III (king, 12th Dyn.)

ḫꜥ.w diadem, crown

Ḫwi=f-wi PN m. Kheops/ Khufu (king, 4th Dyn.)

ḫw unique; *ḥr ḫw=f* apart from him

ḫwsi to pound, beat up; + *ib* to stir; to build

ḫbꜣ hack up, destroy

ḫbsw.t beard

ḫpr to come into being; + *m* to become

ḫpri / *ḫpr.w* form, shape, mode of being, character

ḫfꜥ fist; to grasp, seize

ḫft prep.: in front of, in accordance with (§ 35)

ḫft.y enemy

ḫm to not know, be

ignorant of

ḫm sanctuary

ḫmi to harm, strike (of misfortune)

ḫm.t numeral: 3

ḫni to alight, land

ḫnms friend

Ḫns.w (moon god) Khons

ḫnt front; in front of (§ 35); before, formerly (§ 115)

ḫnt.y s.wt nṯr.w "(he) at the front of the place of the gods" (god Amun)

ḫnti to travel southwards

ḫnd to tread

ḫr prep.: with, under (a king) (§ 35)

ḫr to fall; enemy

ḫrw.y enemy

ḫrw voice; noise, sound

ḫr.t property, possessions

ḫrp to guide, lead

ḫsbḏ lapis-lazuli

ḫsfy travel upstream

ḫt after; through (a land); *m-ḫt* after, behind (§ 36); "the afterwards", the future, posterity; *im.y-ḫt* in the following of

ḫt wood, tree

ḫti to carve, engrave

ḫtm to seal; seal

ḫtm.w bi.ty sealbearer / treasurer of King of Lower Egypt

ḫtm gate

ḫdi to travel downstream (northwards)

ẖ

ẖ.t torso, trunk of body

ẖꜣ.t swamp

ẖꜣ.t corpse

ẖꜣr.t widow

ẖpꜣ navel

ẖnw interior; det. residence, palace

H̱n-ẖn (*H̱n-Nẖn*) GN (the first 7 nomes of Upper Egypt)

ẖni , to row

ẖn.ty statue

H̱nm.w (god) Khnum

ẖr prep.: under (§ 35);

ẖr.y lower

ẖr.t , *ẖr.t-ꜥ.w* property, requirements, wish

ẖr.t-nṯr , necropolis

ẖr.tyw-nṯr stone-masons

ẖr.t hrw.w , daily requirements; *m ẖr.t hrw.w n.t rꜥ.w nb* in the course of every day

ẖr.y-ḥꜣb(.t) lector priest

ẖr.y ḳni porter

ẖrd child

ẖsi be miserable

ẖsꜣ.yt balm, scent

ẖkr.yt ornament

S

si , man; *s.t* woman

s.t seat, throne, place
s.t-ꜥ.w in *im.y s.t-ꜥ.w*: a priestly title; *s.t-ḥr* supervision

sꜣ , son

sꜣ.t daughter

sꜣ-nsw king's son, prince

sꜣ back; *ḳꜣi sꜣ* arrogant
ḥr-sꜣ prep.: behind (§ 36)

sꜣi be sated

sꜣi be wise

sꜣw company, troop

sꜣw herd (elephants)

sꜣw to guard, protect

sꜣw guardian, guard

sꜣr.t wisdom

sꜣḥ to reach

sꜣḥ *tꜣ* to land (trans.);
sꜣḥ m endow with

sꜣtw ground (n.)

si-išš.t why? (§ 34)

siꜣ to perceive

sip to control, assign

sꜥb (caus.) to purify

sꜥnḫ (caus.) to vivify, make live, nourish

sꜥr (caus.) cause to ascend

sꜥḥ rank, dignity

sꜥḥꜥ (caus.) to raise up, erect

sꜥšꜣ (caus.) to multiply

swꜣi (caus.) to pass (*ḥr* by)

swꜣš (caus.) to honour, adore

swꜥb purify; restore

swr > swi to drink (§ 10 c)

swhi (+ *n*) to boast of

swsḫ (caus.) to widen, extend

swt indep. pron. "he" (§ 26, like *ntf*)

swt encl. part.: but (§ 38)

sb.t cargo, load

sbi to go; det. to perish; *sbi n.y sḏ.t* "that of the flame which perishes": burnt offering

sbi to rebel

sbꜣ , gate

sbꜣ.yt teaching

sbḥ to call out, shout, laugh; cry (n.), laughter

sbt to laugh (*n* / *m* at); laughter

sp occasion, matter; (blameworthy) act

spi to remain, be left over
dmi n.y sp resting place

sp.t lips

spꜣ.t nome (province)

spr arrive (*r* at); reach s'one

spr to plead, make a petition

spr.ty petitioner; plea

sf yesterday

sfn be kindly, merciful

sfṯ to slaughter, make a sacrifice

smꜣ to unite
smꜣ-tꜣ to land; be buried

smꜣ.y comrade, fellow

smꜣ to slaughter, kill

smꜣꜥ (caus.) to make an offering

smi (caus.) to report, complain, announce

smn (caus.) to make firm, establish, perpetuate; record

smn goose

smnḫ , (caus.) to advance, embellish; to endow (a tomb)

smr "companion" (a court title)

sn brother

sn.t sister

sn.nw , second

Sn-nfr PN m. Sennefer

sn to kiss

snb be healthy

Snb PN Seneb

Snfr.w Snofru (king, 4th Dyn.)

sns praise

snṯr (√*nṯr*) incense

snḏ to fear, be afraid; fear (n.)

snḏm (caus.) to dwell

sr ram

sr prince, official

sr to foretell

srwḫ (med.) treat; treatment

srḫ to accuse, charge

sḥ hall, booth

sḥ counsel, plan

sḥtp (caus.) to please, propitiate

Sḥtp-ib-Rᶜ.w PN Amenemhet I (king, 12th Dyn.)

sḫw (√*wsḫ*) width

sḫ.t field

sḫ.ty peasant

Sḫ.t-ḥm3.t GN Wadi Natrun

sḫ3 (caus.) to remember, call to mind; remembrance

sḫp (caus.) bring into being

sḫm be mighty

sḫm.ty double crown

sḫmḫ enjoy; *sḫmḫ ib* delight the heart, entertain

sḫnti (caus.) advance, promote

sḫr (caus.) to overthrow, cast down

sḫr plan; nature

sḫsḫ to hasten, run

sẖr (*sḫr* / *sšr*) , to brush over, overlay

ssbi (caus.) to send

ss dust, ash

ss3i (caus.) to sate

sš marsh, nest

sš (*sẖ3*) to write

sš (*sẖ3.w*) script

sš (*sẖ3.w*) scribe

sš3 see *šs3*

sš3i to beseech, pray

sšm , (caus.)

to lead, guide; guidance

sḳni (caus.) to make strong

Sḳni-n-Rꜥ.w PN m. Sekenenre (king, 17th Dyn.)

sḳr-ꜥnḫ prisoner

sḳdi to travel (by ship or chariot)

sḳd.w sailor

skꜣ to plough

ski to perish

skm (caus.) become grey

sksk to destroy

sgr (caus.) to silence; calm (n.)

sti smell

stw.t rays

stp to choose, select

stp.t.. choice cut of meat, choice offering

stp-sꜣ palace

stkn (caus.) allow to approach

Sṯ.t mythical term for Asia

Sṯ.tyw Asiatics

sṯꜣ to pull; usher in

sd tail

sḏ to break, smash

sḏ.t flame

sḏꜣw.ty bi.ty see *ḫtm.w bi.ty*

sḏm to hear, listen, obey

sḏr to sleep

sḏsr (caus.) consecrate, sanctify

sḏd (caus.) to recount

š

ši lake, pool

šꜣꜥ to begin; beginning

šꜣwꜣb.ty shabti (funerary figurine)

šꜣd to dig

šꜥ to cut off

šꜥy sand

šꜥd to cut

šw sun, light

šw.t > šy.t , shadow, shade

šwi be empty

špsi, špss be rich, noble

špss wealth

šfy.t respect, majesty

šfdw ⸻ papyrus roll

šm (inf. *šm.t*) to go

šmw dryness, summer

šms to follow

šms.w follower

šni to encircle, surround

šnᶜ to turn back, detain

šnᶜ storeroom, labour establishment

šnb.t chest

šri child

šr.t nose

šsȝ (also *sšȝ*) be skilled, conversant with; skill, experience

šsp to receive

šsr arrow

štȝ secret; difficult

šdi to take/tear away; dig (a lake etc.), cut out; rescue; read

šdw raft, skiff

ḳ

ḳȝi be tall, high, exalted
ḳȝi ḫrw loud voiced

ḳȝi sȝ arrogant (lit.: high backed)

ḳȝᶜ to vomit

ḳȝb middle; coil

ḳᶜḥ bend (esp. the hand while offering)

ḳᶜḥ corner

ḳbb be cool, happy

ḳbḥ be cool

ḳmȝ > ḳȝm to create without : throw

ḳni be strong, brave

ḳn.t strength, bravery

ḳni to embrace; open arms

ḳni baggage

ḳnb.t council of magistrates or officials

ḳri storm

ḳrs to bury

ḳrs.t coffin

ḳs bone

ḳsn difficult

ḳd to build

ḳd character

ȝ i ᶜ w b p f m n r h ḥ ḫ ẖ s š ḳ k g t ṯ d ḏ

Ḳdm GN Qedem (locality east of Byblos)

ḳdd to sleep; sleep

k

kꜣ "*Ka*", life force, spirit

kꜣ.w food

kꜣ bull

kꜣ.w (pl.) unripe fruit (of the sycamore)

kꜣ.t work

kꜣi (Nubian) ship

kꜣp to cover; roof (n.)

kꜣmw vineyard

Kꜣš GN Kush (Nubia)

ky other (§ 25 c)

kyw ape

Kpny GN Byblos

kfi , to uncover

km to complete

km.t completion

Km.t GN Egypt (Black Land)

Km-wr GN (region around the Bitter Lakes)

Kry GN (region in the Sudan)

ksw bowing down (n.)

ktt be small

g

gꜣw need, lack (n.)

gꜣb arm

gwf small monkey

Gbtyw GN Coptos

gmi to find

gmꜣ temple (of head)

gmḥ catch sight of, espy

gmgm to smash, break, break off

gr, grt , encl. part.: but (§ 38)

gr be silent

grḥ night

grg lie, untruth

grg to order, create, found, establish, settle

gs side

rḏi ḥr-gs show partiality

gs-pr.w temple

gs.y neighbour

gsty scribe's palette

t

t bread

t-ḥḏ white bread

t3 land

T3-mri GN Egypt

T3-mḥw the Delta

T3-sty GN Nubia

t3š border

ti non-encl. part. (§ 37)

Ty PN f. Tiy (queen, 18th Dyn., wife of Amenhotep III)

tišps tree (camphor tree?)

twt be like, resemble

twt.w , statue, image

Twt.w-ʿnḫ.w-Ỉmn.w Tutankhamun (king, 18th Dyn.)

tp head, top

tp Šmʿ.w GN "top" of Upper Egypt (area around Elephantine)

tp-ʿ.w before

tp-rd instruction, regulation

tp.t-r3 utterance

tp.y first (month)

tp.w personnel

tm be complete; neg. verb § 134

(Ỉ)tm.w (god) Atum

tnm to go astray

tri to respect, worship

thi to go astray, transgress

tḫ plummet (of balance)

tḫn obelisk

tkn (+ *m*) to approach, draw near

ṯ

ṯ3i to take, steal

ṯ3w air, wind

ṯ3.ty vizier

Ṯ3nwny PN m. Tjanuny

Ṯwi3 PN f. Tjuia

ṯm3 mat

ṯni to distinguish

ṯnw number; + noun: every

ṯnṯ3.t throne

ṯs to tie (a knot)

ṯs.w speech, utterance

ṯs.t.. speech

ṯs.w commander

ṯs.t troop

ṯs.w taxes (pl.)

ṯsm hound

d

d3.t netherworld, the beyond

d3b figs

d3r > d3i , to control, subdue (§ 10.3)

dw3 to awake (in the morning)

dw3 to praise

dw3-nṯr to thank

Dw3.wy-r-nḥḥ PN m. Duawy-er-neheh

dwn to stretch out

dbḥ to ask for, beg

dp.t taste

dp.t ship

dm to pronounce (a name); sharpen,

dm3 bind together

dm3 stretch out

dmi to touch; reach (a place)

dmi town

dni.t dam

dns be heavy, important

dr to expel; subdue

drp to offer (to a god)

dhn to appoint, promote; + *n* bow to

dḥr leather

dšr red

dšr.t the red land, desert, foreign land

dšr.t the red crown of Lower Egypt

dgi to look, see

dgi , to hide

dgm castor-oil plant

ḏ

ḏ.t eternity

ḏꜣ fire drill

ḏꜣi to ferry (across water)

ḏꜣi to extend, stretch out;
ḏꜣi-rꜣ argue (*ḥr* over, about)
ḏꜣi-ḥr have fun, enjoy oneself (*n* / *m* with)

ḏꜣy.t wrongdoing

ḏꜣy.w see *rꜣ*

ḏꜣw.t in *r-ḏꜣw.t* accordingly

ḏꜣm.w troop, youths

Ḏꜣhy GN Syria

ḏꜣt.t estate

ḏꜣḏꜣ head

ḏꜥ storm

ḏꜥm fine gold, electrum

ḏꜥr to seek

ḏw to be bad, evil

ḏw.t evil (n.)*ḏw* mountain

ḏb.t brick

ḏbꜣ to block up

ḏbꜥ finger; numeral: 10,000

ḏnḥ wing

ḏr prep.: since, until (§ 35)

ḏr.w border, boundary
r-ḏr + suffix-pronoun: to (its) end, limit; entire, whole

ḏr.t hand

ḏrḏr > *ḏrḏy* foreign, foreigner

Ḏḥw.ty (god) Thoth

ḏs + suffix: self, own (§ 28)

ḏsr , to dedicate; make way; be splendid, holy; to be separate

ḏd to speak, say

INDICES

1) GRAMMATICAL INDEX

The numbers refer to the paragraphs. Table 1 – p. 50, Table 2 – p. 83, Table 3 – p. 85.

2) INDEX OF VERB PATTERNS

The numbers refer to the paragraphs.

3. Index to the Hieroglyphic Sign List

A. Men

1 2 3 4 5 6 7 9 10 12 13 14 15 16 17 19 21 22 23
24 25 26 27 28 29 30 32 33 34 35 36 40 41 42 43 44 45 46 47 49 50 51
52 53 54 55

B. Women

C. Anthropomorphic Deities

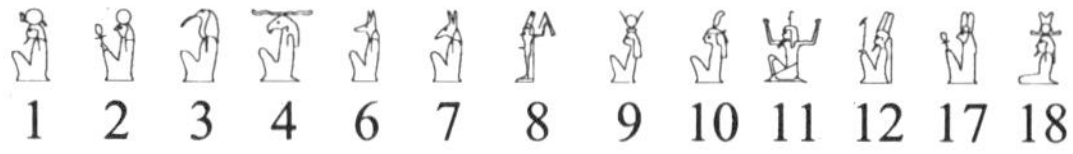
1 2 3 4 6 7 8 9 10 11 12 17 18

D. Parts of the Human Body

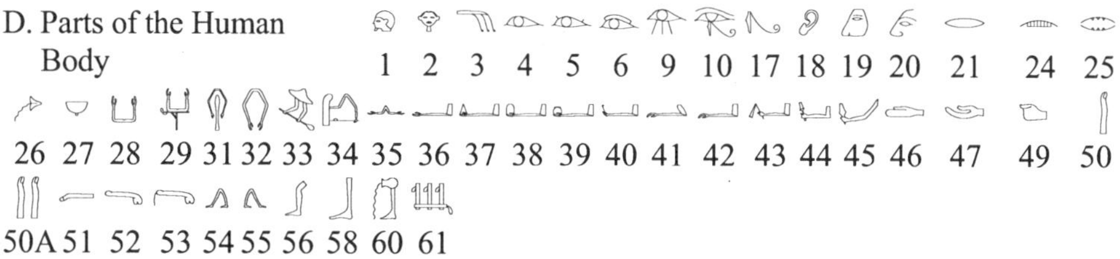
1 2 3 4 5 6 9 10 17 18 19 20 21 24 25
26 27 28 29 31 32 33 34 35 36 37 38 39 40 41 42 43 44 45 46 47 49 50
50A 51 52 53 54 55 56 58 60 61

E. Mammals

1 2 3 6 7 8 9 10 12 13 14 15 16 17 18 20 21 22
23 24 26 27 31 34

F. Parts of Mammals

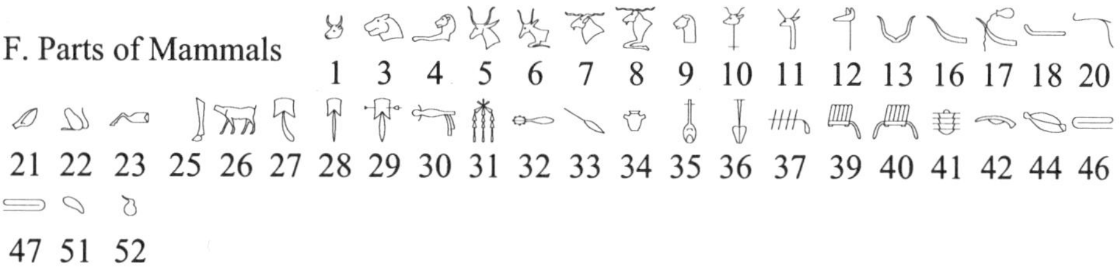
1 3 4 5 6 7 8 9 10 11 12 13 16 17 18 20
21 22 23 25 26 27 28 29 30 31 32 33 34 35 36 37 39 40 41 42 44 46
47 51 52

G. Birds

1 4 5 7 7A 8 9 10 11 14 15 16 17 21 22 23 24 25 26
27 28 29 30 31 32 33 35 36 37 38 39 40 41 42 43 47 48 49 51 52 53 54

H. Parts of Birds

1 2 3 4 5 6 8

I. Amphibious Animals, Reptiles

1 3 5 6 7 8 9 10 12 13 14

K. Fish

1 2 3 4 5

L. Insects and Lesser Animals

1 2 6 7

M. Trees and Plants

1 2 3 4 8 11 12 13 15 16 17 18 19 20 21 22

23 24 26 29 30 31 32 33 34 35 36 40 42 43 44

N. Sky, Earth, Water

1 2 4 5 6 7 8 9 10 11 12 14 15 16 17 18

20 21 23 23A 24 25 26 27 28 29 30 31 33 34 35 36 37 40 41 42

O. Buildings and Parts of Buildings

1 2 3 4 6 9 10 11 16 22 23 24 25

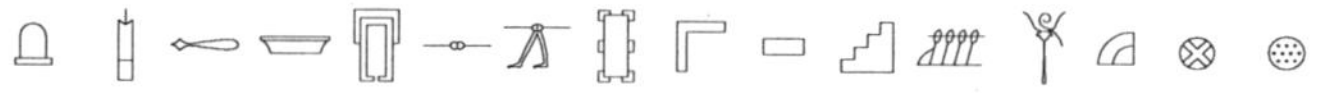

26 28 29 31 32 34 35 36 38 39 40 42 44 45 49 50

P. Ships and Parts of Ships

1 1A 2 3 4 5 6 8 11

Q. Domestic and Funerary Furniture

1 2 3 6 7

R. Temple Furniture and Sacred Symbols

4 5 7 8 10 11 12 13 14 15 19 22 24

S. Crowns, Dress, Staves

1 2 3 4 5 6 7 8 9 10 11 12 15 18 19 20

22 23 24 27 28 29 32 33 34 35 37 38 39 40 41 42 43

T. Warfare, Hunting, Butchery

1 3 8 9 10 10A 11 12 13 14 17 18 19 21 22

24 25 28 30 31 32 34

U. Agriculture, Crafts

1 6 9 13 15 17 19 21 22 23 24 26 28 30 30A

32 33 34 35 Aa23 Aa24 36 38 39 40

V. Ropes, Baskets, Bags etc.

1 2 4 6 7 10 12 13 15 16 17 19 20 22 24

25 26 28 29 30 31 33 36 37

W. Vessels of Stone and Earthenware

1 2 3 4 5 7 9 10 11 14 15 17 18 19 20

21 22 23 24 25

X. Bread and Cakes

1 2 3 4 6 7 8

Y. Games, Instruments for Writing, Music

1 2 3 5 6 8

Z. Strokes, Geometric Shapes, Signs adopted from Hieratic

1 2 3 4 5 6 7 8 9 11

Aa. Unclassifed

1 2 5 6 7 8 13 17 18 19 20 21 25 26 27 28 30 32

Selection of Signs Ordered By Shape

Tall narrow signs

M40 Aa28 P11 T34 U28 U32 U33 S43 U36 T8 M13 M17 H6 M4 M12

S29 M29 M30 S37 R14 R15 P6 S40 R19 S41 F10 F11 F12 S38 S39

T14 T13 Aa26 Aa21 U39 O44 Aa27 R8 T3 V24 V25 U23 S42 U34 S36

F28 U26 U24 Y8 F35 F36 W19 P8 T22 T23 Z11 Aa25 M44 Aa30 Aa20

V36 F31 M32 L7 V17 S34 Q7 T18 T19 R11 O28 O11 O36 V28 V29

Tall broad signs

V4 U19 U6 F40 D61 O42 Aa18 O40 W4 S28 N2 T25 N35a W17 Y3

M8 M16 M20 M43 R1 R10

Low narrow signs

Q3 O39 Z8 N21 N23 N29 O45 X2 X1 N28 Aa17 I6 W10 R7 M36

N34 U30 W11 T28 N41 V37 M31 F34 W7 V6 V33 V7 S20 V20 V19

Aa19 Aa2 H8 F51 F21 D26 N33 N5 Aa1 O50 O49 X6 S10 N6 N8

S11 N15 M42 V1 Z7 Z9

Low broad signs

N1 N37 S32 N18 X4 N16 N20 Aa11 Aa13 N35 Aa8 V26 R24 Y1 Y2 R4 N11 F42

D25 F20 Z6 F30 V22 R5 O34 V2 S24 R22 T11 O29 T1 T21 U19 U21 T9 T10

F32 V13 F46 F47 U17 Aa7 F18 D51 U15 N31 O31 N36 D21 T30 T31 V30

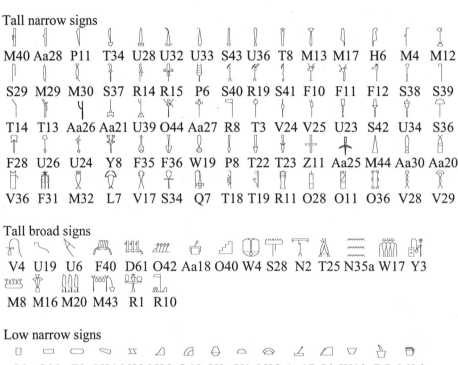

3. Negation: both types of *pw*-Sentences are negated by ....  *n ... is* **§ 55**

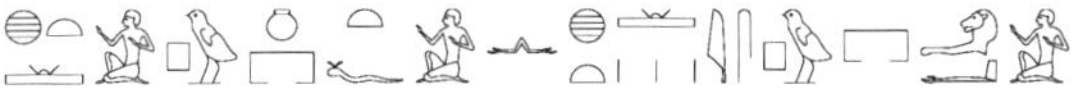 *iḫ.t=i pw n.w pr.w it=i n iḫ.t is pw pr.w ḥꜣ.ty-ꜥ.w* "It is my property of the estate of my father, it is not the property of the estate of the prince."

 *n wr is pw wr im ꜥwn-ib* "The great one there, the greedy one, is no (true) great one."

3) ADJECTIVAL SENTENCES (*nfr sw* - SENTENCES) **§ 56**

WORD ORDER : predicate – subject

Predicate: invariable adjective (§ 22f.) or participle (§ 98–104)

Subject: (1) noun, or (2) dependent pronoun (§ 27, usually 2nd or 3rd person, rarely 1st person).

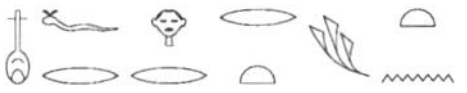 *nfr ḥrr.t tn* "This flower is beautiful." (1)

 *nfr tw ḥnꜥ=i* "You are/will be happy/well-off with me." (2)

Often, the ending , the "admirative *wy*", is appended to the adjective or participle:

 *nfr.wy sw* "How beautiful it is!" (2)

 *rwḏ.wy sw ib=i* "How firm it is, my heart!" (2)

An interrogative (§ 34) can also take the place of the adjective or participle:

 *ptr (i)r=f* (§38) *sw* "Who, then, is he?" (2)

4) THE ADJECTIVAL SENTENCE with  *nn* or  *nn wn* (see also § 59) **§ 57**

In this sentence type,  *nn* ("it does/did not exist") takes the place of the adjective.
WORD ORDER: predicate – subject. The tense is dependent upon the context.

 *nn mꜣꜥ.tyw* (§ 23) "There are no just ones."

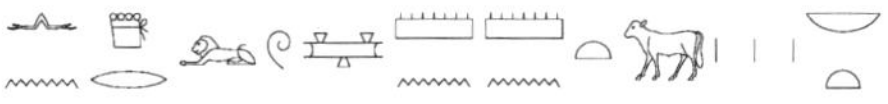 *nn ḏr.w mnmn.t nb.t* "There was no end to all (kinds of) cattle."

 *nn wn pḥ.wy=fy* "His / its end does not exist."